C000078621

The Future of Parliament

Also by Philip Giddings

THE OMBUDSMAN, THE CITIZEN AND PARLIAMENT, 2002 (*co-author with Roy Gregory*)

THE OMBUDSMAN: PRESENT PRACTICE AND FUTURE PROSPECTS, 1995 (*co-editor with Roy Gregory*)

PARLIAMENTARY ACCOUNTABILITY: A Study of Parliament and Executive Agencies, Macmillan, 1995 (*editor for the Study of Parliament Group*)

RIGHTING WRONGS: The Ombudsman in Six Continents, IOS Press, 2000 (*co-editor with Roy Gregory*)

WESTMINSTER AND EUROPE: The Impact of the European Union on the Westminster Parliament, Macmillan, 1996 (*co-editor with Gavin Drewry*)

BRITAIN IN THE EUROPEAN UNION: Law, Policy and Parliament, 2004, Palgrave Macmillan (*co-editor with Gavin Drewry*)

The Future of Parliament

Issues for a new century

Edited for the Study of Parliament Group by

Philip Giddings
Senior Lecturer in Politics
University of Reading

First published 2005 by
PALGRAVE MACMILLAN
Houndmills, Basingstoke, Hampshire RG21 6XS and
175 Fifth Avenue, New York, N. Y. 10010
Companies and representatives throughout the world

PALGRAVE MACMILLAN is the global academic imprint of the Palgrave Macmillan division of St. Martin's Press, LLC and of Palgrave Macmillan Ltd. Macmillan® is a registered trademark in the United States, United Kingdom and other countries. Palgrave is a registered trademark in the European Union and other countries.

ISBN-13: 978–1–4039–9527–8 hardback
ISBN-10: 1–4039–9527–3   hardback

This book is printed on paper suitable for recycling and made from fully managed and sustained forest sources.

A catalogue record for this book is available from the British Library.

Library of Congress Cataloging-in-Publication Data
The future of Parliament : issues for a new century / edited for the Study of Parliament
    Group by Philip Giddings.
       p. cm.
    Includes bibliographical references and index.
    ISBN 1–4039–9527–3 (cloth)
       1. Great Britain. Parliament—History—20th century. 2. Great Britain. Parliament—Reform. I. Giddings, Philip James. II. Study of Parliament Group.

JN550.F88 2005
328.41′09′051–dc22   2005045256

10   9   8   7   6   5   4   3   2   1
14   13   12   11   10   09   08   07   06   05

Printed and bound in Great Britain by
Antony Rowe Ltd, Chippenham and Eastbourne

Contents

List of Tables

Notes on Contributors

Sarah Childs is Senior Lecturer in Politics at the University of Bristol. She has written widely on women and British Politics. Her book *New Labour's Women MPs* was published in 2004.

Stephen Coleman is Professor of e-Democracy at the Oxford Internet Institute and a fellow of Jesus College Oxford. He was formerly Director of Studies and Director of the e-Democracy programme at the Hansard Society.

Byron Criddle is Reader in Politics at Aberdeen University, co-author of *The Almanac of British Politics* and *Parliamentary Profiles*, and a contributor to the Nuffield election series.

Paul Evans has been a Clerk in the House of Commons since 1981. He is the current Chairman of the Study of Parliament Group and has contributed to a number of SPG publications. The fifth edition of his *Handbook of House Commons Procedure* was published by Dod's Parliamentary Communications in 2004.

Matthew Flinders is Reader in Politics and Sub-Dean, Faculty of Social Sciences, at the University of Sheffield. His books include *The Politics of Accountability in the Modern State* (Ashgate, 2001) and *Multi-Level Governance*.

Oonagh Gay is head of the Parliament and Constitution Centre in the House of Commons Library. She joined the Library in 1983 and has specialised in parliamentary and constitutional issues since 1992.

Philip Giddings is Senior Lecturer in Politics at the University of Reading. He has edited and contributed to a number of books on Parliament, including 'Britain in the European Union' (2004). He is a former Secretary of the Study of Parliament Group.

Mark Hutton is currently the Clerk of the Defence Committee. He has previously worked on the Foreign Affairs, Transport and Welsh Affairs Committees. He was one of the Assistant Editors of the 23rd edition of

Erskine May. He is a former Treasurer of the Study of Parliament Group.

Helen Irwin is Principal Clerk, Table Office in the House of Commons. She first joined the Department of the Clerk of the House in 1970. She is a former Secretary of the Study of Parliament Group.

Nevil Johnson is Emeritus Fellow of Nuffield College, Oxford, where from 1969–96 he was Reader in the Comparative Study of Institutions. He has written widely on parliamentary institutions in both Britain and Germany as well as on the British constitution. He joined the Study of Parliament Group in 1964 and is a past chairman of the Group.

Colin Lee has been a Clerk in the House of Commons since 1988 and is a former Official Secretary of the Study of Parliament Group.

John McEldowney is Professor of Law at the University of Warwick. He has written on many aspects of public law including public finance and has advised the House of Lords Select Committee on the Constitution on the new EU Constitution and on the role of Parliament in the legislative process. He has been a member of the Study of Parliament Group Executive and editor of its Newsletter since 1994.

David Miers is Professor of Law, Cardiff University. He has written extensively on the preparation and interpretation of legislation and on the role of Westminster in its making and scrutiny. He is a former Academic Secretary of the Study of Parliament Group and is currently a member of its Executive Committee. He is manager of *Wales legislation online*, a database that analyses the functions devolved to the National Assembly for Wales: http://www.wales-legislation.org.uk.

David Natzler is currently Secretary of the House of Commons Commission, and has been a select committee clerk on and off since 1979. From 2001 to 2004 he was one of the Principal Clerks supervising select committees.

Ralph Negrine is Professor of Political Communication in the Department of Journalism Studies, University of Sheffield. His main interest lies in the relationship between politics, politicians and the media and he has written several books on these topics, including 'Parliament and the Media' (1998).

Philip Norton is Professor of Government and Director of the Centre for Legislative Studies at the University of Hull. He was made a life peer in 1998. He has authored or edited more than 25 books.

Dawn Oliver is Professor of Constitutional Law in the Faculty of Laws, University College London. She has written extensively on constitutional reform, relations between politicians and the courts, and the legislative process.

Michael Rush is Emeritus Professor of Politics, University of Exeter and the author, co-author and editor of a number of books on Parliament. He was Academic Secretary of the Study of Parliament Group 1975–77 and Chairman 1990–93. He has edited and contributed to a number of the Group's books, including most recently, *The Law and Parliament* (1998), and *Conduct Unbecoming: The Regulation of Parliamentary Behaviour* (2004).

Michael Ryle was a Clerk in the House of Commons, 1951–89. He was joint founder (with Bernard Crick) and Secretary of the Study of Parliament Group, 1964, Chairman, 1975–78, and President, 1986–94. He has written, lectured and served as a consultant overseas on parliamentary procedure and reform and was Secretary of the Hansard Society Commission on the Legislative Process, 1991–93. He has edited various SPG publications, including *The Commons in the Seventies*, 1977, and *The Commons Under Scrutiny*, 1988. He is the joint author (with J. A. G. Griffith) of *Parliament: Functions, Practice and Procedures* (first edition 1989; second edition, by Robert Blackburn and Andrew Kennon, 2003).

Colin Seymour-Ure is Emeritus Professor of Government at the University of Kent and was Chairman of the Study of Parliament Group, 2002–05. His publications about political communication include various aspects of Parliament and the media. His latest book is 'Prime Ministers and the Media' (2003).

Donald Shell is senior lecturer in politics at the University of Bristol, and is a former executive committee member and academic secretary of the Study of Parliament Group. He jointly edited the Study of Parliament Group book, *The House of Lords at Work*, and has contributed chapters in several other SPG sponsored works.

Barry K. Winetrobe is Reader in Low at Napier University, Edinburgh. After working for many years in the House of Commons Research Service he was seconded to Edinburgh to assist in the establishment and early operation of the Scottish Parliament's Research Service. He has written extensively on parliamentary and constitutional issues.

Preface

This volume has been put together to mark the fortieth anniversary of the founding of the Study of Parliament Group (SPG). The Group has just over a hundred members, most of whom are either academics with an interest in the Group's work or Parliamentary officials. Its purpose is to study the working of Parliament and Parliamentary institutions, and other related aspects of Parliamentary government and political science, and to advance public knowledge of these subjects.

The Group began life just before the 1964 General Election at a time when, as now, there was much debate about Parliament's effectiveness and how it might be enhanced. On 24th September 1964 a memorandum calling a meeting was drawn up by Sir Edward Fellowes the recently retired Clerk of the House of Commons, Michael Ryle a Senior Clerk in the House of Commons and Dr Bernard Crick of the London School of Economics. They were concerned about the working of Parliament and the fact that, whereas there were many historical studies of Parliament, there were surprisingly few studies of the working of the contemporary Parliament. Part of the reason for this, it was thought, was a lack of regular contact between academic students of Parliament and those interested in such matters within the Palace of Westminster. It was suggested that it would be mutually useful, both for practical and academic reasons, for people in the universities and in the Palace of Westminster interested in the study of the modern Parliament to have the chance to meet each other on some known and regular basis, however informal, to study and to stimulate studies of Parliament. This would provide, it was thought, a helpful forum to develop practical ideas for the reform of Parliament, which was a key interest of some members of the founding group, not least Michael Ryle and Bernard Crick whose initial exchange of letters provided the stimulus for the conversations which led to the memorandum.

Copies of the September memorandum were sent to Kenneth Bradshaw, David Pring and Robert Rhodes James of the Department of the Clerk of the House; to David Holland and Dr David Menhennet of the Department of the Speaker (Library); and to Professor Max Beloff, Norman Chester, Professor John Griffith, Professor Harry Hanson, Professor William J. M. Mackenzie, Dr Peter Richards, Professor William Robson and Professor Victor Wiseman.

Most of these attended the first meeting on 2nd October 1964 at the London School of Economics and constituted themselves the Study of Parliament Group – and invited a number of academics (including Peter Bromhead, Bernard Donoughue, Norman Hunt, Nevil Johnson and Geoffrey Marshall) to join them.

Since that founding meeting the Group has produced, through a variety of study groups, a number of authoritative studies of the workings of Parliament and has given evidence to a number of parliamentary committees. Details of its activities can be found on its web-site at http://www.spg.org.uk/index.htm. Publications are listed in the appendix at the end of this book.

This volume is a collection of essays by members of the Group who were asked to reflect critically on the workings of Parliament and, where appropriate, speculate about Parliament's future and how it might change. The exercise was originally led by Colin Seymour-Ure but he handed over the task of editorship to Philip Giddings in October 2003. Most of the essays were written around the time of the Group's Fortieth Anniversary in the autumn of 2004, though a few have been able to take account of developments since then. I am grateful to all the contributors for their efforts, and we all want to acknowledge the advice and assistance we have received from colleagues in the Group before and during the preparation of this volume. I am particularly grateful to Colin Seymour-Ure for preparing the index and to Simon Patrick for producing the list of publications.

The volume is divided into eight parts. We begin with the views of two of the Group's founder members on changes in parliamentary work and practices over the past forty years and on Parliament's future. We then look at the ways in which the membership and culture of Parliament have also changed and at the challenge to adapt to continuing change in society. Much is made of Parliament's scrutiny role and that forms the basis of the third group of essays, examining different ways in which that role has developed and might continue to develop. The fourth group of essays considers different aspects of Parliament's legislative role in the light of pressure for reform. That is followed by a pair of essays examining the constitutional and legal context in which Parliament now has to operate, particularly with regard to protecting the citizen from abuse of power. The next two groups of essays look at the wider world both within (devolution) and beyond these shores (war, and the European Union) and in terms of the need to adapt to the new world of global and accessible media. The chapters have been written to a common theme – the issues facing Parliament in a new century – but not to a common agenda, so that the authors themselves have been, to use a medical analogy, free to diagnose as well as to prescribe. The result is a combination of informed reflection on Parliament's recent past with realistic insights into the challenges the first quarter of the twenty-first century will bring.

The founding fathers of the SPG who gathered in 1964 saw the long term purpose of the Group to be to study and to stimulate studies of Parliament and to open up thinking on reform. This volume of essays is written in that tradition and dedicated to that objective.

Philip Giddings

Part I
Prospects for Change

1

Forty Years On and a Future Agenda

Michael Ryle

Thinking about another parliament

Imagine the parliament of another country whose function is mainly restricted to debate of government business. Members have little formal contact with the public; there is no broadcasting or televising of proceedings (the Government has restricted radio or television coverage of debates); and the media pay little attention to its work.

The Members are poorly rewarded, with no pension rights and few allowances to cover working expenses. Few ordinary Members have an office, and very few have personal secretaries, so they have to write their letters in longhand. They have no research assistants and the Library research services are minimal. There are no computers, fax or photo-copying machines.

Debate of Government bills is often lengthy and detailed but few changes of any importance are made. Members from both sides can criticise the policies and administration of government in debate, but parliamentary Questions are mainly limited to constituency concerns. There are few opportunities for backbenchers to hold Ministers to account. Select committees are not allowed to consider government policy; do not receive evidence from Ministers; are not allowed to travel overseas and make few outside visits. They cannot employ specialist advisers. All their evidence is heard in private and their reports make little impact.

Some notable figures in this parliament have played major parts in the country's history and speak with authority, but most of its Members

---

[Note: This contribution relates almost exclusively to the House of Commons, although the term 'Parliament' is often used in its popular sense]

are loyal party supporters who are not politically ambitious, speak seldom, and ask few Questions. For many of them, service in parliament is a part-time occupation. Their main political function is to support their party and dissent is rare. In general, this parliament has a long historical tradition and is generally respected. At times of international crisis its voice is heard and heeded, but for much of the time it has, as an institution, little direct influence on the conduct of public affairs.

The parliament thus crudely described is, of course, the House of Commons as it was at the time I went to work there in 1951. It is against that background that, in this chapter, I examine the claim that Parliament is in decline today, with less independence, influence and relevance than it once possessed. My argument is that simple factual comparison with the 1950s and early 1960s shows that Parliament – particularly the House of Commons – plays a more active, independent, and influential role in Britain today than at any time for many years. Important reforms are still needed, but the major advances in the past fifty years should not be derided.

The creation of the study of parliament group

By the end of the 1950s there was a growing awareness that reform was needed which was expressed most convincingly by Bernard Crick in his seminal work, *The Reform of Parliament*, published in 1964. Spurred on by expectations of parliamentary reform if Labour came to power, Bernard and I, with a few like-minded colleagues, founded the Study of Parliament Group with a small membership of university academics and parliamentary officials. Today the total membership is over 140. This book celebrates the Fortieth Anniversary of the Group.

From the beginning the Group had a dual purpose: to strengthen the study of Parliament for the purposes of research and teaching and to provide a forum for advocating parliamentary reform. The Group began this latter work by preparing evidence to the Commons Procedure Committee that was set up in December 1964. The main recommendations dealt with legislation (detailed discussion should mainly be in committees); financial control (with annual reviews of expenditure priorities); scrutiny of policy and administration (appointment of an Ombudsman); specialist advisory committees covering the whole field of Government; and improved research and information for MPs (improved services in the Library of the House).

Looking back, the Group's evidence in 1965 looks strangely unadventurous and little progress was made at first, particularly on legislative scrutiny and proper examination of expenditure plans and priorities. On the other hand the Group's proposals for specialised advisory committees have been implemented by the present departmental select committees with wide remits and more effective powers. Finally, strengthening of the Library research services has gone far further than the Group envisaged in 1965.

Since its inception, the Group has regularly given evidence to parliamentary committees and has pressed for reform in numerous publications. Others have taken up the cudgels. Reform-minded bodies (especially the Hansard Society, the Constitution Unit and certain Conservative and Liberal Democrat working groups) have long campaigned for a more effective and influential parliament. And in recent years the Procedure Committee and, more recently, the Modernisation Committee have become increasingly involved. Individual MPs, academics and journalists have played their part. So the original initiative of the Group, before parliamentary reform became a popular cause, helped to set in train a much broader movement.

The changing Commons

Comparative studies show clearly that Parliament as an institution has changed enormously over the past fifty years. But how significant has this been? Accepting the premise that Parliament does not govern but is the forum for public debate and criticism of the policies and acts of government (as the SPG has always argued), the changes in Parliament should be assessed by their success in providing such a forum and in exercising such criticism.

Effective criticism by Parliament requires three things: adequate opportunities for the participants on both sides of the House to initiate debate on matters of their own choosing; appropriate procedures for different types of business; and access to relevant information.

Over the past fifty years, although the share of opportunities between the Government and the Opposition has changed little, and backbenchers have lost some opportunities on the floor of the House, there has recently been a very significant increase in the debating opportunities available for backbenchers off the floor of the House. Since 1997 meetings in Westminster Hall have provided a new forum for debates on select committee reports and extra adjournment debates.

Turning to procedures, the legislative process is in a state of flux with many changes being proposed (as shown elsewhere in this publication), but the standard debating procedures are – so far – largely unaltered.

Elsewhere there have been major developments. Much the most important change in the Commons procedures has been the extension of select committee inquiry into non-legislative business. In 1979 new departmental committees were appointed, with powers to consider policy, administration and expenditure, to meet in public, and to take evidence from Ministers. Their activities, volume of work and significance have continued to grow. As a result, backbench Members are bringing more – and more important – issues before Parliament. The committees are increasingly willing to raise matters which Ministers would prefer to leave fallow, and to agree to reports which are unwelcome to Ministers. All of this enhances the accountability of Ministers for the conduct of their office.

Parliamentary Questions are an important part of the critical process. The basic procedures have changed little, but there has been a great growth in the number of written questions asking for information, a big shift toward policy Questions to most Ministers, and a major change in the nature of Prime Minister's Question time. In the 1950s, Questions to the PM were frequently not called as time ran out, and supplementary Questions were often not asked at all. By contrast, Prime Minister's Questions today provide a big political occasion for half an hour each Wednesday – highly adversarial, and frequently rowdy – when MPs, especially the Leader of the Opposition, can call the Government to account on what they see as the major issues of the day.

The third requirement for effective criticism is access to accurate information. Here again significant progress has been made since the 1950s. MPs still learn from numerous public sources – not least the proceedings of Parliament itself – but these are now further enriched by briefing by interest groups, research assistants and greatly expanded research and information services in the House of Commons Library. The widespread development of information technology has also opened up sources of information and helped its speedy dissemination (computers, mobiles and pagers were not conspicuous fifty years ago!).

The nature and ways of work of MPs is another crucial factor in the process of change. Members today benefit from improved working conditions with better salaries, pensions and accommodation. The impressive Portcullis House is the most striking demonstration to the wider public of the changing nature of the House of Commons. In addition, in contrast with the Commons in the 1950s, many MPs today come from jobs where words were the tools of their trade – lawyers, teachers, PR men, journalists, advisers, etc. – and Parliament is a natural habitat for such people; they relish it and they are increasingly active. Being an MP is certainly no longer a part time job; many work very long hours.

However with this has come growing concern about extra-parliamentary relationships which are potentially financially beneficial and not related to MPs' parliamentary responsibilities ('sleaze'). These fears (sometimes sadly realised) have led to more severe procedures for investigation of charges that a Member has failed to declare an interest or has behaved improperly in some way.

Parliament, however, must be outward looking. To be fully effective it must both listen to and speak to the public, and be seen to do so. Again there have been major changes. Business in both Houses and their committees is now sound-broadcast and televised. The Library makes parliamentary publications available to the public on the internet. The Public Information Office publishes other material about the House and answers queries from the public. There is an Education Office to help schools and colleges. Working papers have been made more readily available to the public; and notes on clauses of bills are used to clarify their meaning. And above all, the public now submits voluminous evidence to select committees and can present its case orally, and the committees' responses are all published. It is a two-way process.

Sadly, threats to the security of the Palace of Westminster and its inhabitants are growing, but despite very necessary restrictions, it is still relatively easy for citizens to contact MPs at Westminster, to tour the building and to see their Members at work. Recent proposals by the Modernisation Committee aim to make the Commons more 'user-friendly' and the daily throng of visitors remains a striking tribute to Parliament as a living organ of our democracy.

Finally, the life and achievements of Parliament are conditioned by its workload. The volume and range of Government business for which Ministers are accountable has increased steadily throughout the last hundred years, and this involves more legislation, Questions, debate and select committee scrutiny. Parliamentary diligence increases the load still further. The more MPs look critically at the actions of Ministers, the more time is needed to do this. So the net workload of Parliament tends to grow and grow, as has been the pattern over the past fifty years. The demand for more effective parliamentary scrutiny must take account of the additional work and resources required to secure it.

What does it all add up to?

Today there is a constant stream of denigration of Parliament (particularly the Commons), largely orchestrated by the press. This (surprise,

surprise!) results in low respect for Parliament by the public at large as revealed by public opinion polls. The press then say we told you so, which is quite right, they *have* told us so and the general public, with very little real knowledge or understanding of the functions, practice and procedures of Parliament, has believed them. The myth has thus been created that Parliament is in decline and is less effective than it used to be. This is now often stated by journalists – and by some academic writers who should know better – as if it were an accepted and established fact.

The truth, I am firmly convinced, is exactly the opposite. Judged by the way Parliament actually works – the opportunities it gives Members to carry out their critical scrutiny role, the procedures which are now available for these purposes, the amount of work it undertakes, and its contacts with the wider public – as opposed to the way it is portrayed by those who ignore the historic facts, Parliament today is, in my view, more active, more effective and much more significant in the politics of this country than ever before – or at least for a very long time. Some of the facts on which this argument is based are set out in this collection of essays and also, in great detail, in *Parliament: Functions, Practice and Procedures* which Professor John Griffith and I wrote fifteen years ago and of which a second edition was published in 2003.[1] My overall judgement, expressed very personally in this chapter, is also based on my own direct experience, when working for nearly forty years in the House of Commons.

Apart from press bias, I suspect that the main reasons for low respect for Parliament are two. First very few people really appreciate the central function of Parliament as a critical forum, not a governing institution; Parliament does not govern and is therefore wrongly blamed for bad government. Second, paradoxically, the very success of the Commons in improving its effectiveness, and the growing influence of backbenchers, have made the public more aware of some undoubted failures and defects in parliamentary practice and behaviour. These long-standing weaknesses were not commonly criticised fifty years ago precisely because Parliament was so boring and ineffective that the public took little interest in it. No publicity is not always good publicity; more publicity also reveals the warts and blemishes.

What are the consequences of the changes that I have outlined? I begin with the role and influence of backbench MPs because they help to set the mood within which Governments must plan and act. Look at the reactions of Parliament to major international crises such as the war in Iraq, and the Falklands war. In domestic politics as well, dissent has often played a major part in moulding party and Government policy. Witness the influence of the Euro-sceptics on the evolution of Tory policy on Europe under Thatcher, Major and Hague. And consider the influence of Labour dissenters over a range of recent controversial policies including disability payments, foundation hospitals, top-up fees for university students (the latter almost fatal to the Government) and hunting. In each case the reactions of Government would have been considerably different if backbench opinion (support or dissent) had been different. No doubt there will be other examples by the time this book is published.

Perhaps the most remarkable evidence of the growing influence of backbench MPs – and thus of the House – has not been in the chamber but inside the parties. Margaret Thatcher's fall from office was essentially brought about by her own Members' growing concern over her policies (especially the poll-tax and the party rift on Europe) which led them to withdraw their full support when she most needed it. Similar concerns over policies and leadership style weakened backbench support for John Major, William Hague and Ian Duncan Smith and led to the selection of new Conservative leaders. *Pari passu*, the choice of successors to those party leaders was essentially made by the Conservative backbenchers. Similar influences were at work within the Labour Party, which affected the careers of Michael Foot, Neil Kinnock, Gordon Brown and Tony Blair. Not since 1940, and the fall of the Chamberlain Government, have ordinary Members of Parliament exercised such influence and power.

The expansion of third and other parties in the House and in the country has also broken the monolithic hold the leaders of the older parties had over their Members and has given encouragement to dissenting opinion by voters in the country. This has been shown particularly in by-elections and during the continuing arguments over the Iraq war and its outcome. In general, MPs on both sides are much more involved in policy formation than hitherto. This is also shown by the growing significance of select committees, which requires Ministers to heed parliamentary reactions to their policies over an ever-widening field.

Governments can no longer ignore parliamentary opinion. MPs must be heeded or the media will put the Government in the dock for being 'out of touch with the public'. The ability to damage or to improve Ministerial reputations also increases MPs' influence. And at all stages Ministerial accountability is being enforced. None of this is evidence of a Parliament in decline.

Looking ahead

Descriptions of the past and the present reveal an unfinished agenda. Much still needs to be done to restore the standing of Parliament and to augment its influence on public and political life. This is partly a political problem and centres on how Ministers, the Opposition and Members themselves behave in Parliament, treat the House and use their opportunities. But Parliament itself, as an institution, also has a part to play and responsibilities to fulfil. The House of Commons in particular should take itself and its practices more seriously, be sensitive to criticism and consider how to respond to reforms proposed by its own committees or outside bodies. Far too often, proposals for procedural reform have simply been ignored by the Government of the day.

Here, without going into detail, are some suggestions for further reform. First, the legislative process is still far from satisfactory. All bills should be considered by committees with powers to take evidence – and with less haste. This should be done within the framework of a two-year programme for most bills, worked out by an all-party body, as in many other parliaments. And the way delegated legislation is scrutinised is shameful. Reforms should be adopted to enable there to be proper debate, with votes if necessary, on all major statutory instruments.

A second major blemish is the failure to consider expenditure plans seriously. There should be full annual scrutiny, concluding with debates on the floor of the House, of the planned total and balance of expenditure, with emphasis on debate of priorities. Select committees should also report on the priorities of expenditure within the various sectors of government and on major individual investments and projects; the latter should be subject to specific approval in the Estimates.

Third, further thought should be given to the consideration of European legislation. This is of growing importance; at present the details of European legislation are examined seriously by various committees but largely ignored by the House – but are MPs willing to get involved?

Last, a general thought. With the growing pressure for debates on the floor of the House, should routine or less controversial business be taken in large committees, for example debates on regional matters and on more specialist issues? Questions to some Ministers could also be taken in committees. These are the sort of ideas to which the House and its Modernisation and Procedure Committees should give further thought.

Conclusion

Constructive criticism of Parliament and positive proposals for reform are still needed and the primary purpose of this collection of essays is to stimulate new thinking. However I summarise my own position thus: Parliament may not have great power over the executive – that is not its function under our constitution – but it does have increasing influence and could yet be more effective. However, if you still consider that Parliament is in decline, is of little effect and is of diminishing importance to the public, try telling that to Tony Blair.

Notes

1 J. A. Griffith and M. Ryle, *Parliament: Functions, Practice and Procedures*, Sweet & Maxwell, 1989. Second Edition, edited by Robert Blackburn and Andrew Kennon, 2003.

2
What of Parliament's Future?

Nevil Johnson

The cause of parliamentary reform was inspired by the hope of strengthening Parliament. But since it had to proceed within an institutional framework evolved through generations, it had perforce to draw extensively on prevailing practices and values. Most of the reformers too remained relatively conservative in their working assumptions, a position that has not changed much in recent years. There was little inclination in the reform movement to undertake radical reappraisal of basic political relationships in Parliament. Yet the very moderation shown by reformers may help to explain why parliamentary reform has failed to capture the popular imagination and thus help sustain confidence in parliamentary government itself.

First amongst the assumptions on which reformers proceeded was the belief that the House of Commons would continue to discharge its functions within a predominantly adversarial, two-party framework. This had major consequences for the kind of structural changes that can be contemplated. Second, and largely as a consequence of the first point, it was accepted that the passage of legislation must remain within the full control of the Government of the day, so long as it has a majority. Third, it has been almost universally assumed that the key function of Parliament is to call governments to account through the application of scrutiny procedures. And this has been taken in both Houses to require the development and expansion of select committee activity. Fourth, it is generally agreed that the House of Lords should act as a revising chamber where some of the deficiencies in the House of Commons' handling of legislation can be made good. But because it remains uncertain what this revising function really adds up to, it is difficult to reappraise the wide range of powers still formally vested in the Lords. This in turn supports the contention that the chamber's composition must remain based chiefly, if not solely, on appointment (and for life). It has been underlying assumptions of this sort that have usually set the parameters within which parliamentary reform has taken place.

Calling government to account

I turn now to a matter that has been at the heart of parliamentary reform endeavours all along – the business of scrutiny and calling the Government to account. It was argued back in the early 1960s that through the extension of select committee scrutiny Parliament could be strengthened and to some extent at least the imbalance between Parliament and the executive redressed.[1] After some hesitant steps taken in the later 1960s a decisive move towards widening the ambit of scrutiny was taken in the Commons in 1979 when Mrs Thatcher's Government took the initiative by agreeing to a more or less full range of departmental scrutiny committees. This represented a big increase in the range of scrutiny. In addition the terms of reference of the departmental select committees were widened to permit them to raise policy issues rather than remain confined to the administration of policy and the proper expenditure of funds. This pattern has survived, with the number and remits of the committees varying according to the prevailing pattern of departments. In addition further select committees have been charged with looking after activities and functions which cut across or lie outside the boundaries of departments, for example draft legislation emanating from the European Union, issues affecting the public services generally, regulatory reform, and science and technology. Indeed, the 2003 edition of Standing Orders of the House of Commons listed 33 committees,[2] the chairmen of which had a seat on the Liaison Committee of the House. There has been an extension of scrutiny in the House of Lords too, though on a much more modest scale and not related specifically to departments.

In quantity scrutiny yields an immense amount of paper – reports, evidence oral and written, minutes of proceedings, responses of ministers, even draft bills on occasion.[3] But if we ask questions about the quality of these scrutinising activities and their impact, it is very difficult to offer satisfactory answers.[4] The performance of select committees, especially in the Commons, varies according to time and circumstances, the type of topic taken up and investigated, the style and attitude of chairmen, the general quality of the membership, the amount of time spent on each inquiry, and the degree of public and

media interest in the matters under review. The readiness of departments to provide evidence and useful material as well as the experience
and skills of the clerks and special advisers supporting select committees have also to be brought into the equation.[5] In the face of so many
variables it is dangerous to generalise about select committees and their
impact. Perhaps the only safe generalisation about their work is that
their efforts sustain across the board a critical and probing environment within which ministers and officials know they have to operate.
But this falls well short of exerting effective political influence over
major decisions.

The familiar rationale for engaging so many parliamentarians in the
scrutiny function is that it ensures accountability in government. But it
also expresses another rationale that is less often advertised. An adversarial political system leaves many members of both Houses, and particularly of the Commons, without well-defined functions or career
prospects. The shift from part-time to professional full-time politics has
intensified the demand for useful and promising roles within the
parliamentary framework. For some on the Government side there is,
of course, the chance of ministerial office, whilst for a relatively small
number from the opposition parties there may be a front bench
'shadow' role that can be both difficult and frustrating. But for most of
those with few outside professional commitments – and this applied
particularly to many Labour Members after 1997 – work on select committees has offered the best prospect of being kept reasonably busy
until something better comes along. Thus the tendency to expand
committee scrutiny, including to a modest extent joint committees of
both Houses,[6] reflects the fact that this may be the best way of offering
job satisfaction to many Members whilst also allowing them to inform
themselves about what is going on in government.

The interest of professional politicians in securing publicity has also
propelled many select committees – and again chiefly in the Commons
– towards a focus on matters of current political concern. This often
means shorter and more frequent reports, presented by the chairman
at a press conference in the hope of gaining some publicity for them.
But a price has to be paid for turning more readily to current 'political'
topics. Since they are often controversial it becomes harder to secure
agreement within a committee, open dissent in the body of a report
does not inspire confidence, and any way if a minister knows that
a topic has been taken up so that political axes can be ground, he or
she is unlikely to be impressed by the outcome. So the more political –
and partisan – scrutiny becomes, the less influential it is likely to be.

Scrutiny committees in the House of Lords, for example the Select Committee on the European Union and its sub-committees or the Select Committee on Science and Technology, retain a more austerely investigatory style which often secures respect for their reports, even though they too may well have little discernible impact on executive decisions.

Alongside the expansion of select committee scrutiny as a method of calling ministers and officials to account, there have also been other extensions of the opportunities available for backbenchers to seek to reinforce accountability. Adjournment debates still take place regularly, the presentation of Questions, oral and written, remains popular, though except on Wednesdays when the Prime Minister appears attendance tends to be small, and morning debates for backbenchers now take place in Westminster Hall under flexible rules intended to encourage a more consensual atmosphere. All of this continues to impose a substantial burden on the executive whenever Parliament is sitting. But the survival of so many opportunities for backbenchers to question what the Government is doing has to be seen in conjunction with a steady shift towards what might be called procedural rationalisation, a process carried forward by the Modernisation Committee set up in 1997. Procedural rationalisation is not always directed to accountability and the control of the Government, but may also reflect the desire of the executive to get its business through as expeditiously as possible, in particular its legislative programme. The most recent changes made as a result of proposals originating in the Modernisation Committee point on the whole in this direction. The more extensive programming of legislative bills, sensible though this may sound, tends to relax the already modest constraints affecting the progress of Government measures. It is perhaps ironic that in comparison the House of Lords remains procedurally better placed to challenge and question Government proposals than the Commons. And even the rationalisation of Commons sitting times and the move away from going on into the night does not necessarily strengthen Members in their efforts to supervise the executive.

Whilst in recent years there has been a large expansion of accountability processes, especially through the development of select committee scrutiny, far less change has occurred in the way legislation is dealt with. The use of non-specialised small standing committees to take care of the detailed examination and amendment of bills was already well established in the Commons over fifty years ago, and in essentials survives to this day. As these procedures are subject to the rigours of party discipline and shortage of time the outcome is a very inadequate process of legislative scrutiny. Indeed, so defective has the treatment of legislation in the Commons become, that the case for a second chamber is now often based simply on the need to have a place that makes good the deficiencies of the elected House. Hesitant steps have been taken recently to devise methods of meeting this problem, notably through the provision for a bill to be referred to a select committee for study of at least specified parts of it, and for pre-legislative scrutiny of draft bills, also by select committee. Sometimes this procedure may involve reference to a joint pre-legislative committee. But the use made of such methods remains modest and anyway depends on Government agreement. Thus it remains true that apart from the small amount of private Member legislation that still comes forward, law-making in Britain is now almost entirely an executive activity. The parliamentary input to it is strictly limited, and even in the case of the House of Lords many of the numerous amendments passed are in reality the second thoughts of the Government.

The explanation for this state of affairs lies partly in parliamentary procedures, but also in more deep-seated political attitudes. The Commons has always been interested far more in the 'principles' of bills (shorthand for matters about which it is possible to have a noisy debate) than in the practical details of statutory provisions. This is why there is still so much emphasis on second reading debates. There is too the relative shortage of legal knowledge and experience in the chamber as well as the highly technical character of modern legislative drafting.[7] Thus there is hardly a basis for coming to grips with the detailed terms of legislation as happens in some legislatures elsewhere. Parliamentary revolts still occasionally occur – over shop hours under Mrs Thatcher, on university tuition fees under Mr Blair in early 2004. But as the second of these shows, even rebels are generally ready to agree that law-making is really a matter for the Government and to leave the details of schemes of regulation and their implementation to ministers and officials.[8]

Different perceptions of what reform can achieve

In relation to both accountability and law-making there has been substantial procedural change and adaptation. Yet there has also been continuity with pre-existing parliamentary practices and assumptions, and this has worked alongside concrete party interests to dilute the qualitative effects on Parliament of many of the reforms. What might be called the moderate mainstream in the parliamentary reform movement, including many practitioners in politics or in the service of Parliament, has generally been ready to travel hopefully, trusting that piecemeal procedural improvements will eventually ensure that Parliament emerges strengthened in relation to the executive. For the most part too such reformers have accepted traditional ideas about the rationale of Parliament, and in particular its duty to enforce accountability, whilst also often sharing the contemporary faith in the benefits to be gained from re-jigging institutions and 'getting the structures right'. But another, more sceptical view has always co-existed with and within the reform movement. Although rarely firmly opposed to procedural improvements, it has doubted whether in the British political context such reform can ever have the far-reaching impact hoped for by the more enthusiastic reformers. Above all the sceptical voice has noted that most reforms come at a price: more time for one particular activity is likely to mean less for something else. Enthusiastic parliamentary reformers have sometimes forgotten there must be finite limits to what members of both Houses can do and are prepared even to try to do.

Underlying these contrasting judgements on parliamentary reform are different assumptions about the character of parties and political activity generally. If it is assumed, even *sotto voce*, that Britain will retain a predominantly two-party adversarial system, this sets strict limits to what kind of change parliamentary reform can bring about. Indeed, on this basis it might be reasonable to conclude that parliamentary reform has now more or less exhausted the possibilities of useful change within the limits of the present institutions and partisan politics. But for those who hope that one day Parliament will be restored to some kind of golden age when it supposedly held governments on a short leash and often had the last word, the target of reformers should not be parliamentary procedure but parties, the terms on which they operate, and the conditions under which they seek support from the electorate. For only in an elected chamber constituted differently from the present-day Commons would it be likely (though not certain) that political conditions would change sufficiently to open the way to a different relationship between Parliament and the Government. About the merits of such a transformation opinions would, of course, diverge.

Future prospects

So what are the future prospects for Parliament? This question must be considered in the context of the range and diversity of the challenges facing Parliament and parliamentary government. Parliament is no longer unique, set on a lofty pedestal above all other sources of authority. It co-exists with numerous institutions public and private that are in some degree its rivals, and some of which have recently been given functions, for example the courts in relation to the 'redress of grievances', traditionally reserved for Parliament. There is the ever growing impact of professionalised politics on both the kind of people coming into Parliament and their relationships with their parties and leaders. There is the overwhelming presence of the media in all their forms and the power they have to shape public perceptions of political life and the priorities of publicity-hungry politicians. Alongside the conventional media there is the huge growth in methods of electronic communication now open to virtually everyone and on which the functioning of a large part of the economy and the social infrastructure has come to depend.

Social and technical change has indeed become so extensive and pervasive that much of the familiar terminology used to describe and characterise British institutions begins to sound obsolete. There is a constant call for 'debate' on all kinds of issues on which governments apparently seek guidance about what to do. But we must ask what 'debate' can mean nowadays: almost certainly not what still passes for debate in both Houses of Parliament. Indeed, the inability of many Members of Parliament to play an effective part in debate and the embarrassingly low levels of attendance put a question mark over the justification for allocating so much parliamentary time to debate. What is the point if so few want to take part in these rituals?

In what sense can parliamentarians now claim to be 'representatives'? Nearly all accept party discipline and hold themselves mandated to fulfil a party manifesto. Does this mean that they just 'represent' their party or is there still something else that they can claim to represent? Moreover, at some levels of elected representation such as the Scottish Parliament, Welsh Assembly and European Parliament many of those elected no longer have geographical constituencies. So do they too just represent their party or can they claim to represent? And what about accountability and its close relation, responsibility something else? If current methods of seeking to enforce accountability apparently have such modest effects in terms of modifying or checking what Governments do, might it not be necessary to look critically at the priority accorded to accountability and to consider whether there could be other more effective ways of controlling executive action?

And then there is the people – the voters, the stakeholders, the customers, those whose right to choose is nearly always lauded by politicians, except perhaps when their own powers and discretion are at issue. For Parliament direct consultation of the people is a two-edged sword: it acknowledges the ultimate source of the authority claimed by Parliament, yet it also threatens to subvert traditional ideas of representative government by introducing a decision-maker against whose judgement there can be no appeal. And if the *demos* – the people – can be brought in directly and given the last word for some purposes, what justification can there be for retaining a chamber of Parliament whose members are all appointed for life? Might it not be more defensible even to choose them by lot?

There can be no doubt that the environment in which Parliament now has to operate makes it increasingly difficult to see the institution as the fulcrum of political life and government. The ideal of parliamentary government offered by classical liberal theorists like J. S. Mill in the middle of the nineteenth century no longer looks realistic. Even if we start from the origins of the word 'Parliament', a place where the members speak, and by extension parliamentary government as a method of governing through talk and debate, it is clear that the boundaries within which political talk and decision-making now occur are so different from what was envisaged in the past that it becomes difficult even to locate Parliament on something like a map of political talk and argument. In late 2003 the Prime Minister urged people to engage in what he called a 'Big Conversation', a process all too obviously designed to help politicians to get their ideas across to the public. That such exercises were held to be capable of making a useful contribution to rekindling trust as between politicians and the people is a sad commentary on the state of parliamentary government. The danger threatening Parliament is that it is now disconnected in what it is doing and saying both from vital social forces and interests in the society, and from the conditions in which the bulk of people live, earn a living, and help to keep the economy moving and growing.

In the light of such conditions it seems likely that parliamentary reform such as has been pressed forward for the past forty years or so has reached its limits. The challenge is not so much to change the balance of power between the Government and Parliament by yet more effort to reform procedures. We know that within current political parameters that has little prospect of working. Instead the challenge must be to think very hard about what Parliament can do, and what it cannot do, in present conditions. This means standing back from the preoccupations of politicians and officials who work the system as it now is in order to focus instead on ways of embodying the underlying commitment to democratic government by consent in practices that society at large might understand and recognise as meeting some of its political needs.

Uncomfortable questions

No attempt will be made here to offer plans for the future shape of parliamentary institutions whether at the centre in Westminster or elsewhere in the United Kingdom. Instead it might be a more encouraging way forward to ask a range of questions about the limits affecting Parliament in the contemporary political context, including questions about what it need not do. What would be the implications of having a smaller membership in the House of Commons? Does the Commons or indeed the Lords as well need to sit in plenary session so long and so often? Are there not other politically useful activities in which the Members could be engaged, and not all of them at Westminster? Are select committees adequately equipped for an effective and penetrating scrutiny of executive activity? Could they not usefully employ something like expert counsel (not necessarily lawyers) to interrogate on their behalf? Is it really desirable or necessary to have so many ministerial officeholders? Could not officials discharge some of the functions presently reserved for the most part to political appointees, many of whom are ill-prepared for the managerial functions to which they often lay claim? And if the House of Lords is not to contain any elected element at all, on what conditions might it have a chance of enduring for say the next thirty years as an appointed body? Might not this require a reappraisal of what is meant by the revising function as well as of the very notion of part-time legislators retired from active professional life?

Difficult and uncomfortable questions of this sort impose themselves as a result of the pressures generated by a rapidly changing society linked indissolubly to a dynamic world economy. There are clear signs that confidence in traditional political methods and in the dominant class of political entrepreneurs through whom Britain is governed has diminished and is unlikely to be restored by mere palliatives. Nor is Britain alone in facing such challenges: they appear in varying degrees in many countries of Europe, and beyond. At the heart of the contemporary challenge is the need to find methods of reintegrating people who have become little more than occasional spectators of politics into institutional arrangements that secure their interest, support and active engagement. This almost certainly means acceptance of a far more loosely structured and dispersed pattern of government and politics than exists at present. There would almost certainly be a price to be paid for that, perhaps in terms of diminished cost-effectiveness, and certainly in acceptance of a wider range of inequalities in society. Inevitably too in a much more diffused polity no single central institution could expect to play such a paramount part as has been attributed to Parliament for so long. That in turn would call for yet another retreat from the sovereignty doctrine that is still widely held to underpin the claims made by the lower house of Parliament. But if that doctrine were to be substantively modified or even abandoned, then many might conclude that the time had come to give acceptance of a written constitution – a new Instrument of Government – precedence over a seemingly never-ending effort to reform Parliament.

Notes

1 See Bernard Crick, co-founder of the Study of Parliament Group, in *The Reform of Parliament*, Weidenfeld & Nicolson, 1964.
2 *Standing Orders of the House of Commons*, HMSO, January 2003. With the subsequent creation of another departmental select committee, Constitutional Affairs, the number of departmental select committees rose to 18.
3 See *Parliament: Functions, Practice and Procedure*, 2nd edition, R. Blackburn & A. Kennon, Sweet & Maxwell 2003, p. 599.
4 For an early review of the post-1979 select committees see G. Drewry (ed.), *The New Select Committees: A Study of the 1979 Reforms*, OUP for the Study of Parliament Group, 1985.
5 The principles to be observed by civil servants when giving evidence were set out in the Osmotherly rules in 1980. They make it clear that civil servants appear before committees as the agents of ministers, not in their own right.
6 There are, for example, Joint Committees on Statutory Instruments (1973), on Human Rights (2001) and on Reform of the House of Lords (2002). In addition there have been several joint committees on bills, for example on Gambling and Mental Health (2004).
7 The very extensive use made in nearly all modern legislation of provisions for the passage of statutory instruments reflects both the impulse to retain the maximum degree of ministerial discretion over implementation, and the fact that it is not unusual for legislative proposals to be put forward and even passed before the minister and department concerned actually know what the delegated powers will provide for.
8 e.g. the Higher Education Bill 2004, though bitterly opposed by many Government supporters as well as by both opposition parties, completed its committee stage unscathed and unamended. Members had made a lot of noise about certain policy matters but, having received a range of promises intended to meet some of their complaints, left the actual content of the legislation entirely to the executive.

Part II

A Changing Parliament?

Does it matter how representative Parliament is? Does it matter what parliamentarians do? The socio-economic make-up of Parliament, the extent to which it has been professionalised, changes in behaviour and participation, and what MPs think about their role are crucial in seeking answers to such questions. There are no definitive answers but these matters are essential to seeking them, as we shall see in the chapters which follow.

3

The Make-Up of Parliament

*Byron Criddle (Part One), Sarah Childs (Part Two) and Philip
Norton (Part Three)*

Part One: The House of Commons

MPs have long been perceived as middle class, middle aged, male
and white and most Members of Parliaments elected between 1951 and
2001 conformed to this pattern, though subject to three significant
provisos. First, the term 'middle class' is an arbitrary expression extending from high status professionals to public sector teachers and local
government officials and from privately-schooled 'Oxbridge' graduates
to the state-educated products of post-war universities and poly-
technics. A second proviso concerns the greater diversity of Labour
MPs reflected in a significant, if latterly declining, minority drawn
from the ranks of manual workers. Thirdly, by the end of the century,
another significant minority of Labour MPs was female.

Table 3.1, drawn from the Nuffield election studies, compares
Conservative and Labour MPs by occupation, education, sex, race and
age in 1951 and 2001. The first three occupational categories constitute the 'middle class' upon which the Conservative Party has been
almost exclusively reliant for its MPs and in proportions virtually
unchanged from mid-century to end-of-century. But in each of the
three categories there were perceptible changes. Among the professions there was a retreat of the Bar and of military service. At mid-
century 19% of Conservative MPs were barristers, but by 2001 only
11%. As the barristers retreated, in the 1980s, so the proportion of
solicitors rose, from 3% in 1951 to 8% in 2001. Officers in the armed
forces provided one in ten Conservative MPs at mid-century, but only
one in twenty by the elections of the 1980s and 1990s. A professional
category rising slightly over the period was that of teachers (including
lecturers) which doubled, albeit from the very low base of 2% in 1951

Table 3.1   The socio-economic backgrounds of MPs, 1951 and 2001 (%)

	Conservative		Labour	
	1951	*2001*	*1951*	*2001*
Occupation				
Professions	41	39	35	43
Business	37	36	9	8
Miscellaneous	22	25	19	36
Workers	0	1	37	12
Education				
Public school (Eton)	75 (25)	64 (8)	21 (1)	17 (1)
University (Oxbridge)	65 (52)	83 (47)	41 (19)	67 (16)
Women	2	8	4	23
Non-white	0	0	0	3
Median age	47	48	52	50

to 4% in 2001, though it had been as high as 7% in 1987. In the business category there was a trend away from captains of industry to business executives and the self-employed, but no overall diminution in the proportion of Conservative MPs with experience of the commercial world. In the miscellaneous category there was a doubling of the percentage of journalists to 8% and a reduction of farmers from one-in-ten at mid-century to under one-in-thirty by 2001. By the end of the period the party retained its mid-century ethos comprising businessmen and business-related professionals.

The position in the Parliamentary Labour Party was much less stable. The Party's distinct contribution had been to introduce working men into the political elite. In 1951 manual workers comprised 37% of the PLP. Between 1951 and 1987 manual workers averaged 32% of Labour MPs, but thereafter the proportion dropped steeply to 22% in 1992, 13% in 1997, and 12% in 2001. With the retreat of manual workers came the 'white collarisation' of the PLP, but it was a process that still left Labour uniquely reliant for over half the 2001 PLP on MPs drawn from families of working class origin, compared with 6% of Conservatives and 20% of Liberal Democrats.[1] Social mobility had taken these sons and daughters of manual workers into the public sector professions – teaching (24% in 2001, 14% in 1951), local government administration, social work, and politics-related occupations of union official, full-time councillor, party staffer and political adviser –

together comprising the swelling category of 'professional politician', and certain to expand in the years ahead. By 2001 in both parties one-in-ten MPs was classifiable as such, though numerically this accounted for many more Labour MPs. But the basic distinction between the two parties was the divide between public and private sectors, with as few Labour MPs drawn from business backgrounds in 2001 (8%) as in 1951 (9%), a contrast revealed even more starkly in educational backgrounds. Conservative MPs traditionally have been educated at private schools, originally of the most exclusive kind. In 1951 24% of Conservative MPs were Old Etonians; by 2001 Etonians comprised only 8%. Yet when the party was pushed back into its safest seats (as in 1945) in 1997 and 2001, the proportion did not, as one might have expected, rise. The demise of the Etonian Conservative MP reflects a move away from the grander public schools in general and towards the minor ones, a move from older to newer money. It marks too a retreat of the upper middle class from political careers now more arduous because full-time, lower in status and less well paid than in much of the private sector. However, the relative decline of the major public schools as nurseries of the Conservative elite has not destroyed the contrast with the Labour Party: two-thirds of Conservative MPs in 2001 had attended public schools, down from three-quarters in 1951, compared with Labour's limited reliance on private schooling – 17% in 2001, 21% in 1951.

In both parties increased proportions of MPs have attended universities: 83% of Conservatives in 2001, 65% in 1951; in Labour's case, 67% in place of 41%. However, significantly higher proportions of Conservatives are 'Oxbridge' graduates: 47% in 2001, 52% in 1951, compared with 16% for Labour in 2001 and 19% in 1951. In both parties the proportion of all graduates who had attended Oxford or Cambridge has declined, from 80% to 56% for the Conservatives, and from 50% to 24% for Labour, reflecting the post-war expansion of the university system. But further evidence of the retreat of the upper middle class Conservative MP is in the decline of Conservatives with the elitist 'public school and Oxbridge' pedigree: in 1951 49% shared this distinction, by 2001 39%. Labour's expanded graduate base rested more on the provision of free secondary and university education from the 1940s and the social mobility it offered to children of working class parents.

Few women were elected to the House of Commons before the elections of the 1990s. In 1951 of seventeen women MPs, eleven were Labour and six Conservatives. The 5% barrier was not surmounted until 1987, but rose to 9% in 1992 following Labour's mandatory shortlisting of women. The use of all-women shortlists by Labour after 1992 and the landslide of 1997 doubled the number of women MPs. By 2001 the 23% of the PLP who were women (compared with 8% of Conservative MPs), though well short of the parity figure sought by campaigners, was close to the 28% comprised by women of the party's list of approved candidates: the electoral outcome was thus approximately matching the available supply.

Since the election of three Asian MPs, two (one Liberal, one Conservative) in the last decades of the nineteenth century, and one (Labour, subsequently elected as a Communist) in the 1920s, no nonwhite MP was elected until 1987, when four (all Labour) were returned. The total rose to six in 1992 (one of whom Conservative), eight in 1997 and twelve in 2001 – all Labour. With only 5.5% of the population registered as non-white in the 1991 Census, pressure for all-black shortlists was resisted rather more easily than calls for all-women shortlists. Selections of non-white candidates were inevitably confined to constituencies with high concentrations of non-white voters, accounting for eight of Labour's twelve non-white MPs in 2001. To augment numbers of non-white MPs would require the retirement of white incumbents in non-white constituencies, abatement of conflicts in such areas between rival ethnic groups, and the selection of non-white candidates in Conservative-held seats. As it was, in 2001 Labour's 3% of non-white MPs poorly reflected the 11% of non-white candidates on its approved list, confirming that supply far outstripped demand. Nevertheless, as with the number of women MPs, the contrast between the two parties was obvious.

The median age of Conservative and Labour MPs varied little across the half century. Few MPs reached Westminster in their twenties; many in their early forties, increasingly after experience in local politics for Labour and the accumulation of financial assets and the contest of a hopeless seat for Conservatives.

Liberal Democrat MPs have not been included in Table 3.1 because of very low totals of (Liberal) MPs in the early part of the period. In 1951 six Liberal MPs were elected, and numbers remained below twenty until 1987. By 2001 there were 52, of whom 27 (52%) were in the professions, fourteen (27%) from business, ten (19%) in miscellaneous occupations, and one (2%) manual worker. University graduates numbered 36 (70%), of whom fourteen (25%) had attended Oxford or Cambridge; eighteen (35%) had attended public schools, of whom two Eton. These figures placed the party midway between the occupational and educational profiles of the two major parties. No women MPs were elected after 1951 until two under the Liberal-SDP Alliance in 1987; subsequently the totals were two in 1992, three in 1997, and five (10%) in 2001.

Members of Parliament are not a demographic cross-section of society, but does 'unrepresentativeness' matter? Arguably, a widespread perception of an unrepresentative House of Commons might undermine its legitimacy. However, the qualitative question of whether a more representative body would be a more effective one remains unanswered. Moreover, the fact that those seeking to become MPs – the so-called eligibles – are not a cross-section of society, precludes a more representative outcome. At the century's end Labour came closer to producing a relatively balanced range of MPs in terms of their occupation, education, sex and race, but the Conservatives, in an age of collapsed deference, have been slower to adjust.

Part Two: Women in the House

As Table 3.2 shows, three generations after the Parliament (Qualification of Women) Act 1918, the House of Commons remains overwhelmingly male. Though women now constitute 18% of MPs, the gains made are recent, significant relatively, less so absolutely. The great leap forward came in 1997: the numbers of women doubled overnight, from 60 to

Table 3.2 Women elected in general elections, 1945–2001

Year	Con	Lab	Lib	SNP	Others	Total	% MPs
1945	1	21	1	0	1	23	3.8
1950	6	14	1	0	0	21	3.4
1951	6	11	0	0	0	17	2.7
1955	10	14	0	0	0	24	3.8
1959	12	13	0	0	0	25	4.0
1964	11	18	0	0	0	29	4.6
1966	7	19	0	0	0	26	4.1
1970	15	10	0	0	1	26	4.1
1974F	9	13	0	1	0	23	3.6
1974O	7	18	0	2	0	27	4.3
1979	8	11	0	0	0	19	3.0
1983	13	10	0	0	0	23	3.5
1987	17	21	2	1	0	41	6.3
1992	20	37	2	1	0	60	9.2
1997	13	101	3	2	1 (Speaker)	120	18.2
2001	14	95	5	1	4	118	17.9

Source: Amended from J. Lovenduski and P. Norris, *Gender and Party Politics*. London: Sage, 1993.

120, although the upward trend faltered in 2001 as the number fell to 118 – the first decline since 1983. Though only a slight reduction, symbolically, it signifies the difficulties women still face in being selected and elected. Yet, individual women have long been successful in British politics: Margaret Bondfield in the 1920s, Ellen Wilkinson in the '40s, Barbara Castle in the '60s, and, of course, Margaret Thatcher, but have these individual successes had any wider impact?

The determinants of women's numerical representation are socio-economic (women's labour force participation and participation in the professions), cultural (the extent to which there is an egalitarian ideology, degrees of religiosity, and positive or negative attitudes towards the state) and political (the nature of the electoral system, party organisation, quota laws, and the policy formation process).[2] Only 252 women (6% of all MPs elected between 1918 and 2001) have sat in the House of Commons. The record of the main parties is also uneven: more than 60% were Labour MPs.

Women no longer suffer legal barriers to their election, but they face a majoritarian electoral system that is less favourable than proportional representation systems. Supply-side explanations in legislative recruitment 'suggest that the outcome of the selection process reflects the supply of applicants wishing to pursue a political career'; demand-side explanations assume 'selectors choose candidates depending on their perceptions of the applicants' abilities, qualifications and experience'. However, demand, or perceptions of a demand, may also be an important factor in determining who comes forward. Because of the sexual division of labour, it is likely that women will 'have lower resources of time and money, and lower levels of political ambition and confidence',[3] but, if candidates with resources primarily associated with men and masculinity are those desired by party selectorates, women may also suffer from selectorate discrimination.[4]

Selectorate discrimination is the key to understanding the fate of women seeking selection to the Commons. Women have faced gender-discriminatory questions at selection committees; prospective women candidates have suffered from indirect discrimination, where ideas of what constitutes a good MP have counted against women; and there have been discrepancies between the number of women seeking candidatures and the numbers selected. Party is also important, with the Conservative Party suffering both supply and demand-side problems and Labour demand-side problems.

The experience of the 1997 and 2001 general elections throws important light on women's recruitment to Westminster. Not only did the

1997 general election see an unprecedented 120 women MPs elected, but also one party – Labour – employing positive discrimination measures. All-women shortlists (AWS) operated in 50% of its key seats (seats winnable on a 6% swing) and vacant seats, but only in these seats did the Labour manage to select 50% women (see Table 3.3). Yet, in the 2001 general election there were no such measures: the government had failed to deal with the legal situation following the 1996 industrial tribunal ruling that AWS was illegal. Unsurprisingly, the numbers of women MPs fell.[5]

The situation for the forthcoming 2005 election looks a little better. The government belatedly introduced legislation permitting positive discrimination – the Sex Discrimination (Election Candidates) Act, 2002. Though parties can now engage in positive discrimination, only Labour has, despite both Conservative and Liberal Democrat support for the Bill.

The Conservatives have, at last, publicly acknowledged their difficulties in selecting women candidates. Selection procedures have been revised with assessors fully trained and an MP's job description drawn up reflecting the 'reality' of MPs' varied roles. Local associations have been exhorted to select a greater diversity of candidates and greater 'outreach' efforts been undertaken. Nonetheless, of the 132 seats that have so far selected prospective candidates, only 27 have selected women. While an improvement, only two women have been selected in the top twenty most winnable seats.[6] Even if the Conservative party polls 35% of the vote in 2005, (with Labour on 36% and the Liberal Democrats on 22%) the four additional women MPs would not increase the percentage of Conservative women MPs, who would continue to be a mere 9%.

Table 3.3   Labour candidates by type of seat at the 1997 General Election

Type of seat	No. of women	No. of men	Total	% women
Returned Labour Incumbents	36	199	235	15.3
Labour Retirements	11	21	32	34.4
Key Seats	43	42	85	50.6
Unexpected Gains	11	55	66	16.7
Total MPs	101	317	418	24.2
Unwinnable Seats	57	166	223	25.6
Total Candidates	158	483	641	24.6

Source: M. Eagle and J. Lovenduski, *High Time or High Tide for Labour Women*. London: The Fabian Society, 1998, p. 8.

The prospect for more Liberal Democrat women MPs is also slight. With divisions over positive discrimination, the party is limited to a sex quota at the short-listing stage[7] and to trying to ensure that 'confident' and 'trained' women are seen by local selectorates, helped by a Gender Balance Task Force. Yet, just like the Conservatives, women Liberal Democrats are finding it hard to get selected for target seats. So far, less than a quarter of the thirty target seats have selected women. Only one has been selected to replace the five retiring MPs, and she is replacing a retiring woman. Furthermore, even if the Liberal Democrats have a good election – winning, say, thirty more seats – it is unlikely to improve its percentage of women. And if it loses seats the situation gets dire: three of the six sitting women Liberal Democrats are in very vulnerable seats.[8]

Alone among the three main parties, Labour has taken up the opportunities provided by the new legislation. There will be AWS in 'at least 50% of the seats in every region where the sitting Labour MP is retiring' with a target of 35% women MPs in each English and Welsh region. MPs announcing their retirement after December 2002 found their constituency classified as a late retirement and declared an AWS, although the NEC has retained the power to authorise exceptions, so that an increase in women MPs is dependent upon the NEC not doing so.[9] Moreover, although the small swing against Labour in 2001 did not affect many women MPs – having been (s)elected for the safe and winnable rather than the marginal seats in 1997 as a result of AWS – a larger swing will unseat more of them.

In 1981 Jorgen Rasmussen suggested that if 'Margaret Thatcher proves to be a successful Prime Minister, perhaps 10–15 years from now an influx of young women...may be permitted for flow into the political elite.'[10] Both happened, but many of the young women got there not because the party gatekeepers *admitted* them but because they were *forced* to do so. And while there is acknowledgement that British political parties are 'institutionally sexist' and that parity requires 'long-term policies of positive discrimination', only one of the three main political parties has acted in this way.[11] In all likelihood, the 2005 election will, at best, maintain the level of women MPs. If there is a big swing away from Labour, a decline is likely. In short, the lessons from the last century, and particularly the last two general elections are, though simple not yet learnt: where parties introduce positive discrimination and demand is artificially created, women are selected in greater, if not proportionate, numbers; where such measures are absent, women are neither selected nor elected in significantly greater numbers.

Part Three: The House of Lords

The House of Lords has seen two major changes in composition. The first resulted from the Life Peerages Act 1958. Before its enactment, apart from Bishops and Law Lords (the latter forming the original version of life peerages),[12] members inherited their seats on the death of their fathers. Many had interests outside politics and did not devote much time to the House; some attended infrequently, some not at all. The creation of life peerages – the peerage and the consequent entitlement to a seat in the Lords expiring on the death of the holder – had a dramatic impact, both quantitatively and qualitatively. The membership not only increased in number, but the life peers were disproportionately active in the House.[13] They also brought in additional expertise. Table 3.4 shows the occupational background of peers in 1981, 23 years after life peerages were introduced. The data records multiple occupations and it was possible to identify the occupational background of only a proportion of hereditary peers. However, it is clear that life peerages resulted in the influx of more members drawn from the civil service, the law and the teaching (particularly the universities). They also resulted in a greater proportion of those who had served as MPs becoming members of the upper house.

Life peerages also resulted in more women and in members from ethnic backgrounds. The first of the latter was Dr David Pitt, a West Indian, elevated to the peerage in 1975. He has since been joined by

Table 3.4   The occupational experience, hereditary and life peers 1981

Occupation	N	Hereditary peers (%)	Life peers (%)
Full-time trade union official	20	–	4.9
Civil/diplomatic service	114	6.2	16.1
Legal (judge/barrister/solicitor)	120	5.9	18.3
Banking/insurance	121	11.6	7.8
Engineer	25	1.6	3.2
Accountant/economist	25	1.9	2.4
Scientist	9	0.4	1.5
Medical (surgeon/doctor/dentist)	19	0.6	3.4
Teaching (school/university)	103	3.4	18.8
Industry	208	3.0	34.9
Politics	166	3.0	34.9

Source: N. Baldwin, 'The House of Lords: Behavioural Changes', in P. Norton (ed.), *Parliament in the 1980s* (Oxford: Basil Blackwell, 1985), p. 105.

other non-white members. Although women had been eligible to sit in the Commons since 1918, and in the Lords only since the passage of the 1958 Act,[14] the Lords soon boasted more female members – both absolutely and proportionately – than the Commons. In 1970, there were 42 women in the Lords: 23 women life peers and 19 peeresses. Twenty years later, there were eighty women in the House, constituting just under 7% of the membership. Only in 1992 did the Commons pass the Lords in the proportion of its non-white and female membership.

The second fundamental change occurred in 1999, with the passage of the House of Lords Act. With effect from the new session in November 1999, all bar 92 of the hereditary members of the House were excluded from membership. This affected the composition of the House not only numerically – more than 600 peers ceased to be members – but also in terms of age and background.

Life peerages tend to be conferred on those who have achieved some particular distinction in their chosen sphere. This brings in a range of expertise but it also means that the House is not a young one. The age profile was occasionally leavened pre-1999 by a number of hereditary peers succeeding to their titles at a very early age. Lord Freyberg (b. 1970), for example (who remains in the Lords as one of the 92 hereditary peers chosen to stay on), entered the House at the age of twenty-three; he remains the youngest member. In 2004, the median age of MPs was just under 50, compared with a mean of 67 for members of the Lords.

The change also had an effect on the proportion of women in the House. In 2000, there were 105 women in the House (100 life peers, five elected hereditary peers), up by three on the number of the previous year. The increasing number of women appointed to the House, coupled with the removal of most male hereditary peers, meant that the proportion of women in the House increased from under 8% to more than 15%. With the number of women appointed to the House since 2000 being greater in proportion to males appointed – and with the number of women MPs looking likely not to increase notably in the near future – the upper house is likely to overtake the Commons again in its proportion of female membership.

The biggest change in the background of members has been political rather than social. The occupational background has changed, but not significantly. An analysis by McNeill (Table 3.5) shows that the proportion working in banking and insurance has declined compared with 1981, but otherwise the largest change appears to be the disappearance of

Table 3.5 The occupational experience of members of the House of Lords, 1981 and 2000

Occupation	1981(%)	2000 (%)
Full-time trade union official	2.2	4.9
Civil/diplomatic service	12.3	10.4
Legal (judge/barrister/solicitor)	12.9	16.2
Banking/insurance	13.0	2.4
Engineer	2.7	2.4
Accountant/economist	2.7	4.4
Scientist	1.0	1.3
Medical (surgeon/doctor/dentist)	2.0	3.8
Teaching (school/university)	11.1	11.2
Industry	22.4	29.8

Source: J. C. McNeill, *Is the reformed House of Lords a more representative chamber?*, Unpublished Undergraduate Dissertation, University of Hull: Department of Politics and International Studies, 2003, p. 23.

those for whom no occupational background is given. The figures have to be treated with some caution as different methods have been employed for compiling the two sets of data, but they are sufficient to indicate no paradigmatic change in the particular occupational categories employed by Baldwin.[15]

The biggest change has been political. Before November 1999, most hereditary peers sat either as Conservatives or as crossbenchers. Their departure had the effect of removing the Conservative preponderance in the House – in existence since Pitt the Younger created a large number of Tory peers – and nearly equalising the figures for the two main parties. The effect was to leave the balance of power with the Liberal Democrats and the remaining crossbenchers.

Notes

1 Andrew Roth and Byron Criddle, *Parliamentary Profiles*, various volumes, 1998–2001.
2 See J. Squires and M. Wickham-Jones, *Women in Parliament*, (Manchester: Equal Opportunities Commission, 2001).
3 Pippa Norris and Joni Lovenduski, *Political Recruitment: Gender, Race and Class in the British Parliament*, (Cambridge: Cambridge University Press, 1995) p. 15
4 Ibid., p. 14
5 The Labour Party had a sex quota for candidate shortlists – there were equal numbers of women and men on candidate shortlists, with at least two of each sex on each shortlist – but this had little effect.
6 In contrast in the bottom 20 seats, there are 7 women candidates. In its 8 retirement seats, the Conservatives have selected 2 women – again

an improvement on 2001, when not one woman was selected for a Conservative retirement seat.

7 Subject to their being a sufficient number of applicants of each sex, short-lists of three or four must include at least one member of each sex and shortlists of five or six must include at least two members of each sex (the One-third Rule).

8 Of the 110 seats that the Liberal Democrats have already selected forty have selected women (an improvement from 22% to 36% the last election).

9 *The Guardian*, 10 and 29 January 2003.

10 Jorgen Rasmussen, 'Female political career patterns and leadership disabilities in Britain', *Polity*, 13, 1981, p. 620.

11 L. Shepherd-Robinson and J. Lovenduski, *Women and Candidate Selection* (London: Fawcett Society, 2002) p. 1.

12 Law lords were created under the provisions of the Appellate Jurisdiction Act 1876 and sit for life. The two Archbishops, the Bishops of London, Durham, and Winchester, and the 21 most senior bishops in the Anglican church sit for the period that they hold their appointments.

13 C. Grantham and C. M. Hodgson, 'The House of Lords: Structural Changes' in P. Norton (ed.), *Parliament in the 1980s* (Oxford: Basil Blackwell, 1985), pp. 130–1.

14 Peeresses in their own right were admitted under the Life Peerages Act 1963.

15 Baldwin allowed for multiple entries for an individual who has pursued more than one occupation. McNeill confined each entry to the occupation pursued for the longest period of time by the individual. The different methodologies affect particularly the figures for those listed under the heading of 'politics', making it difficult to regard the two figures as comparable; as a result, that category has been excluded from the table.

4
Career Patterns and Professionalisation

Michael Rush

Career patterns in the House of Commons

British politics is dominated by two major parties, Conservative and Labour, especially in Parliament. Of course, a significant proportion of members of the House of Lords sit as crossbenchers – 27.1% in 2004, plus the Law Lords and former Law Lords, but this still leaves more than two-thirds with party affiliations, although no party has an absolute majority. In any case, politically the Commons is much more important than the Lords. In 1945 eight MPs were elected as independents, but six sat for university seats abolished in 1950. Between 1950 and 1997 a handful of candidates managed to defy the party machines standing as 'Independent Conservative' or 'Independent Labour' (or 'Democratic Labour' in one case), but Martin Bell (Tatton) in 1997 and Richard Taylor (Wyre Forest) are the only true independents. Between 1945 and 1970, 97.9% of MPs were either Conservative or Labour. Third parties, mostly the Liberals, had their by-election successes, but tended to fall back at general elections. However, since 1970 third parties have had greater success at general elections, so that the proportion of Conservative and Labour MPs between February 1974 and 2001 fell to 92.3%, falling further to 88.4% in 1997 and 87.7% in 2001. Consequently, a number of Liberal Democrat, Scottish Nationalist and Plaid Cymru MPs have had parliamentary careers comparable in length to most Conservative and Labour Members. Many of the latter, however, have had ministerial careers denied their third party colleagues. Nonetheless, for most MPs political careers include the possibility of ministerial office and, of course, parliamentary office as Speaker or one of the now three Deputy Speakers. The expansion of the select committee system provides an additional or alternative career path.

Political careers start outside Parliament, of course, and the cynical but sound advice to the would-be MP is, 'First choose your party!'. In spite of the heavy defeats of 1997 and 2001, the Conservative Party remains one of the two major vehicles for a parliamentary career. The party label is crucial but party membership is not enough; active party membership over a number of years is the norm. For many, this involves local government experience, either electoral, serving as a local councillor or both. Indeed, serving as a councillor before becoming an MP has become increasingly common, but more so with Labour than the Conservatives. In 1950 54.9% of Labour MPs but only 20.2% of Conservatives had been local councillors. However, by 1970 it had reached a third and was more than two-fifths between 1983 and 1992, but the heavy defeats of 1997 and 2001 reduced Conservative local government experience back to a bare third. Meanwhile, Labour MPs with local councillor experience now constitute more than three-fifths of the PLP – 62.5% in 1997 and 64.1% in 2001. For their part, the Liberals/Liberal Democrats increasingly used local government as a training ground for national politics and in 1997 56.5% and 2001 59.6% of their MPs had been local councillors.

Local government is thus a common career path to Westminster, but not the European Parliament nor the devolved legislatures in Scotland and Wales. Only a few MEPs have made the transition to Westminster. As for the Scottish Parliament and the National Assembly for Wales, traffic has been from rather than to Westminster. The Northern Ireland Assembly is different – here dual mandates are more common, even triple mandates in a few cases with the European Parliament, but this is a reflection of Northern Ireland politics.

Another obvious type of experience is fighting elections, even though the chances of being elected are often poor to non-existent. Elections to the European Parliament and the devolved legislatures can provide such experience but not to the extent that local elections can, although for would-be politicians options may remain open unless or until they are elected to one or other of the available legislatures. The most relevant electoral experience is gained fighting Westminster elections and the proportion of Conservative MPs who fought one or more parliamentary elections before election to Westminster has steadily increased from less than a third in 1950 to two-thirds in 2001. The trend for Labour MPs was similar, but in more recent elections an increasing proportion has not previously fought Westminster elections. Thus, in 1992 only two-fifths had and less than a fifth of the newly-elected Labour MPs in 2001 had done so. This suggests either

that competition for winnable seats is now greater among the Conservatives or that the greater local electoral experience of would-be
Labour MPs is seen as an adequate substitute, or some combination of
the two. However, as noted earlier, local government experience
among Conservatives had become more common until the elections of
1997 and 2001. Not surprisingly, among Liberals and their Liberal
Democrat successors, the experience of unsuccessfully fighting other
elections before winning a seat at Westminster has become increasingly common, applying to more than half since 1964 and as many as
four out of five in the 1970s and two-thirds in 1992 and 1997.

Some occupations also lend themselves more readily to a political
career than others. Traditionally, this has long been the case with
the legal profession, especially barristers, but, as Byron Criddle notes,
the number of lawyers has declined. Other occupations, such as journalism, teaching and business, provide either skills, time or both
which facilitate developing a political career, sufficient to offer a
partial explanation for their over-representation in the Commons but
not to the significant exclusion of many other occupations. However,
more specific political career paths have long existed. In the Labour
Party the trade unions have always provided a career path for MPs,
notably through financial sponsorship, formally abolished in 1995
though still significant through the financial support given to particular constituency parties, but also through the selection of trade union
officials. For most of the period since 1945 one Labour MP in eight
was a former full-time union official; in 2001 it was still one in twelve.
Party officials have been another but generally smaller source of
MPs. In the Conservative Party there has been a steady stream of individuals whose early political careers included posts in Conservative
Central Office or the Conservative Research Department, some of
them later to become Cabinet ministers – Enoch Powell, Iain Macleod,
Reginald Maudling, David Howell, and Tony Newton, for example.
This particular route has been less open to would-be Labour MPs,
however, because of party rules restricting the selection of party
officials, although a few, such as Denis Healey and Peter Shore, gradu-
ated from the old Transport House party headquarters. An increasingly common precursor to election is serving as a research assistant
to an existing MP or, more importantly, as a political adviser to a minister or a frontbench spokesperson. In 1992 fourteen of the 53 newly-
elected Conservatives had been research assistants to MPs or political
advisers to ministers. Political advisers in particular, however, have
become more important sources as their numbers have increased,

especially under Labour since 1997. The 2001 election saw similar proportions of Conservative and Labour MPs who had been political advisers elected – 10.8%, but numerically they comprised eighteen Conservatives and 44 Labour Members, including three who had served as aides to Tony Blair as Prime Minister – David Miliband, Jon Cruddas and James Purnell.

Most parliamentary careers start later than a normal career and few MPs are elected under the age of 30. Most enter the Commons between the ages of 35 and 45: the median age of newly-elected MPs in 2001 was 41 – 38 for Conservatives, 41 for Labour, 48 for Liberal Democrats, and 45 for other parties. Electoral landslides, such as those of 1983 and 1997, tend to bring in more first-time MPs under 30 but also more of 50 and over, as the winning party captures seats it would not normally win and brings in younger and older candidates who would not normally be elected. How long individuals remain MPs depends on a number of factors, not least the fortunes of their parties, and, although turnover has averaged 20% since 1945, it has ranged from the massive 40% of 1997 to the minuscule 7% of October 1974. Thus, the number of MPs whose Commons' careers are brought to a premature end (or in a few cases are interrupted by defeat) varies from election to election, from the 132 (126 of them Conservatives, including seven Cabinet ministers) in 1997 to the thirty defeated in October 1974. Other MPs resign between general elections for various reasons, such as appointment to a position incompatible with continued membership or because of ill-health. A few decide to leave Parliament prematurely at a general election, again for various reasons: in 2001, this could be said to be the case for two Conservatives and four Labour MPs, one of the former for family reasons, the other 'a disaffected Eurosceptic',[1] at least three of the latter because they were disillusioned with political life at Westminster.[2] In addition, the former Labour MP, Ken Livingstone, expelled from the Labour Party after running against and defeating the official Labour candidate for Mayor of London, also 'retired'. Also in the run-up to the 2001 election, one Labour MP was deselected[3] and one Conservative 'virtually deselected'[4] and, as already noted, a number of Scottish and Welsh Members migrated to the devolved legislatures and left the Commons in 2001. Most MPs, however, end their parliamentary careers at or near normal retirement age, with a handful continuing their careers in the House of Lords. The median age of those who retired from the Commons in 2001 (excluding those elected to the Scottish Parliament or the National Assembly for Wales) was 65 – 66 for Conservatives and Liberal Democrats, 63 for Labour and 64 for other parties. This practice has been much facilitated by the introduction of the MPs' pension scheme from 1964. Although length of service varies considerably, mainly because some MPs are defeated rather than retiring, the mean number of years served for those leaving the Commons was 17.6 – Conservatives 22.3, Labour 18.6, Liberal Democrats 13.3, and other parties 11.4. The average length of service has been growing since 1945 and now stands at nineteen years. In short, a parliamentary career is now much like a career outside Parliament: starting later than a normal career but ending at or near normal retirement age after nearly twenty years – all part of the professionalisation of politics in Britain.

Achieving ministerial office, especially Cabinet office, is widely regarded as the pinnacle of a political career and for MPs the opportunities of doing so are much greater now. The figures in Table 4.1 reflect two important trends: first, the increase in the number of ministerial posts and, second, the growing proportion of those posts held by MPs rather than peers. In 1950 the number of ministerial posts was 81 and 2004 114, plus the Speaker and three Deputy Speakers. In addition, the number of Parliamentary Private Secretaries (PPSs) – MPs acting as unpaid aides to ministers and widely seen as the first rung on the ministerial ladder – rose from 27 in 1950 to 55 in 2004. The proportion of ministerial posts held by MPs has varied, usually being lower under Conservative and higher under Liberal and Labour governments, but has been around four-fifths since 1945 (45% in 1900). Ironically, the Blair government actually has a higher proportion of peers (19.3% in 2004) than its Labour predecessor under Attlee (16.0% in 1950), but the increase in the number of ministerial posts between these dates means that under Attlee 68 MPs were ministers, compared with 92 under Blair, although the number of peers holding ministerial office was thirteen in 1950 and 22 in 2004. Of course, much depends on party and long periods of Conservative rule from 1951 to 1964 and 1979 to 1997 deprived Labour MPs of ministerial office, just as Conservatives must wait for the end of Labour's 1997 hegemony before any hopes of ministerial office can be realised.

Table 4.1 MPs achieving ministerial or parliamentary Office, 1945–97

Period	Conservative	Liberal	Labour
1945–97	39.0	0.0	31.3

Source: Michael Rush, *The Role of the Member of Parliament since 1868: From Gentlemen to Players*. Oxford: OUP, 2001, Table 5.10.

Table 4.2   The importance of serving as a minister or chair of a select committee (%)

Serving as	Very important/ quite important	Not important/not at all important
Cabinet minister	49.6	35.0
Junior minister	48.3	37.4
Chair of a select committee	36.8	41.1

Source: Report of the Hansard Society Commission on Parliamentary Scrutiny: The Challenge for Parliament – Making Government Accountable, London: Vacher/Dod, 2001, Appendix 4, Table 3.11.

Do MPs think holding office is important? And are they ambitious for ministerial office? Table 4.2, from a Hansard Society survey conducted in 2000, provides an answer to the first question.

Unfortunately, the survey does not distinguish between parties, but it is clear that nearly half those responding thought serving as a minister was important, although a substantial minority did not. Not surprisingly, more thought serving as a Cabinet minister 'very important' (30.9%) than as a junior minister (24.5%) and chairing a select committee as less important than either. As for ministerial ambitions, surveys of newly-elected MPs by the Study of Parliament Group in 1992 and 1997 found Conservatives were more ambitious than Labour MPs: 64.1% of Conservatives in 1992 and, in spite of the electoral debacle, no less than 92.9% in 1997 hoped to achieve office; in contrast, this was true of 43.1% of Labour MPs in 1992 and 48.1 in 1997. Moreover, no newly-elected Conservative denied ministerial ambitions, but 18.2% of Labour MPs in 1992 and 18.5% in 1997 did.[5] The increasing use of select committees has provided an alternative career path in Parliament, whether involving active membership of a committee or leading a committee as chair, a career path recognised in 2003 by the introduction of a salary for the latter. How far it will develop as a true alternative to a ministerial career remains to be seen, but of the select committee chairs in 2004 only four out of 24 had been solely backbenchers; of the rest, eight had been ministers (five as opposition frontbenchers as well), nine opposition frontbenchers, one a government whip, and two PPSs.

The House of Lords

Until the passage of the Life Peerages Act 1958 membership of the House of Lords was almost exclusively hereditary. From 1958, a

growing proportion were life peers, appointed either for their emi-
nence and expertise or as party appointees (or a mixture of both), in
number of cases after long service in the House of Commons. About a
quarter of the members of the House of Lords are former MPs, of
whom half have been Cabinet ministers. However, ministerial opportunities are limited in the upper house and, whereas at any one time
about one MP in seven is a minister, this is the case for only one
in thirty peers, even though the two Houses now have similar numbers
of members. Furthermore, not only must the Prime Minister and
Chancellor of the Exchequer be members of the Commons by constitutional convention, but few heads of government departments are
members of the upper house. In 2004, only the Secretary of State for
Constitutional Affairs (and Lord Chancellor), Lord Falconer, was in
the upper house (plus, of course, the Leader of the House), although
the government's senior law officer, the Attorney General, Lord
Goldsmith, was also in the Lords. The view generally is that heads of
departments should be in the Commons so the elected representatives
of the people can hold them accountable. The minimum number of
Cabinet ministers required in the Lords is two – the Lord Chancellor
and the government's business manager in the Lords, the Leader of the
House, although the Government Chief Whip in the Lords has
attended Cabinet meetings since 1997. Nonetheless, only three departments – International Development, the Northern Ireland Office, and
the Treasury – had no representation in the upper house in 2004, but it
was more commonly at under-secretary than minister of state level:
only 10.3% of ministers of state were peers, compared with 21.6% of
parliamentary under-secretaries. In addition, only two ministers in the
Lords were former MPs – Lord Grocott, the Government Chief Whip,
and Lord Rooker, Minister of State in the Office of the Deputy Prime
Minister, all others having started their parliamentary careers in the
upper house.

Since four-fifths of the members of the House of Lords are now life
peers, those who have not been MPs generally start their parliamentary
careers later than members of the House of Commons and the average
age of members of the upper house in 2004 was 67. Indeed, because as
many as a quarter are former MPs, the upper house has been called a
'retirement home for MPs', but many remain active parliamentarians
well beyond normal retirement age. The House of Lords thus provides,
on the one hand, an extension of their political careers for those
former MPs made life peers and, on the other, a limited but not necessarily short and by no means unrewarding parliamentary career to
those whose careers are confined to the upper house.

The professionalisation of Parliament

MPs and the House of Commons

> By professionalisation of the MP is meant the development of the full-time Member [of Parliament] in both attitude and practice, the provision of a level of salary sufficient to sustain such a Member financially, accompanied by appropriate resources to support the performance of parliamentary duties, and...the development of career patterns which reflect these developments.[6]

Although MPs have been paid since 1912, it was not until 1972 that a proper distinction was drawn between salary and expenses. A proportion of the salary was treated as a tax-free allowance to meet expenses and MPs received free travel between their constituencies and Westminster from 1924, but any additional costs incurred in carrying out parliamentary duties had to be met from the salary or private income. This led to a significant minority of better-off MPs legitimately claiming the whole of their parliamentary salary against tax. Change came but it was a long time coming: in 1969 a secretarial allowance was introduced and MPs were allowed free telephone calls and postage in the UK on parliamentary business. Then, in 1971, the Top Salaries Review Body (TSRB) (now the Senior Salaries Review Body (SSRB)) observed, 'By any reasonable standard...most Members must be regarded as working on a full-time basis, and we consider the level of remuneration should be assessed accordingly.'[7] More importantly, it recommended that a clear distinction be drawn between salary and expenses. Its recommendations were implemented in 1972 and the range of allowances now includes subsistence costs, particularly for MPs outside London, a substantial staff allowance, the costs of running a constituency office, staff travel and IT equipment.

Information now published in the annual Register of Members' Interests shows that a significant number of MPs continue to earn income from non-parliamentary work and others from acting as parliamentary advisers or consultants to pressure groups or other organisations outside Parliament. Between 1975, when the first register was published, and 1995 the number of MPs employed as parliamentary advisers or consultants rose from 86 to 234, but fell to 59 following the banning by the House of Commons of 'paid advocacy'. Surveys going back to the first TSRB report show that the time that MPs spent on outside work was limited in most cases and, moreover, that during the parliamentary session in 1971 they spent an average of 63 hours per week on parliamentary work and 70 hours in 1996.[8] Two of the surveys, those of 1982 and 1996, also covered parliamentary work during recesses and in 1982 found that the average per week was 40 hours for backbenchers and 50 for opposition frontbenchers and in 1996 50 and 53 hours respectively.[9]

The SPG surveys of MPs in the 1992–97 and 1997–2001 Parliaments found that 87.6% and 88.8% respectively believed that the job of being a Member of Parliament should be full-time, many arguing that it could not in practice be otherwise, although a substantial minority of Conservatives thought that ideally it should be part-time and have outside occupations that 'kept them in touch with the real world'.[10] This recognition and acceptance of the full-time role constitutes the completion of the professionalisation of the Member of Parliament, but it has been accompanied by a professionalisation of the House of Commons itself.

The House of Commons has, of course, long had staff to assist it in performing its functions, but the institutional professionalisation of the House is a much more recent development. Furthermore, for most of its history the Commons has not had control over its own budget, although it has always been the case that staff are servants of the House, not civil servants. In 1965 the situation began to change and control of most of the Palace of Westminster passed to the Speaker and the Lord Chancellor, advised by select committees, though financial responsibility did not. Then, in 1978 the House of Commons (Administration) Act set up a House of Commons Commission consisting of the Speaker, as chair, the Leader of the House and Opposition 'Shadow' Leader, and three MPs appointed by the House, none of whom may be a minister. It is responsible for the House's budget and exercises overall strategic responsibility. Co-ordination of the work of the House lies with a Board of Management, comprising the heads of the five departments of the House, but the departments retain a considerable degree of autonomy.

The 1978 Act was based on the recommendations of a select committee chaired by a senior ex-minister, Arthur Bottomley,[11] which had itself been set up following an earlier report by Sir Edmund Compton, a former senior civil servant. Compton[12] had recommended a unified House service and a centralised system of career management; his model, in essence, was a government department. The report was severely criticised by staff, the most damning indictment being that 'it virtually ignores the existence of Members of Parliament', though few showed any interest in it!

In 1990 a further review, by Sir Robin Ibbs, a former head of the Central Policy Review Staff, took place and reported that the financial management of the House was inadequate, lacking satisfactory control of substantial areas of expenditure. To remedy these deficiencies, the House of Commons Commission should adopt a more pro-active strategic role, advised by a Finance and Services Committee to include the chairs of five domestic advisory committees covering the range of services and facilities provided by the House. The overall management responsibilities of the Clerk should be clarified, and Directors of Finance and of Works should be appointed to strengthen control of finance and facilities. Finally, House of Commons expenditure should be subject to review by the National Audit Office and the Commons' Public Accounts Committee.[13] These recommendations were accepted and most of the new arrangements put in place. In particular, the Parliamentary Corporate Bodies Act, 1992 made the Clerk of the House (and his Lords' counterpart, the Clerk of the Parliaments) corporate officers so that they could assume the necessary legal responsibilities.

Yet a further review, by Michael Braithwaite, a management consultant, took place in 1999. The Braithwaite Report noted that, while most of the Ibbs recommendations had been implemented to varying degrees, more change was necessary, particularly to improve the audit function, provide more effective centralised management and better strategic planning. It proposed that the Clerk should be made Chief Executive of the House Service (but retaining the traditional title) and that heads of department should be responsible to the Clerk for their departments, an Office of the Clerk be set up to assist with the Clerk's executive responsibilities, an Audit Committee established, and a Communications Adviser be appointed.[14]

The implementation of Braithwaite has resulted in a more integrated organisation of the House of Commons, but, crucially, one achieved with the co-operation of staff and the recognition that they are there to serve the House and its members. Whereas MPs showed little interest in Compton, both Ibbs and Braithwaite were to an important extent driven by Member-dissatisfaction. Of course, it could be argued that Compton has been realised by a different route over a long period of time, but that would be to misunderstand the strongly dirigiste nature of the Compton proposals, on the one hand, and the service-oriented ethos of the House of Commons Service, on the other. This is clearly reflected in two of the core tasks set out in strategic plan of the

House of Commons administration for 2001–06, a search for which in the Compton Report would be in vain:

• Supporting the House and its committees.
• Supporting individual Members (and their staff).

Much has changed since the House of Commons first achieved a degree of control over its own affairs in 1965: financial control and accountability has been transformed and strategic planning introduced where little or none existed, but Bottomley, Ibbs and Braithwaite were not just about organisational and managerial reform; they were a means to the end of improving the ability of MPs and the House as a whole to fulfil its functions by providing appropriate and adequate resources. In terms of services and facilities, much would be recognised by MPs of earlier post-1945 Parliaments; what would strike them is their extent. The two most visible changes have been in accommodation for Members, epitomised by Portcullis House, and the number of staff employed by individual Members, but other services and facilities have expanded enormously. Excluding the Refreshment Department, for which figures were not available in 1972, the number of staff increased by 215% between 1972 and 2004, and the total staff (including the Refreshment Department) in 2004 was 1,517. The staff of the House of Commons has long been professional in attitude; what has changed is that organisationally and managerially the departments of the House of Commons have become increasingly professionalised, though what may be termed institutional professionalisation has yet to be achieved.

Professionalisation: peers and the House of Lords

Peers and the House of Lords could be seen as the amateur part of Parliament: MPs are paid, peers are not (apart from a few office-holders or unless they are ministers); MPs are full-time, some peers are but most are not; and the scale of services and facilities available to peers pales beside that available to MPs. Of course, like the Commons, the Lords has long had full-time staff, to whom the term 'amateur' would not be appropriate, but it would not have been a unreasonable term to apply to the upper house generally before the 1958 Life Peerages Act and for some time after. Today, its use is misleading and the Lords has experienced and continues to experience a process of professionalisation. The upper house is now a much more active body: it now meets as often as the Commons and attendance has increased from fewer than a hundred in 1950 to more than four hundred before the removal of most of the hereditary peers in 1999. There has been a small decline since, but the pre-1999 attendance amounted to more than third of the membership, post-1999 attendance to more than half. The Lords has become a busier place, expanding its legislative and scrutiny roles on and off the floor of the House. Services and facilities have been extended, partly through the introduction of a range of allowances, beginning with limited travel allowances for rail travel in 1946 and now covering more extensive travel, day and overnight subsistence, secretarial help, telephone and postage, and by the provision of accommodation and increases in staff. As recently as 1988–89, only 150 desk spaces were available to backbench peers, but by 2003 they were available for 90% of peers, though mostly in shared rooms. Although the number of Lords' staff is less than a third that of the Commons, it still reflects a significant growth: in 1988–89 there were 198 staff, in 2003 was 416. Like the Commons, the most important staff are the Clerks and the librarians, of whom there were 76 and 33 respectively in 2004.

Organisationally, too, the House of Lords has undergone significant change. Following the relinquishment of control of most of the Palace of Westminster by the Lord Great Chamberlain in 1965, services and facilities became the responsibility of the House of Lords Offices Committee. There was no equivalent of the Ibbs Report for the Lords, but in 2000 the Offices Committee recommended that Michael Braithwaite undertake a management structure review which would also cover its committee structure, but, following a debate, the matter was referred back and eventually the House agreed to set up a Steering Group on Management and Services, rather than appoint an outside consultant. The Steering Group recommended that the Offices Committee and its sub-committees be replaced by a 'slimmed down' House Committee, with general administrative responsibility delegated to a Board of Management and more decisions left to staff of the House. It also recommended the appointment of a full-time Principal Finance Officer and an Audit Committee. These proposals were accepted and implemented at the beginning of the 2002–03 session. The House Committee consists of the Chairman of Committees, who is ex officio chair, the leaders of the party groups in the House and Convenor of the Crossbench Peers, and six backbenchers. It has overall strategic responsibility and is advised by four other specialised committees. The Board of Management comprises the Clerk of the Parliaments, by whom it is chaired, and other senior officials, who have day-to-day responsibility. These arrangements largely parallel those operating in the House of Commons, but they illustrate, neither for the first nor the last time, that the House of Lords 'does its own thing' and in that regard is unlikely to change.

The professionalisation of the Lords will undoubtedly continue and there will be growing demands for better and more extensive services and facilities. Those who wish to reform the Lords will be ill-advised to ignore them; failure to heed them will disadvantage peers and damage the ability of the House of Lords to carry out its functions fully and effectively.

Notes

1 Byron Criddle, 'MPs and Candidates' in David Butler and Dennis Kavanagh, *The British General Election of 2001*. London: Palgrave, 2002, p. 185.
2 *Ibid.*, p. 184.
3 *Ibid.*, p. 183 and 188–9.
4 *Ibid.*, p. 185.
5 Unpublished research by members of the Study of Parliament Group, supported between 1992 and 1997 by a Nuffield Foundation grant and between 1997 and 2001 by an ESRC award (R0000222474).
6 Rush, *The Role of the Member of Parliament*, p. 112.
7 Top Salaries Review Body, *First Report: Ministers of the Crown and Members of Parliament*, Cmnd. 4836, December 1971, para. 25.
8 *Ibid.*, Appendix A, Table 6 and SSRB, *Report No. 38*, Cm. 3330-II, July 1996, pp. 30–31.
9 TSRB, *Report No. 20*, Cmnd. 8881-II, May 1983, Section 1, Table 4 and SSRB, *loc. cit.*
10 Unpublished SPG research 1992–2001.
11 *House of Commons (Administration). Report to Mr Speaker*, HC 624, 1974–75.
12 *Review of the Administrative Services of the House of Commons. Report to the Speaker by Sir Edmund Compton*, HC 254, 1974.
13 *House of Commons Services. Report to the House of Commons Commission* (the Ibbs Report), HC 38, 1990–91.
14 *Review of Management and Services. Report to the House of Commons Commission* (the Braithwaite Report), HC 745, 1998–99.

5
A Changing Culture

Michael Rush (Part One and Part Two), Sarah Childs (Part Three)
and Michael Rush (Part Four and Part Five)

Part One: Party cohesion in Parliament[1]

In 1965 an eminent academic observer of British politics, Samuel Beer, suggested that party cohesion 'was so close to 100% that there is no longer any point in measuring it.'[2] Yet, as Table 5.1 shows, already there were signs of change: the 1959–64 Parliament witnessed 120 rebellions by government backbenchers, ten times the rate in the previous two Parliaments. In the next normal length Parliament, 1966–70, the number was 109, rising to more than 300 in 1974–79, when the Labour government had either a small majority or no majority at all. In the succeeding Parliaments there

Table 5.1 Number of rebellions by government MPs, 1945–2001*

Parliament	No. of rebellions	Governing party
1945–50	79	Labour
1951–55	11	Conservative
1955–59	12	Conservative
1959–64	120	Conservative
1966–70	109	Labour
1970–74	204	Conservative
1974–79	309	Labour
1979–83	159	Conservative
1983–87	203	Conservative
1987–92	198	Conservative
1992–97	174	Conservative
1997–2001	96	Labour

*Excluding the short Parliaments of 1950–51, 1964–66 and March–October 1974.
Source: P. Cowley & Mark Stuart, '"In Place of Strife": the PLP in Government, 1997–2001', *Political Studies*, 51, 2003, p. 3.

were fewer rebellions, but there continued to be many more than between 1945 and 1959.

Of course, the number of actual defeats suffered by governments was much smaller, depending largely on the size of the government's normal majority, so that the largest numbers occurred in the 1974 and 1974–79 Parliaments, when the Labour government was particularly vulnerable (see Table 5.2). More particularly, the eleven defeats between 1945 and 1970 all occurred in two short Parliaments with small government majorities, 1950–51 and 1964–66, and none was the result of deliberate attempts by government backbenchers to defeat the government, but were the result of 'poor organisation by the whips or deliberate opposition ploys' to catch the government out in the division lobbies,[3] whereas later defeats resulted from government back-bench rebellions. Not surprisingly, the Labour government elected in 1997 with a massive 179-seat majority suffered no defeats in the 1997–2001 Parliament, though it has been defeated once in the 2001 Parliament, when the government sought to exclude two senior Labour backbenchers from continuing as chairs of departmental select committees, and came within five votes of defeat in 2003 over proposals to increase university tuition fees. Indeed, during the first two sessions of the 2001 Parliament, one or more government backbenchers rebelled in 18.8% of divisions, more than in any other Parliament since 1945.[4]

What explains this growth in dissent? A variety of explanations have been put forward – poor party leadership, changes in the types of individuals elected to the Commons, and the realisation that, contrary to the conventional wisdom, governments do not normally fall if defeated in the House of Commons. Poor leadership probably explains some rebellions, especially where there is evidence that the leadership has not listened sufficiently to backbench disquiet, since the government

Table 5.2 Number of government defeats in the House of Commons, 1945–2001

Period/Parliament	No.	Parliament	No.
1945–70	11	1983–87	2
1970–74	6	1987–92	1
Mar–Oct 1974	17	1992–97	4
1974–79	42	1997–2001	0
1979–83	1		

Source: D. & G. Butler, *Twentieth Century British Political Facts, 1900–2000*. London: Macmillan, 2000, p. 201.

often seeks to 'buy off' as many rebels as it can. Although no clear evidence has been found to suggest that MPs drawn from particular socio-economic backgrounds are more likely to defy the whips, it is possible to detect a significant change in MPs' attitudes towards them. In the 1950s and earlier, both major parties had solid blocs of loyal MPs on whom the whips could rely. For the Conservatives it was the 'knights of the shire', MPs from mostly safe, rural constituencies, with limited political ambitions; for Labour it was the trade union sponsored MPs, again mostly sitting for safe seats and also with limited ambitions. If either group showed signs of serious discontent, the whips quickly informed the government and steps would normally be taken to respond to their concerns: rebellions were unnecessary and largely unthinkable. Both were gradually replaced by MPs on both sides of the House not content with a largely passive role and politically more ambitious. Crucially, it has become increasingly apparent that government defeats rarely brought about a dissolution of Parliament or the resignation of the government and, on those occasions when governments made a particular vote a matter of confidence, they normally survived. In addition, potential rebels among government backbenchers found that they could extract policy concessions from the government, especially on legislation, and governments became adept at containing rebellions by making concessions. In short, there has always been a certain amount of give and take between the government and its backbenchers, but dissent and threatened dissent have increased the amount of give and take, and dissent has become more common and more overt. At the beginning of the twentieth century party cohesion was the norm; at the beginning of the twenty-first century it remains the norm, but significantly tempered by backbench dissent.

Party cohesion in the House of Commons and the House of Lords is remarkably similar, although the available data on the upper house is limited to recent sessions. In the Lords, in which nearly three quarters of peers accept a party whip and the remaining quarter – mostly crossbenchers – do not, intra-party dissent occurred in about a quarter of divisions (see Table 5.3); in the Commons, backbench dissent is usually less – around a fifth of divisions (see Table 5.4). Put another way, party cohesion is high in both Houses, but somewhat higher in the Commons.

Government defeats in the Lords, however, are significantly higher than in the Commons, attributable mainly to the absence of an overall majority for any single party in the upper house, particularly since the removal of most of the hereditary peers in 1999 but also before then

Table 5.3 Divisions in the House of Lords involving intra-party dissent, 1999–2002 (% (n))

Party	1999–2000	2000–01*	2001–02†
Conservative	7 (13)	12 (4)	14 (22)
Labour	19 (36)	18 (6)	19 (31)
Liberal Democrat	3 (6)	3 (1)	7 (11)
Total§	23 (42)	24 (8)	29 (47)

* Short session due to the dissolution of Parliament for the general election of 2001.
† Long session, following the general election of 2001.
§ Totals do not equal the sums of the column as some divisions involved intra-party dissent by members of more than one party.
Source: Philip Norton, 'Party Cohesion in the House of Lords', Table 1.

Table 5.4 Number of government defeats in the House of Lords, 1974–2001

Parliament	No. of defeats	Government party
1974–79*	362	Labour
1979–83	45	Conservative
1983–87	62	Conservative
1987–92	72	Conservative
1992–97	62	Conservative
1997–2001	109	Labour

* Including the 1974 and 1974–79 Parliaments.
Source: www.parliament.uk.faq/lords_govtdefeats.cfm, except for 1974–79.

among regular attenders in the Lords. Thus in both Houses, party cohesion is the norm, tempered by similar levels of dissent, with government defeats far more frequent in the Lords but caused mainly by the party balance in the upper house, rather than failures in party cohesion.

The growth of dissent and explanations of it have been discussed in relation to the Commons. In the case of the Lords, the survival of the government does not arise, although peers may be influenced by the possible consequences of rejecting a government bill or significantly amending it against the government's wishes. There is prime facie evidence that, since 1999 a substantially non-hereditary House of Lords has regarded itself as more legitimate. It is more meaningful, in fact, to discuss the Lords in terms of party cohesion rather than dissent. Unlike the Commons, where various 'sticks' and 'carrots' are used by the whips to encourage MPs to toe the party line – the prospect of ministerial office, patronage appointments, honours (including peerages), select committee membership, accommodation at Westminster, membership of overseas delegations, withdrawal of the whip, and deselection – are either not available in the Lords or of limited use. This leads Norton to describe the upper house as 'essentially a discipline-free environment'.[5] It is more pertinent to ask of both Houses, why is party cohesion so strong? It would, of course, be naïve to suggest that MPs are not influenced by the whips, not least because of the constitutional and political dependence of the government on the Commons. But it is not unreasonable to argue that most of the time MPs and peers vote with their party because they want to, not necessarily in the sense that they agree with the party on every position or occasion but in that they need to feel strongly about a matter before declining to support the party line. Norton argues that the explanation for peers is 'prior socialisation', which he defines as 'an emotional or intellectual commitment to a particular party'.[6] Such an explanation is no less credible for explaining party cohesion in the Commons, with the higher level of cohesion among MPs being explained to a significant extent by the more serious consequences of dissent. Government defeats in the Commons may be rare, but few if any MPs wish to be blamed for real or apparent splits or disagreement in their party. Of course, MPs and peers are aware that dissent or the threat of it can extract concessions from the government, but all MPs bar one in each of the last two Parliaments and three-quarters of peers are party adherents who normally expect to support their party.

Part Two: A growth in backbench participation

Measuring legislative participation presents a number of problems, particularly in drawing a distinction between quantitative and qualitative participation. What follows focuses entirely on quantitative analysis, using *Hansard* indexes for the parliamentary sessions concerned. The sessions used were 1947–48 and 1994–95, both mid-Parliament sessions to avoid any distortion that might be caused by the immediate aftermath or imminent prospect of a general election. Three measures were used – participation in debates in the Chamber, committee attendances, and the number of parliamentary Questions asked for both oral and written answer.

The data in Table 5.5 show high levels of participation by both government and opposition backbenchers in debates and the asking of parliamentary Questions, with committee attendance becoming much greater in 1994–95, reflecting the increase in the use of com-

Table 5.5 Participation by government and opposition backbenchers, 1947–48 and 1994–95 (%)

	Govt. backbenchers		Opp. backbenchers	
Type of participation	*1947–48*	*1994–95*	*1947–48*	*1994–95*
Debates	88.8	97.1	96.0	99.4
Committees	66.1	94.7	69.5	85.8
Parliamentary Questions	87.0	96.3	96.5	97.2
Overall	96.6	99.6	99.5	100.0

Source: Rush, *The Role of the Member of Parliament*, Tables 6.8, 6.9 and 6.10.

Table 5.6 Participation by government and opposition backbenchers, 1947–48 and 1994–95 (means)

	Govt. backbenchers		Opp. backbenchers	
Type of participation	*1947–48*	*1994–95*	*1947–48*	*1994–95*
Debates	18.0	21.0	37.8	23.4
Committees	9.2	25.1	8.1	20.8
Parliament Questions	29.0	37.0	56.7	111.2

Source: Rush, *The Role of the Member of Parliament*, Tables 6.8, 6.9 and 6.10.

mittees, especially select committees. Overall, participation rates in the two sessions were very similar, involving virtually all MPs, but analysis of earlier sessions suggests that, while opposition backbench participation has long been high – at least 90%, government backbench participation tended to be lower.[7]

If mean figures are analysed (see Table 5.6), a more detailed picture emerges: in debates there was little change among government backbenchers, but a marked decline among opposition backbenchers in participation in debates, reflecting a clear trend through the post-war period; not surprisingly, committee attendance reflects the growth in committees; but parliamentary Questions showed a considerable increase, particularly among opposition backbenchers. These same trends are found when the proportion of backbenchers with more than twenty interventions in debates, committee attendances or parliamentary Questions asked are examined, except for a substantial increase in debates by government backbenchers (see Table 7.5).

Third party MPs tend to have higher scores than government or opposition backbenchers in participation in debates and asking Questions, though not in committee attendance, presumably reflecting

Table 5.7   Participation by government and opposition backbenchers, 1947–48 and 1994–95 (scores of 20 or more (%))

Type of participation	Govt. backbenchers		Opp. backbenchers	
	1947–48	*1994–95*	*1947–48*	*1994–95*
Debates	29.4	42.8	53.5	42.6
Committees	17.0	59.2	13.5	65.3
Parliament Questions	35.2	56.7	62.0	75.0

Source: Rush, The Role of the Member of Parliament, Tables 6.8, 6.9 and 6.10.

a need for them to be more active, to shout louder, to make themselves heard, the Speaker's protection of minorities no doubt helping in debates.

The data shown in these Tables 5.5–5.7 support the picture drawn earlier of the growth of the full-time MP, but even in 1947–48 MPs were fairly active in Parliament; by 1994–95 they could be said to have become very active. It is hardly surprising, therefore, that they should have demanded and gradually received more and better services and facilities, thereby extending and completing the process of the professionalisation of the House of Commons.

It is likely that were an analysis undertaken of the parliamentary activity of members of the House of Lords, a similar picture would emerge, but would likely show that the upper house is a full-time legislative body consisting of mostly part-time members and that the professionalisation process has been underway for some time but has some way to go.

Part Three: The impact of women MPs in the House of Commons

The story of women and Parliament is not just about how women get into Parliament, but also about what they do when they get there, and more recently, particularly what they do *for women*. In reviewing the history of women's presence in the House of Commons, there are many 'key' moments over which historians and political scientists could long debate. Undoubtedly, it is Margaret Thatcher's 'first' as Prime Minister that is likely to trump other claims. Though the nature and effect of her governments have been much debated, less has been said about what she and her governments represented for women. Symbolically, Mrs Thatcher represented, above all else, that a woman could do the top job. Yet, what seems significant is not so much her premiership *per se*, but what came after. Once she had left the political stage, women's absence from the heart of British politics was, perhaps for the first time, noticed *and* considered problematic.

Post-Thatcher, women's presence in politics is seen to matter, not just for reasons of justice or meritocracy – although these are good enough reasons in themselves – but because women's voices *should* be at the centre and not the margins of politics.[8] The focus of contemporary academic and public attention is less on the success of individual women MPs and more on their collective actions, particularly whether they act *for women*. There is an expectation – very much to the fore after 1997 – that women representatives will substantively represent women. Such assumptions seem reasonable and are widely held by ordinary women and men and by MPs of both sexes. They derive from common-sense, history and from feminist political theory. (Auto)biographies of women MPs, as well as early studies of women in Parliament, reveal a tradition of women MPs, individually and collectively, raising women's concerns. More recently, surveys have found consistent attitudinal differences between women and men MPs with women 'more likely to take a pro-woman line than men'.[9] With an unprecedented number of women MPs in the 1997 and 2001 Parliaments, are women better substantively represented than they were when few of them sat in the House?

To establish this *tout court* is, however, difficult. In the past it was said that there were simply too few: women did not constitute a critical mass and were unable to make a difference even if they had wanted to. But the increase in the numbers of women since 1997 allows for more systematic research to occur, although methodological problems remain: critical mass, with its simplistic assumption that feminised change will occur as soon as a certain, but as yet unspecified, percentage of women are present, has been widely criticised. There is also the problem of what constitutes proof of feminised change. Is it sex differences in MPs' attitudes and behaviour? But what if men change their behaviour to mirror women's as a consequence of women's presence? What would the absence of sex differences infer? Unfortunately, the kind of research that will answer such questions – large multi-method research projects and longitudinal studies – will take time and money.[10] In the meantime, there are some indications that there has been feminised change in Parliament since the 1997 election. Howsever, because of the imbalance in the numbers of women from the main political parties elected since 1997 – 101 Labour women, thirteen Conservative and three Liberal Democrat in 1997, 95, fourteen and five, respectively in 2001 – and the impact of party cohesion, it is a question of whether Labour's women MPs have substantively represented women.

According to many of Labour's women MPs (both new and old) there has been a feminisation of the House of Commons since 1997. Interviews with more than half the Labour women MPs first elected in 1997 shows that one-third in 1997, and nearly two-thirds in 2000, consider that they have articulated women's concerns (such as violence against women, forced marriages, sexual harassment, childcare, caring, breast cancer, and emergency contraception) in the House. They also claim that, in addition to making a difference in debates, Questions, in committees, and through Early Day Motions (EDMs), that they have acted 'behind the scenes', by holding private conversations with ministers about women's concerns, raising them in backbench groups (particularly the PLP's women's group), and re-gendering select committees.

MPs' claims to be acting for women, though rich, are self-reported and open to question. To capture better the 'story' of women's substantive representation requires analysis of women's MPs' actual behaviour as well as their attitudes and perceptions. Analysis of the Labour women's voting records and signing of EDMs in the 1997 Parliament provides such data, while analysis of the passage of the Sex Discrimination (Election Candidates) Act provides case study material.

Labour's women MPs, and especially its new ones, have been routinely charged with having been too loyal to Blair and of failing to rebel against the government. Analysis of over 1,300 parliamentary divisions in the 1997 Parliament shows that there was indeed a sex difference: the new women were less than half as likely to rebel against the party whip as the rest of the PLP, with those who did rebel doing so around half as often.[11] Even after controlling for a range of factors that might have explained this difference, an MP's propensity to rebel continues to be influenced by their sex, although the difference was not statistically significant.

According to the new women (or, rather, half of them) this sex difference is to be explained by their preference for a different style of politics, one that eschews macho posturing in favour of acting 'behind the scenes'. The belief in a different women's style of politics – held by more than two-thirds of the new Labour women MPs interviewed in 2000 – may constitute another difference Labour's women have made to Parliament since 1997. In respect of rebellion, however, other MPs, query the women's views and it is simply not possible to test these differing interpretations.

If the analysis of MPs' voting behaviour shows that Labour's new women MPs behaved differently from the men (although not necessarily *for* women), analysis of the signing of EDMs shows that Labour's permanent backbench women MPs not only behaved differently from the men but acted *for* women.[12] Comparing the sex of MPs who signed 'women's' and feminist 'women's' EDMs (those that have as their primary subject matter women and/or their concerns) shows clear sex differences, with women more likely to sign 'women's' and feminist 'women's' EDMs. While men are more likely to sign EDMs in general, the opposite was true of 'women's EDMs. Over the Parliament, women signed an average of 43.3 'women's' EDMs compared with 38.6 for men. However, Labour's women MPs were significantly more likely to sign 'women's' EDMs as a percentage of all motions they signed. Similarly, with feminist 'women's' EDMs – women signed an average of 28.7 compared with 23.4 for men. Moreover, the proportion of feminist 'women's EDMs signed is also higher for the women. In sum, there is hard evidence that Labour's women MPs (or rather its permanent backbench women MPs) did act for women by signing for women in the 1997 Parliament.[13]

Analysis of the passage of the Sex Discrimination (Election Candidates) Act in 2001–02 supports the claim that women MPs are more likely to act for women than male MPs. In this instance, women MPs from all the main parties (and incidentally, women members of the Lords) spoke disproportionately in the debates with male Members (especially backbenchers) conspicuous by their absence. Moreover, the parliamentary debates also reveal the role of party identity. Though women of all parties acted for women by speaking, qualitative content analysis of the debates revealed that those MPs most likely to favour positive discrimination and to draw on the concept of substantive representation to support the legislation were Labour (both male and female). In contrast, those MPs who spoke against the legislation, who were hostile to positive discrimination and rejected substantive representation were mostly Conservative.

The presence of women MPs in the House of Commons in the last 85 years has made a difference, but that made by Labour's women MPs since 1997 is much clearer. Though the presence of women in Parliament represents many things – women's equal ability to serve as MPs, the legitimacy of the institution, and political equality – it is whether Labour's women MPs have acted for women by feminising British politics that remains the key question. The House of Commons may not have been turned upside down since 1997 but there is evidence that

that women's substantive representation has been one effect of the presence of Labour's 101 women MPs.

Part Four: A question of attitude

No amount of theorising about the roles of Members of Parliament (or for that matter, peers), will determine what they do and what they think about what they do. This is not to devalue theorising but to argue that for theory to become practice necessitates parliamentarians accepting the theory. MPs, it can be argued, are expected to fulfil three roles – those of the partisan, the scrutineer and the constituency representative. For all except the rare independent, the partisan role is one MPs accept, having been selected by their party and elected as party candidates. The constituency role is one that is thrust upon all MPs, regardless of party: all MPs expect to advance and defend the individual and collective interests of their constituents. The scrutiny role lies at the heart of parliamentary government, seeking to enforce the constitutional responsibility of the executive to the legislature, but it is a role that can be played in whole or part in a partisan fashion or less so, according to the inclinations of individual Members. Only two of these roles apply to peers, since they do not have constituencies, and even the partisan role does not apply to those who eschew a party whip. In this respect, the scrutiny role looms larger than in the Commons, partly because of the different constitutional and political standing of the two Houses and partly because the House of Lords has increasingly carved out such a role since 1958. Unfortunately, data on the attitudes of peers towards their roles is not available, but it is for MPs.

It is quite clear from the data in Table 5.8 that the constituency role is of great significance to MPs, especially in the form of protecting the collective interests of the constituency and in dealing with the grievances of individual constituents, whether measured as 'very important' or 'quite important' or 'most important'. Nonetheless, in terms of the first two measures, 'voting with my party' is also regarded as important, though regarded as 'most important' by only 2.6%. Indeed, the scrutiny role is regarded as more important that the partisan role. As noted earlier, the Hansard Society survey does not distinguish between parties, but surveys conducted by the Study of Parliament Group SPG) in the 1992–97 and 1997–2001 Parliaments do. The question asked was similar, though not the same.[14] MPs ranked the constituency role first, then the scrutiny role, followed by supporting their party and

Table 5.8 *Question*: How important are the following roles in your work as an MP?

Response	Very important	Quite important	Neutral response	Not very important	Not important at all	Most important	n
Protecting interests of the constituents	67.4	26.3	4.6	1.1	0.6	21.4	175
Dealing with grievances	54.3	36.5	8.0	0.6	0.6	17.5	175
Holding govt. to account	53.1	30.3	13.7	1.7	1.1	38.4	175
Examining legislation	41.1	30.9	21.1	5.1	1.7	14.9	175
Voting with party	24.0	44.5	24.0	6.9	0.6	2.6	175
Informing constituents	20.0	42.9	20.6	11.4	5.1	0.6	175

Source: Hansard Society, *Report of the Commission on Parliamentary Scrutiny*, London, 2001, Appendix 4, Table 3.2. Various other responses have been excluded.

influencing or changing party policy. However, not only did views differ between the parties, but, rather like the differences in participation between government and opposition backbenchers, so views also depended on whether the party was in government or opposition, as Table 5.9 shows.

Although both Conservative and Labour MPs placed much the same emphasis on the constituency role in 1999, the scrutiny role ranked first among Conservatives, having been fourth in 1994, when the party was in government, and there was a decline in the proportion of Labour MPs placing scrutiny first or second in 1999, when their party was in government. It is also clear that both in 1994 and 1999, the partisan role ranked more highly for Labour than Conservative Members. This was confirmed in response to another question, in which respondents were asked to place in rank order who they regarded themselves as representing. Although representing constituents ranked first, regardless of party, Conservatives consistently placed representing the nation second and their party third, whereas for Labour MPs the roles were reversed, with party second and the nation third. Essentially, the Hansard and SPG surveys present similar pictures, but with the latter drawing attention to differences between parties. In particular, MPs

Table 5.9   The most important part of the job of being an MP, 1994 and 1999

A. % of MPs ranking helping constituents/dealing with constituency issues first or second.

Party	1994	1999
Conservative	60.5	76.9
Labour	71.2	78.6
All MPs	64.7	80.2

B. % of MPs ranking supporting their party first or second.

Party	1994	1999
Conservative	42.9	30.8
Labour	54.9	61.5
All MPs	48.7	50.0

C. % of MPs ranking parliamentary scrutiny first or second.

Party	1994	1999
Conservative	31.7	82.0
Labour	45.8	35.0
All MPs	42.5	50.5

Source: Rush, *The Role of the Member of Parliament*, Table 8.2.

generally stress the importance of the partisan, constituency and scrutiny roles. At first sight, the Hansard survey appears to give the scrutiny role – 'holding the government to account' – much greater emphasis, but if protecting the interests of the constituency, dealing with grievances and informing constituents are taken together, they rank marginally above the scrutiny role (39.5% v. 38.4%).

The constituency role has become a major role for MPs to the extent that for most it now takes up more time than any other single part of their job. However, important as it is for all MPs, it looms larger for Labour Members and Liberal Democrats than it does for Conservatives. This is reflected in the growing tendency for local Labour parties to select candidates directly connected to the constituency, often though not always through local government: although in 2001 47.5% of MPs had direct local connections, this was the case for 58.0% of Labour Members, 67.3% of the Liberal Democrats but only 12.0% of Conservatives. It is also important to distinguish between the constituency and other roles in that it is a largely separate role, carried out in a non-partisan manner. Of course, MPs of different parties will be more or less sympathetic to various collective interests, but most will seek to advance and defend most of those interests and, in particular, take up individual grievances regardless of party. The partisan and scrutiny roles overlap and MPs vary in their attitudes towards them, some markedly more partisan than others, some more heavily involved in scrutiny than others. There is also a potential and sometimes actual conflict between the three roles. On the one hand, they compete with each other for MPs' time and attention and, on the other, partisan intensity may undermine effective scrutiny, while assiduous scrutiny may weaken partisan commitment.

Part Five: A changing Parliament

Parliament has changed and is changing. It has changed in socio-economic composition, with the Commons becoming increasingly middle class, the socio-economic gap between the parties lessening, and the number and proportion of women increasing dramatically, though only recently. The House of Lords has become a more meritocratic body, especially as the introduction of life peerages began to have an impact and with the removal of most of the hereditary peers. Both Houses and their members have been subject to a professionalisation process, the Commons more so than the Lords: being a Member of Parliament has become and is regarded as a full-time job, with commensurate pay and resources; peers, while mostly not full-time or paid, have become more fully involved in the work of the upper house and resources have increased, though falling far short of those available to MPs. Crucially, however, these changes have been accompanied by changing attitudes: gone are those two significant blocs, the Conservative's 'knights of the shire' and Labour's trade union MPs, and their replacements see themselves as career politicians faced with role conflicts that were less of a problem for their predecessors. Their attitudes towards their roles are partly driven by party but also by whether the party is in government or opposition. Women have undoubtedly made an impact, even though it is neither as great nor as fundamental as some observers hoped. The House of Lords has become increasingly active because enough of its members are willing and the removal of most of the hereditaries appears to have given it a more widespread sense of legitimacy. However, it is a moot question how long it can remain a full-time House with part-time members and limited resources. The short answer may be indefinitely; the longer-term answer relates both to its composition and its functions.

Functions lie at the heart of the future of Parliament. The partisan role is unlikely to disappear, nor is the constituency role for MPs – how it would affect peers were some or all elected is an open question, but if the scrutiny role remains at its present level, even more so if it were to become more important, the more important the question of who is in Parliament becomes. Would a more representative Parliament in socio-economic terms be a more effective Parliament? Not necessarily, but if Parliament were widely perceived as unrepresentative, its legitimacy could be seriously undermined. On the other hand, an elected second chamber might become more partisan than the current House of Lords, not so much in terms of party cohesion but more in terms of attitude and operation. Of course, it can be argued that functionally an appointed or substantially-appointed second chamber would be more effective than an elected chamber. Similarly, in representational terms, if the House of Commons were widely perceived as not reflecting electoral opinion and, with it, public opinion, the pressure for changing the electoral system would grow. To divorce composition from functions for either the Commons or the Lords is unwise. To put it simply but crudely, what is expected of Parliament and are we getting the MPs and peers who can do the job?

Notes

1 This account is taken from Rush, *Parliament Today*, Chap. 11 and from Philip Norton, 'Party Cohesion in the House of Lords', paper presented to the Sixth Workshop of Parliamentary Scholars and Parliamentarians, Wroxton College, Banbury, 31 July–1 August 2004.
2 Samuel H. Beer, *Modern British Politics: A Study of Parties and Pressure Groups*. London: Faber, 1965, p. 350.
3 Philip Norton, *Dissension in the House of Commons 1945–74*. London: Macmillan, p. xviii.
4 Philip Cowley and Mark Stuart, 'More Bleak House than Great Expectations', *Parliamentary Affairs*, 57, 2003, p. 211.
5 Norton, 'Party Cohesion in the Lords', p. 2.
6 *Ibid.*, pp. 17–18.
7 See Rush, *The Role of the Member of Parliament*, Tables 6.8, 6.9 and 6.10.
8 A. Phillips, *The Politics of Presence* (Oxford: Clarendon Press, 1995).
9 Joni Lovenduski, 'Gender politics: a breakthrough for women?', *Parliamentary Affairs*, 50, 1997, p. 719.
10 S. J. Carroll and D. J. Liebowitz, 'New Challenges, New Questions, New Directions' in S. J. Carroll (ed.), *Women and American Politics* (Oxford: Oxford University Press, 2003), pp. 1–29.
11 Philip Cowley and Sarah Childs, 'Too Spineless to Rebel? New Labour's Women MPs', *British Journal of Political Science*, 33, 2003.
12 Labour's permanent backbenchers are those MPs who were on the backbenches for the whole of the Parliament. Sarah Childs and Julie Withey, 'Sex and the Signing of Early Day Motions in the 1997 Parliament', *Political Studies*, 52.
13 In most cases these differences were statistically significant.
14 The question was: 'Which of the following aspects of the job of being an MP do you think are the more important? (Rank order: scrutinising or keeping a check on the government and the civil service/supporting my party and helping it achieve its policy objectives/influencing or changing my party's policy/helping constituents with their problem and dealing with constituency issues/other).

Part III

Watching the Government: Parliament and Scrutiny

6
Objects and Questions

Philip Giddings and Helen Irwin

In this section we reflect on the different ways in which Parliament 'scrutinises' the work of Government and the State. Scrutiny, and the associated concept of accountability, have become more and more prominent in the work of Parliament in the last half-century. It might, superficially, be thought that the increased emphasis on 'scrutiny' is a consequence of the diminished significance of other roles, reflecting a decline in the power and prestige of Parliament. That may be an over-simplification but it does give us a clue to the meaning of 'scrutiny' in the Parliamentary context because it draws on what scrutiny is *not*. It is not to control, but to review; not to countermand, but to comment; not to command to do, but to invite to reflect. It is logically dependent upon action taken, policy announced or intended – even the apparent exception of pre-legislative scrutiny is the scrutiny of a document (the draft bill) produced by the government.

Scrutiny is closely associated with accountability because it is a form of holding government and state authorities to account by requiring them to explain what they have done, and what they have not done. But it is more than simply explanation because the account given is subject to cross-examination, exposed to criticism and counter-argument, in response to which further explanation and on occasion justification will be invited. The process is thus essentially an *interchange* between the scrutineer and the object of scrutiny, an interchange which may, or may not, affect the way in which either or both act subsequently. In that way the scrutiny process is closely associated with notions of *responsibility* and *responsible government*. An effective process of scrutiny by the legislature embodies *part* of the mechanisms in a democratic political order for ensuring the responsibility of those who govern and exercise public authority to those who are governed and subject to that authority. In a system of parliamentary government such as has evolved in the United Kingdom, scrutiny is thus a fundamental element of Parliament's constitutional function. It is a basic part of what Parliament is there to do.

When assessing accountability mechanisms, one needs to ask who is accountable, to whom, for what, and with what consequence. In parliamentary terms, this means, in the first place, who can be asked to explain and defend what has or has not been done. Generally speaking the answer is Ministers, and officials who respond on their behalf. The second question translates in parliamentary terms into to which part of Parliament are responses made. Normally this will be either the House itself (Commons or Lords); or some committee thereof; or an individual, such as the Comptroller and Auditor-General or the Parliamentary Commissioner for Administration, acting on behalf of Parliament. With the third question – on what matters can explanations be sought – the answer varies considerably according to the topic, the aspect of government concerned (the rules are different for departments of state, executive agencies and other public bodies) and the person answering, partly but not only because of the conventions of individual and collective ministerial responsibility. The answer to the fourth question is more problematic still. The direct 'consequences' will depend on who assesses them and what powers are available to those assessors (the contrast between a vote of censure at one extreme, and, at the other, a critical comment in a report which may not be debated), their willingness to exercise those powers, and the willingness of others, particularly the whips, to allow those powers to be exercised (ministers and whips will be anxious to avoid embarrassment to the Government). Often more significant are the indirect consequences of a successful or unsuccessful 'defence' which flow from (for example) the conclusions drawn by Ministers and/or senior officials about continuing or changing the course of action concerned.

It is clear from the previous paragraph that the systems of scrutiny and accountability are complex and varied but the key elements hold good across the range of complexity. Sir Derek Morris, giving evidence to the House of Lords Constitution Committee enquiry into the regulatory sector of government, identified three key elements to the accountability arrangements for regulators: the duty to explain; exposure to scrutiny, including cross-examination; and independent review, which in this context meant the possibility of changing a decision.[1] 'Independent review' is in fact a specific form of the *consequence* of scrutiny: an alternative consequence of the cross-examination aspect of scrutiny might well be a decision by the regulatory authority to review and change its procedures or organisation, or, no doubt exceptionally, the resignation of an individual or individuals.

Interpreting independent review as consequence, then, Sir Derek's three elements can usefully be applied to the scrutiny of all kinds of public body, including departments of state. The object of scrutiny is to require *explanation*, to expose that explanation to *cross-examination*, and by virtue of that process to achieve a beneficial *consequence* in terms of the quality of government and administration. This was well put at the beginning of the last century by President Lowell of Harvard University, commenting upon Question Time. He wrote, 'the system provides a method of dragging before the House any acts or omissions by the departments of state, and of turning a searchlight upon every corner of the public service ... it helps very much to keep the administration of the country up to the mark, and it is a great safeguard against neglect or arbitrary conduct'.[2] Today many would consider that an over-optimistic view of Question Time, but it well expresses the scrutiny trio of explanation, cross-examination and consequence.

An important additional parliamentary safeguard against arbitrary conduct by public officials has been the creation of the Ombudsman Office, set up in 1967 as part of the parliamentary reforms of the Wilson-Crossman era.[3] Although there was strong resistance from the Whitehall-Westminster establishment to the importation of this Scandinavian administrative device to the UK's unique constitutional order, the Wilson Government insisted on driving the policy through, albeit with some significant changes to accommodate MPs' sensitivities.

The Parliamentary Commissioner for Administration, as the Ombudsman is still formally styled, was initially mocked as a 'toothless tiger' and a 'watchdog on chains'[4] but has become an established feature of the system of parliamentary control of the administration – 'part of the fabric of the United Kingdom's unwritten constitution'.[5] The Ombudsman is empowered to require explanation – having, unlike MPs, the statutory power of access to departmental files and to summon and take evidence on oath from witnesses – and cross-examine the explanation in detail. Although the Commissioner's statutory duty is to investigate and report, he is empowered to comment upon the government department's response to his findings of maladministration, particularly when it has not accepted his recommended remedy.

From the Office's first great triumph in the Sachsenhausen case,[6] through slaughtered chickens,[7] Barlow Clowes,[8] the channel tunnel link railway[9] and the yet-to-be-completed sagas of the Child Support Agency and Equitable Life, MPs and their constituents have had cause to be grateful for the ability of this instrument of parliamentary scrutiny to obtain remedies for maladministration. A significant feature of the Parliamentary Ombudsman scheme is the backing the Office receives from the Commons Select Committee appointed to oversee it, originally dedicated solely to the work of the Office but in recent years subsumed into what is now the Select Committee on Public Administration (PASC).

Notwithstanding the victories the Ombudsman has won, there remain features of the scheme which many observers, including recent holders of the office, consider need reform, including the MP filter. On 20 July 2001 the Government formally accepted the recommendations of the Collcutt Review and PASC for the creation of a new Public Service Ombudsman Scheme to which citizens would have direct access.[10] But in the age-old Whitehall formula for delay if not obstruction of reform, parliamentary time has not been found for the necessary legislation to accomplish it.

In subsequent chapters we shall be looking at the development of other instruments of parliamentary scrutiny. We devote a separate section to the scrutiny of *law-making*[11] and in this section John McEldowney and Colin Lee[12] review financial scrutiny, and particularly audit, which has antecedents in the reform era of the nineteenth century. More recently, and the subject of a separate chapter,[13] the House of Commons has developed a system of departmentally-related select committees, part of whose function is to scrutinise the policy, administration and expenditure of the government departments within their remit. This system, established in 1979, has continued to evolve during the Blair Government's 'modernisation' process and remains the vehicle for many reformist ambitions for enhancing the ability of House of Commons to re-assert its control of the Executive, ministerial reluctance notwithstanding.[14]

The 'departmentally-related' select committees necessarily have a strong departmental focus but from the start they were also empowered to monitor the work of 'associated public bodies' – quangos, regulators, agencies and the like. As the occasional description 'fringe bodies' indicates, many of these are not considered central to public policy and administration. However, this form of administration has been of growing significance in the last thirty years and looks likely to continue to grow. We therefore give these bodies explicit consideration in chapter nine.

Much of the rationale for scrutiny and accountability draws on concepts of representative government in its elected form and therefore has a clear focus on the work of the House of Commons as the elected chamber of Parliament. However, as through the twentieth century the primacy of the Commons was exerted more and more forcefully, so more and more emphasis was placed upon the scrutiny role of the non-elected chamber, the House of Lords – so much so that it might now be considered to be a chamber of scrutiny. Thus the Wakeham Commission identified as one of the key roles of a modern second chamber 'to assist Parliament as a whole to provide *better scrutiny* of the Executive' (emphasis original) and went on to say, 'Given the Government's enormous power in our system, it seems to us important to have a second chamber able and willing to complement the House of Commons in its essential work of scrutinising the Executive and holding the Government to account.'[15] This is the theme of chapter 10.

But first let us return to the most famous aspect of scrutiny and accountability – Questions, and specifically Commons' Questions. Hailed by eminent constitutionalists and former Prime Ministers as of the greatest constitutional significance,[16] Question Time is often the best attended part of the Commons' procedure and yet also the most widely criticised for its raucous, adversarial style and lack of substance. Question Time, and specifically Prime Minister's Question Time, is, of course, only the most visible part of the Question process, which is a key part of Parliament's armoury of instruments of scrutiny.

Members' use of parliamentary questions has greatly increased since 1964. The tables below (Table 6.1 and 6.2), taken from the Order Paper and Hansard for the dates in question, show the number of questions on the Order Paper of the Commons for oral and written answer in

Table 6.1   Number of Questions on Commons Order Paper, 22–25 June 1964

1964	Mon 22 June	Tues 23 June	Weds 24 June	Thurs 25 June
Oral Questions on Order Paper	71	45 + 10 to PM	77	68 + 12 to PM
No. answered orally at Question Time	29	27 + 7 by PM	35	26 + 8 by PM
Written Questions on Order Paper for answer that day	60	54	60	26

Table 6.2   Number of Questions on Commons Order Paper, 21–24 June 2004

2004	Mon 21 June	Tues 22 June	Weds 23 June	Thurs 24 June
Oral Questions on Order Paper	25	25	14 + 15 to PM	24
No. answered orally at Question Time	15	14	7 + 6 by PM	13
Written Questions in Questions Book for answer that day	286	135	150	233

two similar weeks in June in 1964 and 2004 and the number of questions for oral answer which were answered orally by a minister in the allotted hour (Question Time) each day. Questions to the Prime Minister are separately distinguished.

The tables above show that far fewer Members tabling questions for oral answer (orals) can expect to receive an oral answer from a minister during Question Time than in 1964. In 1964 the system of giving notice of oral questions was much less regulated than today. In particular, Members could table more than one question for oral answer to a particular minister and expect to receive an answer. Questions 1 and 2 to the Minister for Public Building and Works on Monday 22 June 1964 were both asked by Jim Boyden and questions 3 and 4 were asked by Willie Hamilton. This even applied to questions to the Prime Minister: on 25th June George Wigg had two successive questions to the Prime Minister, about related subjects, which were answered together, after which the Speaker allowed Mr Wigg two supplementary questions. Questions were listed in the order in which they were tabled and a maximum notice period was yet to be introduced. (This came in 1965.) Ministers answered according to a rota, but several ministers were listed each day, and reached. On 22 June 1964 two ministers replied to questions within the hour; on 23 June questions to three were reached in the forty-five minutes before the Prime Minister's appearance.

In 2004 the number of questions receiving an oral answer was less than half that in 1964, mainly because answers and, crucially, supplementary questions were much briefer in 1964 and the Speaker only very infrequently called opposition frontbenchers to ask supplementary questions, something that is now routine at every Question Time. This applied even to questions to the Prime Minister: during that week in 1964 the Leader of the Opposition (Harold Wilson) was called only once, on the Thursday. In 1964 Prime Minister's question time took place twice in the week, for fifteen minutes each Tuesday and Thursday. Since 1997 the Prime Minister has answered once each week, for half an hour on Wednesdays and it has become the pattern that during that half hour the Leader of the Opposition is called to put up to six questions to the Prime Minister, all without notice. The Leader of the Liberal Democrats gets two questions and if they are present, leaders of other parties may get called too.

Question Time in 1964 was overwhelmingly a time for backbenchers; in 2004 it is a significant part of the battle between the main parties. In addition to the participation of opposition frontbenchers, it has also become the practice for parties to hand out suggested questions and supplementary questions to their backbenchers. This practice, which came to be known as 'syndication', was described by the Procedure Committee in 1990 as an 'abuse', and the Committee proposed rule changes to try to discourage it. In 2001–02 a questionnaire to Members elicited that requests to table questions from whips or party advisers were still frequent: 30% of Members received such requests at least once a week and as many as 52% of respondents stated they occasionally acceded to such requests, only 20% saying they never did so.[17] In 2002 the Procedure Committee offered no judgment on the practice and made no proposals to try to end it.

The figures in the table for 2004 for the number of oral questions greatly understate the number of oral questions tabled. As the figures for 1964 show, there was a good chance then of getting an oral answer to a question tabled for oral answer. Increased numbers of Members seeking to ask oral questions led, over time, to increasingly tight rules about how many questions might be tabled and the maximum and minimum notice required. The questions rota now lists only one minister to answer during each allotted period and over time the maximum and minimum notice periods became effectively the same thing. All questions tabled at the first opportunity (until 2002, ten sitting days ahead of the date for answering) were subject to a random selection process (known as the 'shuffle') to determine the order in which they were answered. Questions tabled on a subsequent day were too far down the list to be reached.

Traditionally, questions not reached at Question Time received a written answer which was published in Hansard the next day. In 1990, in recognition of the fact that only a limited number stood a chance of being answered orally, the Procedure Committee recommended that only a limited number of questions should be printed.[18] This accounts for the smaller number of questions printed in 2004 than in the same week in 1964, even though anything up to a hundred Members may submit oral questions for answer by one of the large Departments of State and up to 200 submit questions to the Prime Minister each week. With the introduction of this new rule about printing, the House also agreed that questions not printed should fall, though Members may request that a lost oral question be reinstated as a question for written answer.

In 2002 questions were examined by both the Procedure and the Modernisation Committees. As part of a package of proposals aimed at increasing the topicality of question time and making tabling of questions more convenient for Members, the House agreed that the notice period for oral questions should be significantly reduced. In 1991 the Procedure Committee had recommended a minimum notice period of five sitting days (instead of ten) to allow greater scope for 'topicality'. The then Government rejected this, but in 2002 the Leader of the House (Robin Cook) himself put forward a proposal for a reduced notice period. Now, for all but the regional Departments (Scotland, Wales and Northern Ireland), Ministers receive only three sitting days' notice.[19] This means that some questions are now tabled at the very last minute and may relate to very topical matters – this is particularly helpful to Members in the case of questions to the Foreign Secretary or the Secretary of State for Defence. However, a related change made in 2002 removed the previous need for Members personally to attend in the Table Office on the day of the shuffle to table an oral question. Questions may now be sent in by post, or electronically, or handed in in person at any time in the period between question time to a particular minister and his or her next appearance, and then held till the date for the relevant shuffle. Thus some oral questions may have been handed in almost a month before they are answered,[20] counterbalancing to some extent the increased topicality of others. Other instances of the recent emphasis on topicality were the decision in 2002 to rename Private Notice Questions as 'Urgent Questions' (although the rules for such questions remained otherwise the same as hitherto) and the earmarking of time in the House of Lords on two days each week for 'topical questions' selected by ballot.

The desire for greater topicality is also a factor in a change in the wording of oral questions. In the case of questions to the Prime Minister, during the 1960s Members looked for questions which would not be transferred by the PM to the Minister responsible for policy in the area concerned and the House has for many years accepted the 'engagements' formula: 'If he will list his official engagements for [the day the question is answered]', to which virtually any supplementary may be asked as the normal method of asking a question of the Prime Minister.[21]

Such open questions are not in order to other ministers and supplementary questions must be within the scope of the original question. The Speaker will haul up a Member who tries to put a supplementary which goes wide of the question on the paper. But for various reasons, the type of oral question tabled to departmental ministers has become briefer and closer to an open question, though the rule is enforced that a question may not be so open as to allow any supplementary. The fact that only questions successful in the shuffle are printed means that Members may not want to waste time and effort in drafting questions which may fall. Even with the shorter notice period Members may not want to narrow down the range of possible supplementary questions far in advance of question time. Also, where questions are handed to Members by their parties, the line on any supplementary may not have been decided when the question is tabled. Thus the order paper has become, with some exceptions, a list of brief and very general questions – pegs on which backbenchers and opposition frontbench spokesmen hope to hang their topical supplementaries.

The number of questions for written answer has increased dramatically since 1964. The numbers for 2004 in Table 6.2 above are relatively low: on some days the Table Office may receive over 500 questions for written answer. Despite the increase in numbers, virtually all are answered, and most within the time period recommended to ministers in government guidance,[22] although from time to time some Departments miss these targets – for example when there is a very large number of questions on a single issue, such as the foot and mouth epidemic or the war in Iraq. Not all answers satisfy the Member asking the question and the Speaker is frequently called upon by Members raising points of order about replies they consider inadequate. Successive Speakers have consistently resisted being brought into such debates, pointing out that the content of answers is a matter for which ministers alone are responsible. The PASC has made it its practice each year to examine those questions where Ministers refuse information and has taken up some complaints by Members about answers.

Some categories of written questions, such as round robin questions asking the same question of each government department, were quite unusual in 1964 but now fill a significant amount of the pages of

Hansard each day. Some Members table hundreds of written questions; others use the device very sparsely. A factor behind the seemingly inexorable increase in the number of written questions is the
increased number of staff Members may employ. One category of
question has all but disappeared: the planted or 'inspired' question
to enable a minister to make a written announcement has been
replaced since 2002 by a new category of written ministerial statement, of which notice appears on the Order Paper, a change intended
to increase transparency.[23]

Question Time remains a time when Members, ministers and their
shadows can and do seize opportunities to shine. The conventional purposes of parliamentary questions: to obtain information or to press for
action are less in evidence at oral questions than party rivalries and campaigns. However, though many backbench supplementary questions,
particularly from the government side, are clearly expected, some are
emphatically not and Question Time remains a significant prime-time
opportunity for backbench Members. Although attendance is lower than
it used to be, Question Time, particularly on Wednesdays, is the time
when the House is fullest, apart from during major statements and a few
very high-profile debates. There is one complete novelty since 1964:
since 2003 oral questions are sometimes taken in the House's parallel
debating chamber in Westminster Hall, on cross-cutting themes, with
junior ministers from several departments answering together. Arrangements for these sessions are still experimental and few Members have so
far taken part.

How the use of Questions may develop in future is difficult to predict
and their interaction with the Freedom of Information Act which came
into force in 2005 as yet uncertain. But what is clear is that Members,
from both front and backbenches, continue to see them as an important part of their armoury in exposing the Government's policies and
administration to scrutiny and cross-examination on the public record,
on occasion in the most (tele-)visual form.

Notes

1   Sixth Report of the Constitution Committee, 2003–04, *The Regulatory State:
    Ensuring its Accountability*, HL 68, 6 May 2004, para 75 and Vol 1, p. 320 at
    Q901.

2   A. L. Lowell, *The Government of England*, 1919, Vol 1, p. 332, cited in D. N.
    Chester and N. Bowring, *Questions in Parliament*, Clarendon Press, 1962,
    p. 269.

3   Parliamentary Commissioner Act 1967. For an authoritative history of the
    Office, see Roy Gregory and Philip Giddings, *The Ombudsman, the Citizen
    and Parliament*, Politico's, 2002.

4 See W. B. Gwyn, 'The British PCA: Ombudsman or Ombudsmouse?', *Journal of Politics*, 35, 1973.

5 First Report from the Select Committee on the PCA, 1990–91, HC 129, p. xiii.

6 Parliamentary Commissioner for Administration, Third Report, 1967–68, HC 54, December 1967.

7 Third Report from the PCA Select Committee, 1992–93, *Compensation to Farmers for Slaughtered Poultry*, HC 593, April 1993.

8 See Roy Gregory and Gavin Drewry, 'Barlow Clowes and the Ombudsman', Parts I and II, *Public Law*, Summer and Autumn 1991.

9 See Gregory & Giddings, *op. cit.* pp. 343–351 for a summary of this complex case.

10 Philip Collcutt and Mary Hourihan, *Review of the Public Sector Ombudsmen in England*, Cabinet Office, April 2000; Third Report from the Select Committee on Public Administration, 1999–2000, HC 612, July 2000.

11 Below, chapters 11 to 14.

12 Below, chapter 7.

13 Below, chapter 8.

14 See, for example, *Shifting the Balance: Unfinished Business*, First Report of the House of Commons Liaison Committee, 2000–01, HC 321, March 2001.

15 Report of the Royal Commission on the Reform of the House of Lords, *A House for the Future*, Cm 4534, January 2000, para 1.3 and 3.10.

16 Sir Ivor Jennings, *Parliament*, Second Edition, 1957, p. 99; Stanley Baldwin, giving evidence to the Procedure Committee in 1931, said 'There is no more inalienable right ... than that right of putting questions to the Ministers' [Q312].

17 Third Report of the Procedure Committee, HC 622, 2001–02, *Parliamentary Questions*, Annex B.

18 A useful summary of the development of the rules for questions can be found in the Third Report of the Procedure Committee, HC 622, 2001–02, *Parliamentary Questions*, paragraphs 6–16.

19 Notice for questions to ministers in the regional departments is currently five sitting days.

20 Up to a week in the case of Prime Minister's questions.

21 See Mark Franklin and Philip Norton, Eds. *Parliamentary Questions* (Oxford: Clarendon Press, 1993), pp. 52–59.

22 Generally within a working week unless the Member specifies a named day for answer.

23 See Procedure Committee, *Parliamentary Questions*, Third Report of Session 2001–02, HC 622, TSO, 2002.

7

Parliament and Public Money

John McEldowney and Colin Lee

Parliament often seems at its weakest in the control and scrutiny of public money. Taxes and duties are raised, and public money is spent, with formal parliamentary authority. However, such authority is almost invariably granted in the form proposed by the Government. While suggestions for reform have often focused on ways to give the House of Commons a greater institutional involvement in these processes, progress has been more marked in the retrospective scrutiny and audit of Government's expenditure decisions. Scrutiny is now much more complex and sophisticated, although parliamentary mechanisms have struggled to keep abreast with the growing range and complexity of the taxation system and public expenditure.

For at least the last forty years the financial procedures of the House of Commons have seemed ripe for reform. In the 1960s, Bernard Crick characterised Parliament's scrutiny of government finance as 'badly under-developed', not so much in relation to the detail of expenditure, but 'of priorities and value for money'.[1] These weaknesses have been only partly tackled in the last forty years. This chapter examines the main mechanisms at the disposal of Parliament for the control and scrutiny of public money – the formal decision-making processes of the House of Commons, the information analysis and scrutiny functions of select committees and the audit and value-for-money work of the National Audit Office (NAO) and the Committee of Public Accounts (PAC). The chapter concludes that progress has been made in the scrutiny of public money in relation in particular to value for money, but that Parliament does not have, and perhaps should not be expected to have, capacity for systematic analysis and sustained influence on priorities between taxation and expenditure and within expenditure itself. Given the complexity and technical aspects of financial information and government accounts, it is likely that Parliamentary scrutiny by its nature has to be broad brush, relying on the value of independent audit and the expertise of the NAO. The PAC provides an important role in monitoring. But there is a constant need for financial information to be distilled into a workable form to enable a broad spectrum of financial work to be undertaken by all select committees.

'Ways and Means' and 'Supply'

There are two main aspects to the formal authorisation of public finance by Parliament, which are characterised in the procedures of the House of Commons as 'Ways and Means' and 'Supply'. The former relates to taxes and duties, which are generally authorised through the passage of the Finance Bill and the resolutions that give rise to such Bills passed at the conclusion of the Budget debate. The amount of time devoted to such business by the House of Commons has fallen markedly in recent years, despite or perhaps because of the growing size and complexity of Finance Bills. In Session 1963–64, for example, the Finance Bill was debated in the House for more than twenty days; in recent sessions, there has tended to be five days debate on the floor of the House on the Finance Bill.[2] In debating such Bills the House has found it increasingly difficult to disentangle novel measures arising from the Budget from the 'tax management' elements, such as measures to counter tax avoidance. The timetable for a Finance Bill – usually introduced in April and receiving Royal Assent in mid-July – militates against systematic analysis by select committee from which many other Bills now benefit. Paradoxically, the fullest analysis of Finance Bills is now undertaken by a select committee of the House of Lords, even though that House does not seek to amend Finance Bills.[3] Proposals from the Hansard Society and others for separate Taxes Management Bills have been resisted by the Treasury.

Until the early 1980s, around 30 Commons sitting days a session were devoted to 'Supply days', which were formally concerned with the authorisation of public expenditure. In reality, the subjects chosen for debate, principally by the Opposition, bore little relation to financial scrutiny.[4] Following the report of the Select Committee on Procedure (Finance) in 1982, the reality was recognised when 'Supply days' were replaced, principally by 'Opposition days', by specific debates on the armed forces and on public expenditure, and by three 'Estimates days' each session. These Estimates days usually represent the only opportunity for the House to debate and amend the proposals for authorisation of the Government's ordinary annual expenditure, which are otherwise agreed to without debate, a process which has been characterised by one MP as 'rubber-stamping tablets of stone handed down by the Executive of the day'.[5] Moreover, the subjects chosen for Estimates day debates are generally policy topics examined in select committee reports, usually tenuously connected to the actual proposals for authorisation before the House.

Select committees

In principle the House has a choice between asserting direct control over levels and patterns of public spending and concentrating on indirect control and influence.[6] In reality such success as Parliament has achieved in relation to public money has come not in exerting formal control, but in exercising influence, the main vehicles for which have been the select committees of the House of Commons generally, and the combination of the NAO and the PAC. NAO-PAC and departmental select committees individually and collectively – through the Liaison Committee composed of chairmen of select committees – have worked together to increase almost exponentially both the quality and the quantity of the financial information provided by the Government in relation to its expenditure plans. Although formal authorisation continues to be based on Estimates documents, these are now complemented by departmental annual reports, which set out departments' expenditure plans in the context of policy objectives, and autumn performance reports, which seek to give provisional information on both financial outturns and policy outcomes. The Treasury also publishes volumes accompanying the Estimates and departmental annual reports which explain the relationship between the different sets of figures and provide some thematic information.[7]

Scrutiny of expenditure by departmental select committees has become more systematic. It is now established as one of the core functions of each departmental select committee, and those committees now almost invariably undertake annual inquiries into the relevant departmental reports. These annual inquiries help in the development of broader knowledge about the expenditure plans and administration of each department, and sometimes throw unexpected light on details of expenditure, such as the inadequately planned move of the Ministerial suite of the Ministry of Agriculture, Fisheries and Food to a new building.[8]

Developments in audit

However, the progress by departmental select committees has arguably been out-stripped by developments in audit. The role of auditing in the control of public expenditure has a long history and has received considerable attention concerning its reform. In the 1960s the main focus of reform was to improve the Office of Comptroller and Auditor General.[9] In addition it was hoped to move auditing from the 'candle ends and cheese-paring examination' established by Gladstone in the nineteenth century to a more rigorous and substantive review. This included settling ambiguities about the Exchequer and Audit Acts 1866 and 1920. It also involved clarification of the role of public audit of the nationalised industries. There was considerable concern about the quality of public audit and it was hoped that a broader and more analytical approach might be adopted beyond the technical certification of accounts. The 1970s was a period of pressure to consolidate the audit system including the principle that all public money should be capable of public audit and a quality assessment of the efficiency and effectiveness of expenditure.[10] These reforms were advocated by select committees of the House of Commons, most notably the Expenditure Committee, the Procedure Committee, and the PAC.[11] Members of the Study of Parliament Group in a variety of ways contributed to the reform of audit and expenditure, focusing on the work of select committees in their ability to handle financial matters.[12] Members of the Group have been active in giving evidence to select committees and preparing memoranda and publishing analysis and assessment of reforms.[13]

The strengthening of audit and financial scrutiny is one of the successes of the 1980s. Coincidental to the government's policy intended to improve the efficiency of public services in general, auditing attracted the attention of Norman St John-Stevas, who, as Leader of the House of Commons had been instrumental in the introduction of the departmental select committees in 1979. In Session 1982–83 as a backbencher he introduced with cross-party support the bill which became the National Audit Act 1983. The 1983 Act made the Comptroller and Auditor General an Officer of the House of Commons, established a new revamped Exchequer and Audit Department, now the NAO. That Act stopped short of providing a unitary system of audit, as local government audit fell under the authority of a revamped District Audit system under the newly established Audit Commission. Nationalised industries were also excluded, though with the advent of privatisation this omission has not proved a problem.

The NAO's reports are scrutinised by the PAC and the work of that Committee may stimulate the NAO to undertake an investigation. One recent example was the evidence taken by the Committee following a critical report by the NAO of the Millennium Dome.[14] There is an annual report summarising the reports undertaken by the NAO in the past year.[15] It is estimated that currently the NAO undertakes the audit of more than 600 accounts.[16] On the basis of each NAO report the PAC takes oral evidence from the relevant departmental Accounting Officer. Information provided by the NAO sometimes also underpins scrutiny of the Executive by other select committees. The funding of the Pergau Dam project in Malaysia[17] and the Sale of Rover to British Aerospace[18] are some of the examples where the NAO provided important and critical analysis in their reports.

It is difficult to calculate the real cost savings of the NAO's work. Over the past three year period the NAO itself has estimated that savings amounted to '£1.54 billion, an average of £512 million each year'.[19] There are some recent specific examples of savings. Recommendations from the PAC and the NAO allowed the Ministry of Defence to recover £75 million from the United Nations for the United Kingdom's contribution to peace keeping in Bosnia.[20] The work of the NAO is usually reactive rather than proactive. Large scale projects, such as the Millennium Dome and complex technical defence contracts appear to cost more than when they are first planned, have a tendency to overrun on cost and take longer to complete than expected.

NAO reports provide a system of vigilance, but preventative measures appear more difficult to plan and implement. The NAO audits bodies over which there are inspection rights, certain health service bodies or any public body that receives more than half its income from public funds. One substantial limitation is that, under company law,[21] the NAO cannot audit Company Act companies as the NAO is not a qualified auditor under the relevant legislation. Lord Sharman recommended that this limitation should be removed, subject to its compatibility with European company law.[22] The Government agreed to that recommendation in March 2002.[23] Lord Sharman's Report also made recommendations for improving the system of internal audit and reinforced the principle that all public money should be capable of being traced and audited by the NAO. While this will undoubtedly strengthen the importance of audit and the role of the NAO, will this lead to a strengthening of *parliamentary* scrutiny?

Expanding the role of audit provides the means for government *and* Parliament to exercise greater control than in the past. Government interest in ensuring that public money is spent wisely and prudently will in most cases complement parliamentary concern about account-ability. However, the resulting audit culture has a habit of developing a life of its own. Auditors and consultants are employed by government departments in ever-increasing numbers to help pre-empt any prob-lems that may arise through the audits undertaken by the NAO in their value for money investigations.[24] Audit and scrutiny have had to become more complex and sophisticated, as Parliament has sought to develop forms of scrutiny to deal with the increasing complexity and variety of Government expenditure initiatives.

The Private Finance Initiative

Take, for example, the Private Finance Initiative (PFI) formally launched by the Government in 1992 to achieve closer co-operation between the public and private sectors.[25] A variety of possible PFI projects were identified in the National Health Service, roads, prisons, tunnels, light railway systems, major equipment, and office accommodation. PFI developed the twin objectives of encouraging value for money in any public sector expenditure and placing the financial risks on the private sector. Since 1992 PFI, which was overseen by a Treasury task force, has undergone a number of important changes, including the Government Resources and Accounts Act 2000 which transferred the task force's role to *Partnerships UK*, a private sector company drawn from a wide cross-section of the financial services industry with access to private and public finance. It is intended to bring greater financial know-how into the management of PFI ventures.

PFIs are often controversial when concerned with matters such as the London Underground, the high-speed rail link to the channel tunnel, toll bridges, prisons, schools, and hospitals. PFI has grown in scale since 1992.[26] Currently there are estimated to be at least £30 billion worth of PFI projects and over 400 PFI contracts currently in force.[27] Taken as a whole it has been estimated that 'investment in the private sector under the PFI is equivalent to 17% of total public sector investment under the three-year period covered by the Com-prehensive Spending Review'.[28] Parliamentary scrutiny of PFI has been *ad hoc* – mainly relying on the NAO to draw attention to any impropriety. In this area as in others, select committee scrutiny tends to be spasmodic and reactive. PFI arrangements set new challenges for Parliament in examining a technically complex and difficult subject.

The European Union

The development of the European Union, especially the adoption of a single currency (euro) and the stability and growth pact, also sets new challenges for Parliament. One such challenge is over the future role of the Bank of England, another is the responsibility for departments to monitor and scrutinise the expenditure of EU funds. Both challenges question the future of Parliament's scrutiny powers over developments that, though often perceived as external to the United Kingdom, have major consequences for the economy and prosperity of its citizens.

The Bank of England is the United Kingdom's central bank, and with the other major banks is a member of the clearing system. The Bank of England acts also as a banker to the government. A radical innovation was introduced by the new Labour government, four days after the General Election on 6 May 1997. The Chancellor of the Exchequer announced that the Bank of England would be given operational responsibility for the setting of interest rates to meet the government's inflation target. This reform is now contained in the Bank of England Act 1998. In formal terms any action required to achieve a set target on inflation is taken by the Monetary Policy Committee of the Bank which meets on a monthly basis. Accountability for the new arrangements is through a report to the Treasury Select Committee and to the House of Commons. The Bank also issues a quarterly Inflation Report and an Annual Report of its activities. In extreme economic circumstances the government retains the right to override the Bank, but subject to ratification by the House of Commons.

The Bank of England's Framework for Monetary Policy has twin objectives to deliver price stability through the government's inflation target and to support the government's economic policy. This may appear straightforward in periods of high growth in the economy, but is less easy in periods of recession. The new arrangements under the current favourable economic climate are largely untested. The Bank's role in the control of public expenditure through determining interest rates and influencing general economic policy has greatly increased. The overt political manipulation of interest rates by the Government of the day appears less easy under the new arrangements as compared to the past.

Speculation remains rife as to whether the UK will adopt the Euro. It remains to be seen whether full independence will be granted to the Bank of England and this raises the question of Parliament's role. Membership of the EU provides flows of funds in terms of income and expenditure. This means that funds must fall under the Estimates and meet the requirements of Resource Accounting Manual. Various responsibilities fall on the relevant UK department under the UK's financial arrangements.[29] There is a monthly requirement for departments to inform the Treasury of any EU transactions, the requirements of audit and monitoring apply. Again all these changes have been gradually incorporated into the existing arrangements for financial control.

Control or scrutiny?

Criticisms of the formal financial control exercised by Parliament are partly justified. It must be admitted that the mechanisms for the authorisation of taxation plans have struggled to cope with the growing complexity of tax law. But such criticisms are partly misplaced. Government will always be better placed than the House of Commons or its select committees to make expenditure planning decisions. The significance of formal authorisation of expenditure is as a means, not as an end; Parliament establishes the benchmarks in relation to which audit takes place. Formal authorisation of expenditure matters as a gateway to scrutiny.

Overall, Parliament and its agencies do more financial scrutiny than ever before and do it better. That scrutiny covers a greater range of public expenditure than ever before. That process of scrutiny, and the audit and value-for-money work of the NAO in particular, provides high levels of assurance about propriety in expenditure. Parliament and the public have a clearer picture than ever before of the Government's overall spending plans, but Parliament has struggled to keep abreast with the different ways in which money is spent as these have diversified. Expenditure is and should be subordinate to policy and administration. The focus in the future will need to be not only changes to the financial procedures of the House of Commons but on taking forward financial scrutiny as part and parcel of analysis of policy and administration.

Notes

1 B. Crick, *The Reform of Parliament* (1968 edition), Weidenfeld & Nicolson, pp. 238–39.
2 Sessional Diary of the House of Commons, 1963–64: Finance (No. 2) Bill.
3 Third Report from the Economic Affairs Committee, Session 2002–03, *Finance Bill 2003*, HL 121-I; Second Report from the Economic Affairs Committee, Session 2003–04, *Finance Bill 2004*, HL 109.
4 M. Ryle, 'Supply and other Financial Procedures', in S. A. Walkland, ed., *The House of Commons in the Twentieth Century* (1979), pp. 329–425.
5 Andrew Mackinlay MP, HC Deb, 3 December 2002, col 87.

6   Report from the Select Committee on Procedure (Finance), HC (1982–83) 42-III, pp. 10–17: Evidence submitted by Dr Ann Robinson in collaboration with members of the Study of Parliament Group.

7   For overviews of the financial information currently available, see Seventh Report from the Treasury Committee, Session 2001–02, *Parliamentary Account- ability of Departments*, HC 340-I; First Special Report from the Treasury Com- mittee, Session 2002–03, *Parliamentary Accountability of Departments: The Government Response to the Committee's Seventh Report, Session 2001–02*, HC 149; *Erskine May's Treatise on The Law, Privileges, Proceedings and Usage of Parliament* (23rd Edition, 2004), pp. 858–866.

8   First Report from the Agriculture Committee, Session 1997–98, *MAFF/ Intervention Board Departmental Report 1997*, HC 310, para 23; First Report from the Agriculture Committee, Session 1998–99, *MAFF/Intervention Board Departmental Report 1998 and the Comprehensive Spending Review*, HC 125, paras 12–14.

9   E. L. Normanton, *Accountability and Audit in Governments* (Manchester, 1966).

10 Minutes of Evidence taken before the Expenditure Committee (General Sub Committee), Session 1977–78, HC 661.

11 Eleventh Report from the Expenditure Committee, Session 1976–77, HC 535, and Twelfth Report from the Expenditure Committee, Session 1977–78, HC 576; First Report from the Select Committee on Procedure, Session 1977–78, HC 588; First Special Report from the Committee of Public Accounts, Session 1980–81, HC 115.

12 In the area of the financial role of select committees see Ann Robinson, 'The Treasury and Civil Service Committee' in G. Drewry, ed., *The New Select Committees* (2nd Edition, Oxford, 1989) pp. 268–318; Ann Robinson, 'The Financial Work of the Select Committees' in G. Drewry, ed., *The New Select Committees* (2nd edition, Oxford, 1989), pp. 307–318; P. Baines, 'Financial Accountability: Agencies and Audit' in P. Giddings, ed., *Parliamentary Accountability: A Study of Parliament and Executive Agencies* (London, 1995), pp. 95–118; Ann Robinson, *Parliament and Public Spending* (London, 1978).

13 Ann Robinson, 'The House of Commons and Public Expenditure', in S. A. Walkland and M. Ryle eds., *The Commons Today* (London, 1981) pp. 154–174; Ann Robinson, Memorandum to the Select Committee on Procedure (Finance), Session 1982–83, HC 42-II.

14 HC 936, 1999–2000 and HC 989-I 2000–01.

15 National Audit Office, *Financial Auditing and Reporting* (London, 2003).

16 David Heald and Alasdair McLeod, 'Public Expenditure' in *The Laws of Scotland: Stair Memorial Encyclopaedia* (London, 2002), para. 520.

17 Third Report from the Foreign Affairs Committee, Session 1993–94, HC 271.

18 First Report from the Trade and Industry Committee, Session 1990–91, HC 34.

19 National Audit Office, *Corporate Plan 2003–04 to 2004–06* (London, 2002), para. 1.2.

20 NAO, *Helping the Nation Spend Wisely*, Annual Report 2002–03 (London, 2003).

21 Section 25, Companies Act 1989.

22 Lord Sharman of Redlynch, *Holding to Account: The Review of Audit and Accountability for Central Government* (London, 2001).

23 *Audit and Accountability in Central Government The Government's response to Lord Sharman's Report 'Holding to Account'*, March 2002, Cm 5456.

24 J. McEldowney, 'Audit Cultures and Risk Aversion in Public Authorities: An Agenda for Public Lawyers' in R. Baldwin ed., *Law and Uncertainty Risks and Legal Processes* (Kluwer, 1997), pp. 185–210. Also see J. F. McEldowney, 'The Control of Public Expenditure', chapter 15 in J. Jowell and D. Oliver eds., *The Changing Constitution* (Oxford, 2004) pp. 375–400.

25 It replaced the use of 'Ryrie' rules, named after Sir William Ryrie, then Second Permanent Secretary to the Treasury and developed in the 1980s.

26 HM Treasury, *Public Private Partnerships: The Government's Approach* (London, 2000).

27 Estimate taken from NAO Press Notice HC 375 2001–2.

28 *Ibid.*

29 See *Government Accounting 2000*, chapter 19, amendment 1/01 paras. 19.1.1–19.5.6. London: Stationery Office, 2001.

8
Select Committees: Scrutiny à la carte?

David Natzler and Mark Hutton

The establishment of the departmental select committees in 1979 represented an attempt by the House of Commons to expose government to more systematic and more comprehensive scrutiny than had previously been possible. The Procedure Committee in its report proposing the new committee structure recommended –

> There should be a reorganisation of the select committee structure to provide the House with the means of scrutinising the activities of the public service on a continuing and systematic basis.[1]

Over the twenty five years since, the House has consistently restructured the select committees to match changes in the structure of government departments. At the same time the structure has been extended to include a number of government departments which had not been covered originally.

In 1990, in its examination of a decade's experience of the new Committee system, the Procedure Committee concluded that 'the present Select Committee system has provided a far more rigorous systematic and comprehensive scrutiny of Ministers' actions and policies than anything which went before.'[2] In 2001 the Select Committee on the Modernisation of the House of Commons (the Modernisation Committee) reported that –

> ... select committees occupy such a central and crucial role in parliamentary scrutiny that it would be helpful if there was greater clarity about their objectives and greater consistency about how these are discharged. **We recommend that there should be an agreed statement of the core tasks of the departmental select committees.**[3]

The Committee's recommendations were endorsed by the House on 14 May 2002 in a motion which called on the Liaison Committee to draw up the list of core tasks. In June 2002 the Liaison Committee produced a list of objectives and tasks, which was published in 2003 in its Annual Report. The Modernisation Committee had also recommended that individual committees should report annually to the Liaison Committee on how they had performed the core tasks and that list is used as the template for their annual reports.

Departmental Select Committee Objectives And Tasks: An Illustrative Template

OBJECTIVE A: TO EXAMINE AND COMMENT ON THE POLICY OF THE DEPARTMENT

Task 1: To examine policy proposals from the UK Government and the European Commission in Green Papers, White Papers, draft Guidance etc, and to inquire further where the Committee considers it appropriate

This calls for more systematic scrutiny of proposals made. It is not intended to involve formal written or oral evidence as a matter of course, but to ensure that a Committee is at least apprised of proposals and has the opportunity to consider whether detailed scrutiny of them should form part of their programme of work.

Departments must ensure that Committees are informed directly of policy proposals and provided with the necessary documentation, rather than waiting to be asked.
* * * * * * * * * *

Task 2: To identify and examine areas of emerging policy, or where existing policy is deficient, and make proposals

This calls for Committees to identify areas where, based on judgement of Members, views of others etc, a Committee inquiry would be worthwhile.

Ministers must be prepared to give proper consideration to policy proposals from committees. This may involve revision of the practice on instant reaction/rebuttal.
* * * * * * * * * *

Task 3: To conduct scrutiny of any published draft bill within the Committee's responsibilities

This calls for Committees to commit time for necessary oral evidence and reporting, subject to its timetable for other inquiries.

Ministers must ensure that committees are warned early on the likely appearance of draft bills: must consult with committee chairmen on how they are to be handled: and must allow a decent time for committee consideration.
* * * * * * * * * *

Departmental Select Committee Objectives And Tasks: An Illustrative Template

OBJECTIVE A: TO EXAMINE AND COMMENT ON THE POLICY OF THE DEPARTMENT – *continued*

Task 4: To examine specific output from the department expressed in documents or other decisions

This calls for a formal framework for being informed of secondary legislation, circulars and guidance, treaties and previously identified casework decisions, so that they can if needed be drawn to a Committee's attention.

Departments will have to engage in co-operative discussions with committee staff on the best means of ensuring that committees are kept abreast of such outputs.
* * * * * * * * * *

OBJECTIVE B: TO EXAMINE THE EXPENDITURE OF THE DEPARTMENT

Task 5: To examine the expenditure plans and out-turn of the department, its agencies and principal NDPBs

This calls for a systematic framework for committee scrutiny of the Department's Main and Supplementary Estimates: its expenditure plans; and its annual accounts.

Departments will as a matter of course have to produce more explanatory material on financial matters, e.g. on Supplementary Estimates, underspends etc
* * * * * * * * * *

OBJECTIVE C: TO EXAMINE THE ADMINISTRATION OF THE DEPARTMENT

Task 6: To examine the department's Public Service Agreements, the associated targets and the statistical measurements employed, and report if appropriate

This calls for an established cycle of written scrutiny and annual reporting of results.

Ministers must be prepared to be genuinely responsive to committee concerns on PSAs etc
* * * * * * * * * *

Task 7: To monitor the work of the department's Executive Agencies, NDPBs, regulators and other associated public bodies

This calls for a systematic cycle of scrutiny of annual reports. It does not require either written or oral evidence except where a Committee judges it to be necessary.

The bodies concerned must ensure that their accountability to Parliament is recognised by full and regular provision of information, including annual reports and other publications.
* * * * * * * * * *

Departmental Select Committee Objectives And Tasks: An Illustrative Template

OBJECTIVE C: TO EXAMINE THE ADMINISTRATION OF THE DEPARTMENT – *continued*

Task 8: To scrutinise major appointments made by the department
This would call for scrutiny of all major appointments made.

Departments would have to systematically notify committees in advance of all major appointments pending and/or made.

Task 9: To examine the implementation of legislation and major policy initiatives

This would call for a framework of detailed annual progress reports from departments on Acts and major policy initiatives so that committees could decide whether to undertake inquiry

Ministers must be more willing to provide for annual reports on particular pieces of legislation, and departments to provide detailed annual reports on identified policy areas or initiatives.

OBJECTIVE D: TO ASSIST THE HOUSE IN DEBATE AND DECISION

Task 10: To produce Reports which are suitable for debate in the House, including Westminster Hall, or debating committees.

This could call for committees to come to an explicit view when deciding on an inquiry as to whether a debate was in due course envisaged.

Throughout the discussion of the core tasks, in the Modernisation Committee, the House and the Liaison Committee, it was repeatedly emphasised that each committee must retain the freedom to balance its work in the light of the duties of its Department or in response to emerging issues. The annual reports of the committees, although each is produced to the same template, illustrate the diversity of approach to the core tasks. Some committees have clearly taken steps to organise their programmes in a way which reflects the priorities set out in the tasks. Others have taken the principle that committees should approach their scrutiny responsibilities in a systematic way, but have addressed it in different ways. Some committees had already taken steps on their own account to adopt a more systematic approach to their responsibilities. For example, in 1999, the Defence Committee instituted a series of annual reports in which it reported on its activities against a set of objectives which it drew up itself.

Another proposal made in 2002 by the Modernisation Committee was that 'investigative select committees' should be named 'scrutiny committees', since the phrase 'select committee' gave no indication of their true purpose or function. In its March 2002 response, the Liaison Committee concluded that the proposed change was 'at best a case of change for change's sake, and at worst likely to spread confusion where there is now clarity'.[4] The Committee pointed out that 'scrutiny' was a 'useful if ill-defined term to describe one aspect of a committee's responsibilities, but it does not reflect the full breadth of its functions', since committees were not merely reactive but equally 'initiators and promoters of new policies'.[5]

In Westminster-speak, 'scrutiny' means detailed critical analysis of output or outcome. It is generally applied in relation to a handful of specialised committees, charged with detailed scrutiny of documents, including the House of Commons European Scrutiny Committee, the Regulatory Reform Committee, the Joint Committee on Statutory Instruments and the Joint Committee on Human Rights. There are further 'scrutiny' type committees in the Lords, notably the recently established committee on the Merits of Statutory Instruments.

These scrutiny committees have several features in common:

- they do not set their own agenda, which is determined by what the Government or the European Commission choose to bring forward as legislative proposals
- they are relatively heavily dependent on systematic staff work and in particular on specialist staff, including in-House lawyers
- they have a more intimate connection with the legislative work of the House and in the case of the European Scrutiny and Regulatory Reform Committees powers to influence or determine what is or is not debated on the floor or in committees
- they do much of their work in private deliberation rather than in public evidence-taking
- their work is, partly as a result of that, little noticed outside or even inside Westminster.

In contrast, the Standing Order establishing departmental select committees requires them to 'examine' the administration, expenditure and policy of a specified department. Certainly this requires examination in some form of the output of a department (see core task 4, above). Some output is readily accessible. Departments issue circulars or directions or guidelines. They sign contracts and make purchases and sometimes sales. There are formal consultations and official reviews of problem areas: the daily procession of ministerial written statements in Hansard gives an idea of this sort of 'second level' activity. But much of the politically significant output remains tantalisingly intangible. The Liaison Committee in publishing its objectives also asked for help from departments, suggesting that they should engage in co-operative discussions with committee staff on the best means of ensuring that committees were kept abreast of such outputs. Progress in this area, however, seems so far to be patchy.

Occasionally outputs may face more detailed scrutiny. Of particular interest is the so-called Quadripartite Committee, of 4 departmental select committees working together. Since 1999, the committee has each year examined in detail the full indigestible list of the 10,000 or so arms export licences and picked out a number for further detailed inquiry, as well as pursuing policy issues in relation to particular countries or categories of arms.

Detailed scrutiny of this sort is demanding not only of committee staff support but also of government officials time in preparing answers. In the course of its examination of the Reports for 2001 and 2002, the committee experienced some difficulties in getting the detailed information it sought, for example on the reasons for refusal of a number of applications for licences. There are inevitable tensions between the demands of a parliamentary committee for detailed information, not always held in the form requested, and what busy departmental officials can reasonably be expected to provide. An area to watch will be how far other committees identify similar specific outputs to scrutinise on such a 'casework' basis and how departments respond.

Each committee has its own dynamic, and so does each inquiry. Committees deploy their resources of time and influence to different ends, with different objectives. Some go for long detailed inquiries focussed on one policy area: others dart around covering a wide area at less depth. Some inquiries are patently more intended to raise a question than to provide an answer. A universally applicable template for evaluating committee activities, beyond the merely volumetric, is therefore a distant prospect. But it would in principle be feasible for a committee to identify, if only for its own internal purposes, its objectives in relation to particular inquiries and/or its overall programme, and then at some time after completion to consider or ask others to consider how far it had met those objectives.

There are also existing sources of expert advice and practical experience which could be tapped were there a clear desire to do so.

- There is often a prevailing 'parliamentary' judgement among Members and others as to which Committees are the most effective, even in the absence of explicit criteria. Exploration of the preconceptions behind these judgements could produce a useful set of implicit values.

- Committee output or outcome can be formally externally assessed, either by an externally contracted academic assessor – the NAO's value for money studies are reviewed by the London School of Economics – or by a peer organisation, of which there are now several in the British Isles area. There are, however, inherent difficulties in those in one institution understanding the underlying objectives of those in another, and some danger of confusing the efficiency of the process with the output.
- Local authority overview and scrutiny [see below] is already subject to the same examination by the Audit Commission as are other local authority services, although the Commission does not appear to have published the criteria and checklists it uses to reach its judgements.

In 1979 the departmental select committees seemed to be one of a type. The continental European legislatures were evidently the product of a different political system. Commonwealth legislatures seemed by and large to be the recipients of Westminster's wisdom, not alternative models to be learned from. Twenty-five years on it looks very different. There is a mass of accessible learning on European parliamentary counterparts. The larger Commonwealth Parliaments are now comparators and models on at least an equal basis. The establishment of the Scottish Parliament, the National Assembly for Wales and the Northern Ireland Assembly has over the past few years offered different but similar working committee systems within the constraints of the overall UK political system.[6]

Following the 2000 Local Government Act the vast majority of local authorities now have a system of 'cabinet' government: a handful of executive councillors each with a portfolio responsibility, and the rest as 'non-executive councillors' engaged in 'overview and scrutiny' through committees, panels etc. At a stroke, the Act created hundreds of miniature select committee systems all over the country. And as a consequence the questions of the Westminster system hitherto posed by academics or occasional journalists – what is it for? what do you achieve? how do you measure it? what does it cost? – are now also being asked by councillors and the small but growing numbers of dedicated local authority scrutiny staff eager to assess their own performance. It remains to be seen how far the existence of a number of broadly comparable systems leads to renewed interest in the evaluation of committees at Westminster.

Over the years since 1979 the public profile of select committees has increased substantially. Increased levels of public recognition generated an expectation that committees would respond to evidence of public concern over issues across the full spectrum of the responsibilities of the relevant government department. Committees have sought to respond to these expectations. They have picked up topical issues and shown themselves to be responsive to public demands for scrutiny of particular aspects of government. Their chairmen have become authoritative commentators across the whole range of their government department's responsibilities whose views are regularly canvassed in the media. Committees have also developed a range of mechanisms below the full blown inquiry through which they can pursue particular issues. These include one-off evidence sessions, informal briefings and seminars as well as written correspondence with the department. As the public and the press have gradually become more aware of the work of the committees and arguably more interested in their product, committees themselves have become more outward looking, more conscious of the public as an audience for their reports and more concerned to be seen as active and influential participants in the political process.

In recent years this steady if unspectacular trend has accelerated. The House of Commons as an organisation has promoted these developments in two particular ways: the increasing use of electronic media (committee websites, web-casting, e-consultation) and the strengthening of committee resources, including those devoted to media relations.

A new design for the main parliamentary website was launched in 2002. It won a number of accolades. Each committee has its own web-pages, with their publications easily accessible, and news on committees activities. Further modernisation is in course of consideration. From October 2004 all public meetings of select committees have been web-cast live.

In its report on select committees the Modernisation Committee stated that 'If the select committees are successfully to hold to account major Whitehall departments then we need to do more to balance the resources respectively available to Ministers and to those who hold them to account.'[7] It then made two specific recommendations. The first was for the establishment of a central unit of specialist support staff for the Committee Office. This had been proposed by the Liaison Committee in its report of March 2000, *Shifting the Balance*.[8] The second was that the National Audit Office be invited to help assess the need for specialist and other support staff for select committees and to advise on how this could best be provided. The staffing review

which was subsequently conducted made a number of recommendations, one of which was for the creation of three new specialist media
officer posts, each of which would work directly for a group of committees. The first of these posts was filled in autumn 2003, the other two
in autumn 2004.

These posts should not be seen as evidence of a radical shift in
committees' relations with the media. But those relations have to some
extent been formalised: activities which were previously discretionary
have been put onto a more structured basis. In the longer term, and
insofar as committees themselves wish to engage more proactively
with the media, there is the possibility that there will be a very significant increase in the media coverage given to select committee activities. Academic analysis over the coming years of the impact of both the
overall increase in committee staffs and the specific recruitment of
media officers would provide a valuable insight into the continuing
development of the select committees.

A sustained increase in media coverage, while not an end itself,
could be an important aid in the achievement of committee objectives.
First, it would contribute directly to the broader effort to raise the level
of public recognition of select committees and understanding of their
role and work. To quote the Modernisation Committee, 'for parliamentary democracy to thrive the public must understand and engage
with Parliament itself.'[9] In 1988, in the SPG book *The Commons under
Scrutiny*, Nevil Johnson described the principal purpose of the select
committees as being to conduct what he called 'explanatory dialogues'
with their government departments. He went on, 'It must also be
added that their impact outwards on the public is muted.... in general,
select committees rate only a short notice on the inside pages of the
quality newspapers and rarely gain a headline.'[10] Even a cursory survey
of the press today would demonstrate how far the press coverage of
select committee activity has come in the intervening years. Reports
regularly receive headline coverage in both the print and broadcast
media.

Secondly, there is a relationship between media coverage and
influence. It is not a direct relationship, but it is an important one, as is
demonstrated, for example, by the effort and resources which the
Government puts into its own media operations. Select committees'
reports derive their authority from being founded on the evidence
which the committee has taken and which is published with the
report, from the standing and expertise of their members, and from
the coherence and rigour of their arguments. They derive their

influence from that authority and from the levels of public awareness which they achieve. An unreported but authoritative report is likely to be less influential than a similar report which receives wide coverage.

Select committees have come a long way since 1979. Progress has been neither consistent nor uniform. It remains under-evaluated. Two significant trends over recent years have been the more systematic approach in terms of both breadth and depth of coverage and the growth in public awareness and media coverage of committees' activities. The conditions are arguably now in place to allow a significant and mutually reinforcing acceleration of those two trends in the years ahead and for that acceleration to be accompanied by a steady growth in the committees' influence.

Notes

1 First Report, Session 1977–78, HC 588-I, Summary of recommendations.
2 Procedure Committee The Working of the Select Committee System, Second Report of Session 1989–90, HC 19, para 67.
3 Modernisation Committee, *Select Committees*, First Report of Session 2001–02 HC 224, para 33, original emphasis.
4 Liaison Committee, *Select Committees: Modernisation Proposals*, Second Report, 2001–02, HC 692, para 25.
5 *Ibid.*, para 24.
6 See below, Chapter 18.
7 *Op. cit.* para 27.
8 Liaison Committee, *Shifting the Balance*, First Report of 1999–2000, HC 300, March 2000.
9 Modernisation Committee, *Connecting Parliament with the Public*, First Report of Session 2003–04, HC 368, para 6, June 2004.
10 Michael Ryle and Peter G. Richards (eds), *The Commons under Scrutiny*, Routledge, 1988, pp. 183–4. See also pp. 14–19 above.

9
Scrutiny At and Beyond the Fringe

Matthew Flinders

This chapter focuses on Parliament's capacity to scrutinise the machinery of government and governance. As the Hansard Society noted 'The bulk of government activity is now carried out through arm's length executive agencies, quangos and the like'.[1]

The central argument of this chapter is that, despite the recent reforms described in the previous chapter, Parliament remains ill equipped to scrutinise the increasingly diverse structure of the British State, because its scrutiny mechanisms and resources are still largely wedded to a late-Victorian conception of the British State which no longer exists. For the twenty-first century Parliament needs to design mechanisms through which it can scrutinise, and therefore legitimate, the vast array of delegated bodies, public-private partnerships (PPPs), public interest companies and other forms of public policy provider.[2]

Some of these arm's length bodies (ALBs) have gone to great lengths to design and implement new channels of communication with the public. The challenge for Parliament, as the Hansard Society recognised in 2001, is to sit at the apex of these broader accountability structures in order to provide a framework for their activity, publicise their existence and use the information they provide to challenge ministers. It is, however, important to understand two issues. First, parliamentary scrutiny of ALBs has been an unresolved issue for Parliament since at least the middle of the nineteenth century.[3] Second, that the convention of ministerial responsibility, designed to enhance and clarify accountability, can also restrict and control parliamentary scrutiny. David Judge has convincingly demonstrated how the negative executive mentality has largely inverted the logic of the convention of individual ministerial responsibility from an accountability sword to an accountability shield.[4] Moreover, the existence of quasi-autonomous

ALBs has on occasion led to 'blame games' between ministers and chief executives over who is responsible for certain events or errors.[5]

In the mid-1990s a number of senior shadow ministers had committed the Labour Party to implementing reforms that would empower Parliament to scrutinise the extended state.[6] The next section examines developments between 1997 and 2005.

New Labour, Parliament and the extended state 1997–2005

The growth of delegated governance since May 1997 has been documented elsewhere.[7] It is sufficient here to note that Toynbee and Walker's assertion in 2001 that 'the quango state [i]s alive and well' under New Labour is supported by detailed research. Examples of ALBs created under New Labour include the Competition Commission, Qualifications and Curriculum Authority, Financial Services Authority, Retained Organs Commission, National Institute of Clinical Excellence, Statistics Commission, Electoral Commission, Assets Recovery Agency and the Postal Services Commission. Indeed, the growth in ALBs during the 1997–2001 Parliament was such that developments within the 2001–2005 Parliament were largely concerned with pruning and amalgamating the vast number of bodies that the Labour Government had created in its first term, for example the Wanless Review of the health sector and the Haskins Review of rural policy.[8]

The 1997–2001 Parliament

Shortly after its election victory in May 1997 the Labour Government published a consultation paper 'Opening Up Quangos'. The tone of the document stood in marked contrast to pre-election 'anti-quango' polemics. Following that consultation, in June 1998 the government published *Quangos – Opening the Doors*. Although the Chancellor of the Duchy of Lancaster, David Clark, stated in the document's foreword that the 'reform package represents a major breakthrough in an area previously thought of as secretive and closed to the public', the actual proposals were notable for their frailty rather than strength. Indeed, Clark had spent much of the period between the consultation paper and government statement attempting to reduce public expectations and asking for the whole topic of public bodies to be debated in a 'non-hysterical way'. The government's proposals set out a soft-law (i.e. non-statutory) guidance framework rather than a statute-based hard-law system that would empower the public with legally enforceable rights and powers.

Not only did the 1998 proposals cover a limited range of ALBs but the commitments allowed public bodies a great deal of discretion as to whether or not they followed the guidance. Phrases such as 'where practicable and appropriate' did little to foster confidence in relation to a tier of governance that had been subject to concerns about a lack of transparency and clarity for decades. Moreover, the document in which these proposals were made had no practical weight or legal force and was nothing more than a Cabinet Office 'best practice' guidance paper. The weakness of this 'soft law' approach was demonstrated in October 2002 when the Qualifications and Curriculum Authority (QCA) – without ministerial approval and contrary to Cabinet Office guidance – took the unprecedented decision to exclude all journalists from its annual conference.

The Government's proposals received a critical reception. The Public Administration Select Committee [PASC] ridiculed the Government's reforms as 'unambitious, piecemeal and *ad hoc*' and instead proposed a number of reforms that were designed to empower select committees *vis-à-vis* both ministers and ALBs.[9] These included the recommendation that in future ministers should circulate minutes of the meetings that ministers have held with Non-Departmental Public Bodies (NDPBs) and that select committees should be informed in advance that a minister is minded to appoint a certain individual to a senior post in an ALB so that the committee may invite the individual to appear before the committee in advance of their appointment.[10] Rejecting both those recommendations, the Government stated that ministers would decide on a case-by-case basis whether to release minutes of their meetings with NDPBs to select committees and that it simply 'did not believe that involving select committees in the appointment process would be appropriate'.[11]

In March 2001 the PASC returned to the fray. Its research found that the Government's June 1998 code of practice had not led to a significant increase in the transparency of ALBs. For example, between 1997 and 2000 there had been only a very small increase – from 12% to 17% – in the number of NDPBs holding open meetings. The PASC concluded, 'There are more black holes than examples of open governance'.[12] This report was published at a time when a broader debate concerning the appropriate balance of power between the Parliament and the Executive was gaining momentum. Research by the Hansard Commission in 2001 revealed that over 60% of MPs thought Parliament was not effective in scrutinising executive agencies, over 70% thought the same for the utility regulators and 80% for 'quangos'.[13] These findings reinforced a widespread view that Parliament needed to engage more systematically and actively with the work of ALBs and adapt to the changing structures of modern governance. The next section will examine developments during the 2001–2005 Parliament.

Parliament 2001–2005

The 2001–2005 Parliament will possibly be remembered, like the 1979–1983 Parliament, as a 'reforming Parliament'. The main reforms are set out in Box 9.1 Several of these reforms were explicitly designed to improve Parliament's scrutiny of the wider state sector. In May 2002 the House of Commons approved a resolution inviting the Liaison Committee to publish common objectives for select committees (see above, page 89). These objectives, building on the previous work of the Modernisation Committee, were quickly agreed and involve ten core tasks, two of which are particularly concerned with ALBs. Indeed, the Modernisation Committee's main purpose in proposing the core tasks was to ensure that all areas of government activity were subject to proper scrutiny by Parliament.[14]

In addition to the core tasks a comprehensive framework to review the work of the select committee system and address and common challenges was established. This involves each select committee publishing an annual report, in which it accounts for how it has sought to achieve each of the core tasks, and the Liaison Committee publishing

---

Box 9.1   Parliamentary Scrutiny Reforms 2001–2005

- The deadline for tabling oral parliamentary questions was reduced from ten days to three.
- Answers to PQs now provided when Parliament is in recess.
- Written statements replaced 'planted' questions.
- Select committees adopted a framework of core tasks
- Comptroller and Auditor General appointed as the auditor of all Executive NDPBs.
- Scrutiny Unit established to support select committees.
- Select committees empowered to establish sub-committees and joint-inquiries with other committees on their own initiative.
- Committees empowered to exchange papers with the Scottish Parliament and Welsh Assembly.
- Additional payments introduced for select committee chairmen
- Prime Minister to appear before the Liaison Committee twice a year.
- Parliamentary vote on the war in Iraq.
- Ministers take questions on cross-cutting issues each week in Westminster Hall.

an overview. The select committee system has therefore become more coherent and integrated. Although select committee chairs are not formally bound to undertake each of the core tasks during each session the tasks do encourage committees to broaden the scope of their scrutiny beyond ministerial departments and into the deeper waters of delegated governance.

The existence of core tasks 6 and 7 in particular has led to a number of practical developments. Relationships between departments and their respective select committees has become more formalised and the flow of information regarding the creation, merger or abolition of ALBs and senior appointments has improved. Several select committees have also altered their working procedures to enable them to fulfil core task 7, usually through the creation of a sub-committee or through holding a greater number of one-off evidence sessions with ALBs, or even informal meetings, rather than full-scale inquires.

Other reforms may also assist in Parliament's scrutiny of the increasingly diverse British state. In February 2003 the Government accepted the recommendation of Lord Sharman's report that the Comptroller and Auditor General should be the official auditor of all executive NBPBs (a recommendation previously made by both the Public Accounts Committee and the PASC), thereby bringing all executive NDPBs within the purview of the National Audit Office and the Public Accounts Committee.[15] The introduction of additional salaries for select committee chairs may in time create an alternative career structure to ministerial office, thereby reducing the influence of the whips and promoting parliamentary scrutiny as a career in itself. The establishment of a Scrutiny Unit to support select committees is also a positive development.

Despite these reforms it is important to keep in perspective the capacity of select committees as well as the relative balance of power between the Executive and Parliament. The 2001–2005 Parliament has been characterised by reform emanating from backbench frustration with the slow pace of modernisation and the perception that ministers frequently failed to take their duty to account to Parliament seriously during the 1997–2001 Parliament. There has not, however, been a major shift in the balance of power between Parliament and the Executive. As noted above, ministerial responsibility was a convention designed for the most part to prevent Parliament from trawling deeper waters in relation to the British State and ministers have been keen to preserve their gatekeeper role during the 2001–2005 Parliament and have often been unwilling to cooperate with Parliament's attempts to scrutinise the extended state. Task Eight, for example, charges committees to 'to scrutinise major appointments made by the department' and was clearly fuelled by the perceived success of the Treasury Committee in relation to appointments to the Monetary Policy Committee. Other committees have been less successful. In 2002 the Education and Skills Committee and the Home Affairs Committee both reported that they had sought an active role in relation to specific senior appointments, HM Chief Inspector of Schools and the chair of the Independent Police Complaints Commission respectively.[16] The committees' attempts to play a role in these appointments had been categorically rejected by the government. Constitutionally, both committees could have taken this issue to the floor of the House, but the realities of power within the House effectively means that select committees are reliant on the cooperation of the government in cases such as these.

Select committees are also limited in their capacity to scrutinise the British State by a range of practical factors (time, resources, staff) and political issues (influence of the whips, ambitions of the members, party majority, role of the chairman). While the introduction of the core tasks has undoubtedly encouraged select committees to shine the spotlight of parliamentary scrutiny beyond the ministerial department it remains the case that only a small number of generally the largest NDPBs are ever subject to parliamentary scrutiny.

Indeed, the views of the majority of select committee chairmen reflect a degree of institutional apathy and political realism. In February 1999 the Chairman of the Agriculture Committee pointed out:

I'm afraid that there simply is not time for select committees to look at each and every one of the quangos within their remit...select committees simply do not have the time and resources to do what they already do, never mind having their burdens added to. I regard this as disappointing but an acceptance of reality.[17]

The Chairman of the Health Committee suggested that in order for select committees to play a greater role the committee structure and available resources would need to be revised accordingly.[18] And yet select committees remain under-resourced compared to scrutiny committees in similar countries. The Scrutiny Unit, although a welcome development, consists of just 16 staff and their main role is to support select committees in relation to the scrutiny of legislation and financial issues. The introduction of additional payments for committee chairman (£12,500 per annum implemented from the start of the 2003–2004 parliamentary session) has so far done little to raise the status or profile of select committee work. The future of parliamentary scrutiny of the extended British State will be the topic of the next section.

The future of Parliamentary scrutiny of the extended state

Parliament's capacity to oversee and scrutinise the extended state is dictated by the broader balance of power between Parliament and the Executive, and the dominant culture of Members of Parliament. The audit of parliamentary modernisation since 1997 conducted by the Hansard Society in 2005 illustrates that although a number of reforms have been introduced during the 2001–2005 Parliament, there has not been a significant shift in the balance of power. The Executive is unwilling to relax its control of the House and will manage its parliamentary majority accordingly. Moreover, the majority of MPs view their dominant loyalty as being owed to their party rather than Parliament. The failure of the House in May 2002 to approve measures designed to reduce the influence of the whips in the construction of select committee memberships exemplified this. A frustrated Peter Hennessy commented, '...this was a case of kissing-the-chains-that-bind which quite took one's breath away – quite the lowest moment for select committees on the road from 1979. May 2002 really was the poverty of aspirations at its malign worst'.[19]

The recent reforms within the House of Commons have provided useful 'cracks and wedges' that can be built upon and developed in future years.[20] These wedges may well provide the basis of further strengthening and extension and, in time, the gradual accretion of these wedges may begin to alter the balance of power. However, in light of the continued growth in (and role of) ALBs since 1997 and the Labour Government's contemporary commitment to public-private partnerships in a growing range of policy sectors it would suggest that in the sphere of delegated governance Parliament has simply failed to evolve sufficiently. As the Hansard Society emphasised in their 2001 Report, Parliament needs to reclaim its position at the apex of the various scrutiny and accountability mechanisms, but this will only happen if its Members are willing to assert themselves – as they did for example over initial list of select committee members in 2001. There is currently a widespread feeling that the current balance of power between Parliament and the Executive is indefensible. Towards the end of the 2001–2005 Parliament the Government was forced to respond to a growing sense of frustration and dissatisfaction on the backbenches in order to vent and control the parliamentary pressure. The Prime Minister's decision to appear twice-yearly before the Liaison Committee, the decision to hold a vote in the House of Commons over the deployment of troops to Iraq and the willingness to review the current Codes of Practice on the provision of 'persons, papers and records' to select committees were all smoke signals or unofficial acknowledgements by the Government that a momentum for reform had developed and must be responded to.

In terms of the specific issue of Parliament's capacity to scrutinise the increasingly devolved and dynamic British State there are two key issues that are currently on the parliamentary agenda and are therefore open to discussion and reform. First, the House of Commons, *via* the Liaison Committee, should not gratefully accept the minimal revisions to the current Whitehall memorandum on the provision of 'papers, persons and records' to select committees that were offered by the Leader of the House in November 2004. Parliament should take the lead in revising the memorandum, possibly even introducing a direct link between certain major public bodies and the relevant select committee, and seek to take ownership of the rules and enhance their legitimacy *via* a resolution in the House. Second, the House of Commons should consider creating a new select committee, or possibly a joint committee of both Houses, with a specific remit to scrutinise developments in the sphere of delegated governance as recently proposed by the House of Lords Committee on the Constitution.[21]

Parliament does matter. Despite a wealth of largely prosaic literature lamenting its demise, Parliament remains the central locus of legitimate state power in Britain. Analyses that suggest that Parliament has become irrelevant or peripheral to modern government and governance or portray MPs as supine foot-soldiers of political parties simply fail to understand the complexity and dynamics of the relationship between Parliament, the Executive and the British State. Reforms have been implemented but it is vital for the future of Parliament that the reform agenda continues and develops after the next General Election. The danger for Parliament is that the roles of alternative scrutiny mechanisms such as judicial review, regional assemblies and parliaments, the European Commission, public inquiries, tribunals and inspectorates and the media, will further evolve and this may harden the public's misguided perception that Parliament is a peripheral actor within the political system.

Notes

1   Hansard Society, *The Challenge for Parliament*, Vacher Dodd, 2001, p. 1.
2   M. Flinders, 'The Politics of Public-Private Partnerships', *British Journal of Politics and International Relations*, Vol. 7, 543–567.
3   M. Flinders, 'Icebergs and MPs: Delegated Governance and Parliament', *Parliamentary Affairs*, Vol. 57, 767–784 and 'Distributed Public Governance in Britain', *Public Administration*, Vol. 82, 883–909.
4   David Judge, *The Parliamentary State*, Sage, 1993.
5   Philip Giddings, (ed.) *Parliamentary Accountability: A Study of Parliament and Executive Agencies*, Macmillan, 1995; C. Hood, 'The Risk Game and the Blame Game', *Government and Opposition*, 37.1, 15–37.
6   See Ann Taylor, 'New Politics, New Parliament' speech to the Charter 88 seminar on the reform of Parliament, 14 May 1996.
7   C. Skelcher, S. Weir, and L. Wilson, *Advance of the Quango State*. Local Government Information Unit, London, 2003; M. Flinders, 'Distributed Public Governance in Britain', *Public Administration*, Vol. 82, 883–909.
8   Derek Wanless, *Securing Good Health for the Whole Population*, HM Treasury, February 2004; Christopher Haskins, *Rural Delivery Review*, Department of the Environment, Food and Rural Affairs, October 2003.
9   Sixth Report of the Public Administration Select Committee, *Quangos*, HC 209, 1998–99, November 1999.
10 *Ibid.*
11 First Special Report from the Select Committee on Public Administration, HC 317, 1999–2000, March 2000.
12 Fifth Report from the Select Committee on Public Administration, *Mapping the Quango State*, HC 367, 2000–2001, March 2001, para. 34.
13 Hansard Society, *op. cit.*, p. 11.
14 Select Committee on Modernisation, *Select Committees*, First Report of Session 2001–02, HC 224, paras 31–35, February 2002.
15 Audit and Accountability for Central Government: the Government's response to Lord Sharman's report 'Holding to Account', Cm 5456, TSO, March 2002.
16 Select Committee on Education and Skills, *The Work of the Committee in 2002*, HC 359, 2002–03, para. 4; Home Affairs Committee, *The Work of the Committee in 2002*, HC 336, 2002–03, para. 8.
17 Sixth Report of Select Committee on Public Administration, *Quangos*, HC 209, 1998–99 Memorandum 21.
18 *Ibid.*, Memorandum 27.
19 Peter Hennessy, 'An End to the Poverty of Aspirations? Parliament since 1979', First History of Parliament Lecture, Attlee Suite, Portcullis House, London, 25 November 2004.
20 Tony Wright, 'Prospects for Parliamentary Reform', *Parliamentary Affairs*, 57, 4, p. 871.
21 Sixth Report of the Constitution Committee, *The Regulatory State: Ensuring its Accountability*, HL 68, 2003–2004, May 2004, paras 195–202.

10

The House of Lords: A Chamber of Scrutiny

Donald Shell

The House of Lords is a chamber well suited to the activity of scrutiny. As the second chamber, not in the business of contesting power with the Government of the day, it is less driven by the demands of competitive party politics than the Commons. A substantial non-party or cross-bench element has been included within its active membership. And the experience and expertise of its membership is wide ranging.

Over the last forty years the House of Lords has greatly expanded its work of scrutiny. In part this has been simply the result of the House becoming a great deal more active. But in part it has also been the result of changing attitudes, a developing culture of scrutiny, which has accompanied the gradual renaissance that the House has undergone. Forty years ago the House of Lords was beginning to shake off its mid-twentieth century moribundity. By 1965 average daily attendance was twice as high as it had been a decade earlier. Newly created peers were arriving in the House at the unprecedented rate of some 25 a year. The House was sitting longer, voting more frequently and beginning to feel that it could at least regain a role of minor significance in the whole business of parliamentary politics. While the absence of fundamental reform is frequently and rightly emphasised, the House has undergone considerable change over the last 40 years. And this has continued up to and beyond the adjustment in membership brought about by the 1999 House of Lords Act.

The spectre of reform

There has, however, been no settled view about the future of the House. In the 1960s, as in every decade since (and indeed throughout the previous 100 years), the spectre of reform hung over the House.

107

While peers went about their normal routines of business in the House, they were constantly aware of background chatter about reform. If the House took decisions that angered the Government of the day, this chatter intensified with threats of drastic reform or even abolition, as with the Labour Government of the 1970s. Nor has it been difficult to make out a case for change of some kind. A predominantly hereditary chamber, with a vast and motley membership – of dukes and earls, meritocratic life peers and semi-retired politicians, bishops and law lords – inevitably attracted all kinds of proposals for alteration. For the Labour Party there has been a general assumption that the House is in need of fundamental reform, or even outright abolition. The Conservatives while in office have taken the pragmatic view that the House is best left alone, but when in opposition they have tended to prefer bold reform rather than gradual modernisation.

In the 1960s and 1970s the future of the House of Lords was generally seen as a discrete issue, a problem to be resolved, no doubt with some implications for the Commons as far as the management of parliamentary business was concerned, but not a matter of wider constitutional significance. However during the 1980s this attitude altered. A much more general programme of constitutional reform was developed and the Labour Opposition gradually placed itself at the centre of this. As far as the Lords was concerned this change was partly assisted by the growing vigour of the House of Lords as a chamber of scrutiny. When opposition to the Thatcher Government was so very weak in the Commons in the mid-1980s, the House developed something of a reputation as 'the other Opposition'. Though in some areas it caused adjustments in policy to take place, the House never threatened major policy decisions – for example, it allowed the poll tax to go through despite serious public disquiet.

Through this period the future role of the Lords became a vital part of Labour's constitutional thinking. Whereas in 1983 the party had wanted simply to abolish the Lords, by 1992 it proposed reforms to make the House a powerful protector of rights. Though it backtracked from that, in 1997 Labour came into office with a clear policy to reform the House in two stages.

That policy has of course not been fully implemented. Indeed the course of events since 1997 has been a monumental saga of bungling and incompetence. After two terms in office all that has been achieved is the removal of most hereditary peers, a significant proportion of whom were rare or infrequent attenders. According to Baroness Jay, Blair's second leader of the House, this has in itself made the House more legitimate. It has certainly made it more assertive. The Government is defeated more frequently (over 60 times in the most recent session), and the 1949 Parliament Act – having been used only once before New Labour came to office – has been used three times since.

The scrutiny role of the House

The House of Lords now sits twice as many hours as it did forty years ago, and average daily attendance has risen almost three-fold. In the 2001 parliament the Lords has sat on more days than the Commons. The House passes as many amendments to legislation in a single session now as it did in a normal length parliament 40 years ago. The bulk of these are Government amendments. The House affords an opportunity for these to be scrutinised. But peers also press their own amendments, and not infrequently extract alterations or compromises from Government. The chapters on legislation in this volume consider the added value made by the House to the legislative process. The pertinence of the factors discussed there has grown rather than diminished over the years. The quantity of legislation has expanded and the technical quality of legislation as introduced by the Government has declined. This has added to the task of Parliament. One response within the Commons has been routinely to introduce programme motions. Many peers argue that this has increased their own workload. And peers can to a greater extent than MPs set their own timescale for considering detailed points within a Bill. Over 30 years ago Professor John Griffith wrote about some legislation leaving the Commons 'in a state unfit to be let loose on the public'.[1] That is more true today than ever.

But as well as time for scrutiny, the House of Lords brings to bear a different mix of expertise. This includes those with substantial experience of politics and other forms of public service which mixes and blends with that drawn from many other areas of professional and business life to give the House its unusual quality.

The House has also been innovative in respect of the forms of scrutiny used. Sometimes its innovations have not been a success. For example, in the 1980s some peers began to draw attention to the decreasing number of Law Commission Bills being brought before Parliament. It seemed strange that so much effort should go into the preparation of these Bills by the Law Commission, yet they should then languish because Government ministers always found so many pressing reasons for monopolising parliamentary time with new legislation of their own. The Law Commission was eager to see some change that facilitated the passage of its draft Bills.[2] So, the House set up a 'fast-track' procedure for Law Commission Bills, but this had limited success before being abandoned after the withdrawal of the Family Homes and Domestic Violence Bill in 1995.

Another campaign run by some peers was the need to try and develop a greater consistency in the way Acts of Parliament conferred delegated powers. In 1992 this led to the establishment of a new Select Committee on Delegated Powers, which quickly developed a substantial reputation within Whitehall and Westminster. It examined all Bills, and made recommendations concerning the inclusion of delegated powers, which almost invariably were accepted. In 1994 this Committee's terms of reference were extended to include deregulation Orders.

The continuing inadequacy of parliamentary scrutiny of statutory instruments has been widely recognised.[3] A joint select committee provided a technical appraisal, examining the *vires* of instruments, but examination of the policy implications of instruments was weak, with little time for debate and no opportunity for amendment. Meanwhile the importance and complexity of many instruments was growing. Both Houses considered proposals for rectifying this. Eventually the House of Lords went ahead on its own, and in 2004 established a new Scrutiny of Statutory Instruments Committee to examine the merits of instruments. This is a very clear example of the House seeking as a second chamber to plug gaps left by the first in the task of scrutiny.

The House has also used select committees to examine primary legislation from time to time. Sometimes these have been private member's bills that raise significant issues, even if early legislation seemed an unlikely prospect. The committee established to examine Lord Wade's Bill of Rights in 1977 was an early and much quoted example. The Government was very tardy in acting on a report from another select committee appointed in 1979 to consider Lord Halsbury's Laboratory Animals Protection Bill, delaying legislation (and in so doing allowing problems to grow) until the 1986 Animals (Scientific Procedures) Bill. More recently the House has returned to this subject, and has also used select committees to examine other issues, including stem cell research, religious offences and euthanasia – or 'assisted dying'. The Government's surprising announcement that it would establish a new Supreme Court led to the House insisting – against the wishes of the Government – on sending the relevant Bill, the Constitutional Reform Bill, to a select committee early in 2004.

The Lords invested quite heavily in a Select Committee to scrutinise European policy questions in the 1970s, with some 80 peers quickly becoming involved in a structure involving seven subject-based committees, taking evidence widely and reporting on a variety of European related matters.[4] For twenty years until the Commons overhauled its European scrutiny arrangements in the late 1970s, the Lords provided more thorough scrutiny of this area than the Commons, and in so doing the House used a wide range of the expertise found among its members; for example a law lord always chaired one of the sub-committees, dealing with law and institutions. In 1979 when the Commons abolished its Science and Technology Committee in favour of the new comprehensive departmental select committee system, the Lords quickly moved to establish its own Committee covering this subject-area. Both these remain regular sessional select committees in the House. In 1998 a select committee established to examine the monetary policy of the Bank of England was made permanent as an Economic Affairs Committee, and in 2003 this Committee examined aspects of the Finance Bill, an exercise repeated in 2004, when its report was made available before detailed consideration of the Bill began in the Commons.

As part of its two-stage policy of reform, in 1999 the Government appointed a Royal Commission under the Chairmanship of Lord Wakeham.[5] The Commission's recommendations on scrutiny by and large added encouragement to developments already taking place in the House. A select committee on the Constitution was set up in 2001. As well as making substantive reports on a range of topics, the Committee monitors and reports on the constitutional implications of new legislation. Wakeham also thought that a select committee to scrutinise treaties would be appropriate. This is a subject that has attracted some attention and support in the House but has yet to come to fruition. The House has also participated in a number of joint committees, including that on Human Rights, and several set up to examine draft Bills.

It is never easy to provide convincing answers to those who sceptically inquire about the effectiveness of select committee scrutiny. Two aspects have to be considered. One is the effectiveness of select committees in digging out relevant evidence. Commons committees have frequently been criticised for the lack of forensic skill shown by their members in questioning and uncovering relevant evidence and then they have sometimes been further criticised for their failure to appreciate the significance of some of their findings. Obviously the quality of committees in both Houses varies a good deal. But many Lords committees do self-evidently contain a significant proportion of members who have very considerable expertise in the areas they investigate.[6]

The greater use of joint select committees is an interesting development in this context. Not infrequently the House can add real value to a committee because they can nominate members who are in their way authorities on the subject of investigation.[7]

A second criticism made of select committees is their inability once they have reported to ensure their reports receive proper attention within Government. To some extent this depends on the persistence of committee members in following up reports, either as a committee or by other parliamentary means. Peers like MPs can find their reports ignored. But reports may be indirectly influential upon Government. Reports from the Lords EU Committee have at times been more influential in Brussels than in London. And informed opinion can be moulded by reports, which thereby in the long run have an influence upon policy-making.

This obliges us to recognise that through its membership the House of Lords has mobilised into parliamentary roles many individuals who have experience and expertise of a kind not found in the Commons. Furthermore, many of its members continue to follow other occupations. They are neither career politicians of the life long kind, nor are members of the House full-time professional politicians.[8] This is important in considering the role of the House. Debate at its best in the Commons draws out many well-argued speeches of great conviction and persuasive power. Certainly this was true of some of the debates on Iraq. Debate in the Lords does the same, but the voices of senior diplomats, former defence chiefs, senior civil servants, bishops and renowned academics, as well as former senior ministers add value to the quality of debate. This does not give the House any power. But it considerably enhances its influence.

What of the future?

The above analysis suggests there is real value in having appointed members in the second chamber. In particular it is hard to see how non-party peers would arrive there if it were not for appointment. Moreover, the presence of cross-benchers as a kind of fourth party within the House adds value to its work through the expertise and the experience of many who have no party allegiance.

Any approach to Lords reform that does not have as its foremost goal the desire to enhance the standing of Parliament as a whole within the life of the nation should be resisted. Parliament is becoming dangerously marginalised. The electorate are unimpressed with an institution that seems to exist simply to provide a forum in which, to put it bluntly, party politicians can endlessly slag each other off. Electoral turnout has fallen. The Government appears able to take Parliament for granted. The demands of the post-modern continuous election campaign stifle debate within parties and grossly exaggerate debate between parties. No wonder the electorate is unexcited, indeed bored by the present practice of politics.

This is the context against which reform of Parliament as a whole has to be considered. The Commons should welcome a second chamber that can enable Parliament as whole to raise its game. The danger is that instead of that, the Commons in its anxiety to ensure the Lords does not threaten in any way its alleged primacy, carries through reforms that weaken and undermine even the role it manages to play at present.

As society becomes more complex, as the decisions we have to make collectively through politics become more difficult, as the subtle art of governance replaces the older art of government, the contribution of an effective second chamber becomes more rather than less necessary. No doubt party politics is essential to the working of modern democracy. But the technicians of modern elective politics can stifle genuine political debate. Parliamentary democracy becomes distorted into being but an adjunct to the media based battle between rival electoral machines. We need to find a way to make the second chamber a gentle but persistent and firm corrective to this.

Notes

1 *Parliamentary Scrutiny of Government Bills*, G. Allen & Unwin, 1974, p. 231.
2 See *Making the Law: Report of the Hansard Society Commission on the Legislative Process*, Hansard Society, 1992, especially paras 494–500 and Law Commission evidence, para. 5.
3 See also below, chapter 12.
4 See Philip Giddings and Gavin Drewry, *Westminster and Europe: the Impact of the European Union on the Westminster Parliament*, Macmillan, 1996, especially chapter 5.
5 *A House for the Future: Report of the Royal Commission on the Future of the House of Lords*, Cm 4534, January 2000.
6 Lord Richard, writing of his experience as a former EU Commissioner, commented: 'a European Commissioner may think he knows his subject, but to appear before a Lords Committee on which there are two former Permanent Under-Secretaries at the Foreign Office, a clutch of former cabinet ministers, and some genuine experts in the field is to say the least 'concentrative' of the mind'. See Ivor Richard & Damien Welfare, *Unfinished Business: Reforming the Lords* Vintage, 1999, p. 26. See also the analysis of the membership of the Select Committee on Science and Technology provided by Cliff Grantham in

Donald Shell & David Beamish, *The House of Lords at Work*. Oxford: Clarendon Press, 1993, pp. 286–88.

7   For example Lord Puttnam, the film producer, chaired the joint committee examining the Draft Communications Bill 2002, and Lord Slynn of Hadley, the former Lord of Appeal in Ordinary, chaired the joint committee on the draft Corruption Bill, 2003.

8   See above, chapters 3 and 4.

Part IV

Making the Law: Parliament and Legislation

11
Parliament's Role and the Modernisation Agenda

Dawn Oliver, Paul Evans, Colin Lee and Philip Norton

Parliament's role in the legislative process

Acts of Parliament are the highest form of law in the UK, subject only to provisions of European Union law. In the absence of a formal constitutional document setting out limits to the power of Parliament, there can be no provision for a Supreme Court or other external independent body to scrutinise Acts against constitutional or other criteria and to invalidate provisions that do not meet such standards. If an Act were to provide, for instance, for there to be no appeal to the courts against tribunal decisions, even if they were made without jurisdiction or under an error of law (as was originally proposed by the Government in the Asylum and Immigration (Treatment of Claimants etc) Bill 2003/4, clause 10), or for the indefinite detention of foreign suspects without trial (as is provided for in the Anti-Terrorism, Crime and Security Act 2001), the UK courts could not disapply the provision. Under the Human Rights Act the higher courts may declare a provision in primary legislation to be incompatible with rights under the European Convention on Human Rights, but they could not refuse to give it effect. So in the UK the responsibility for scrutiny of legislation lies heavily on Parliament itself.

We now take it for granted that Parliament is the supreme law maker. But it would be wrong to suggest that Parliament's role in making the law has ever been settled either in theory or in practice. The legislative supremacy of Parliament is an invention of the common law which the courts began to develop from the early seventeenth century. Until then it was the King – the Executive – that had supreme law making power. (We may ask ourselves whether things are really so different now.) In the *Case of Proclamations*[1] Chief Justice Coke decided that the King could not change the law in ways that criminalised conduct or interfered with the liberties of the individual without the consent of Parliament. In the case of *Entick v. Carrington*[2], Lord Camden CJ decided that there could be no interference with the property or person of the individual in the name of the public interest without specific legal authority. The Bill of Rights of 1689 in effect transferred most of the remaining law making prerogatives of the monarch – in contemporary terms the Executive – to Parliament. But primary legislation may still be made by Order in Council and such orders, for instance in relation to the civil service, are not normally subject to any parliamentary scrutiny.

The political rationales and justifications, or democratic bases, for Parliament's involvement in the legislative process have also developed over the centuries. From the seventeenth century onwards, the assumption was that the estates of the realm should consent to legislation, and the model was of government under the law, limited by consent of those with particular claims to represent the country. In the nineteenth century, with the extension of the franchise, the model became one of representative government by consent. However, until well into the nineteenth century the business of legislating the general law formed a very small element of Parliament's work – the vast majority of legislation was private (enclosure Acts, establishment of banks or limited companies, railway Acts and so forth). Since the early twentieth century the model has moved to one of party government, in other words government by the party which can command a majority in the House of Commons.

In this model the role of the House of Commons is less to give or refuse consent to legislation than to legitimate and endorse government policy. And yet the rhetoric of representative government endures. The myth is preserved that Parliament is at the apex[3] of the system, when in reality that position is held by the government of the day. Inevitably, the efficiency or effectiveness of the legislative process will be judged by very different criteria when looked at from the perspective of government or that of the non-executive parliamentarian.

Public bills

What, then, are the de facto purposes and roles of Parliament in the legislative process, given the dominance of the Executive in the House of Commons and the limited delaying power of the House of Lords? Even though the government can normally count on a majority in the

House of Commons for its measures, the fact that it knows that it will have to justify its proposals in each House no doubt inhibits it from putting forward measures that will expose it to avoidable embarrassment at the hands either of its own backbenchers or the opposition in the Commons, or in the House of Lords, where it has no majority. One role of Parliament then is as an *inhibitor* of the Executive. But any attempt to analyse the role of Parliament in making the law must take into account the criteria against which scrutiny of bills takes place in the two Houses.

The House of Lords, with its relatively independent membership, is better fitted to the scrutiny of bills against non-partisan standards, including such qualities as workability, clarity of drafting, and conformity with agreed (or sometimes imagined) standards of constitutional propriety or other external criteria. The House of Commons by contrast, being dominated by party and controlled (more or less) by the Government of the day, is less able than the Lords by scrutiny in committee to influence decisions taken by the House in plenary session. The role of inhibitor is, in the Commons, largely conducted within the governing party and away from the formal forums of debate, rather than through the House acting collectively as a constitutional watchdog.

However, another role for Parliament is seen as that of *collaborator* with the Executive in making the law, and much of the drive behind 'modernisation' reforms has emphasised this notion of a corporate effort between the Executive, Parliament and the people (the last largely in the shape of the hugely expanded 'civil society' sector of NGOs and other lobby groups). From this perspective, the role of Parliament is to help make better law.

Perhaps most cynically, the other view of Parliament's role is that it is purely *theatrical*: it is a ritual of confirmation for decisions that have been taken elsewhere. Each of these views of Parliament's role: as inhibitor or constitutional watchdog, as collaborator or corporate partner, or as performer, will tend to be simultaneously at play in most discussions. But for reformers and modernisers, the notion that Parliament's job is to make the law proposed by the Executive better will usually be dominant in their thinking.

Ritualistic or functional?

Have things changed over the years? Even when the Study of Parliament Group was established in 1964, there was a common view

that Parliament's legislative role was a constitutional fiction: it was suggested that Parliament 'legitimated' rather than 'legislated', with the
main process of deliberating about and formulating legislation taking
place outside Parliament, either within Government or by a process of
consultation conducted by Government.[4] There were several aspects
of the parliamentary process then which supported the characterisation of Parliament's role as more ritualistic than functional: the perceived futility of the standing committee stage in the House of
Commons; the vast gulf between the information and expertise available to Ministers and that available to other Members seeking to scrutinise and propose amendments to Bills; and the very limited role played
by the House of Lords in amending Bills.

A number of the weaknesses identified in the 1960s by advocates
of reform can still be found in the contemporary legislative process,
but important changes have taken place. The first Report of the House
of Commons Modernisation Committee in July 1997 referred to the
culture 'prevalent throughout Whitehall that the standing and reputation of Ministers has been dependent upon their Bills getting through
largely unchanged'.[5] There is evidence from both before and after 1997
to suggest that the application of this measure of success is less dominant. Mainly this arises from the scale of amendments now made to
Government Bills in both Houses, although large-scale amendment of
a Bill may as often be a result of inadequate preparation as a definite
sign of Ministerial responsiveness to arguments for changes made in
either House.

In 1965, the use of standing committees as the principal mechanism
for detailed scrutiny of Bills could still be regarded as a relative innovation. (Although introduced originally in the 1880s, it was only during
the immediate post-1945 period that they became fully entrenched as
the method of dealing with the huge increase in the flow of legislation.) Most criticism of the legislative process since the 1960s has
focused on the perceived limitations of standing committee scrutiny in
the House of Commons, although the main weaknesses of scrutiny
through debate in standing committee arguably apply as much to later
stages on the floor of the House of Commons, and perhaps even to the
House of Lords. Standing committees were perceived as being weak in
what Bernard Crick termed the 'information retrieval' function, and
the Study of Parliament Group's initial submission to the Commons
Procedure Committee envisaged the systematic use of select as opposed
to standing committees for 'non-controversial' bills.[6] The preference of
standing committees for ritual over substance was seen as being char-

acterised by the unbalanced, unsystematic and overlong scrutiny to which bills were subject.[7]

The modernisation agenda

Since 1997, the 'modernisation' agenda with regard to primary legislation has drawn selectively upon the reform proposals made between the mid-1960s and the 1993 Report of the Hansard Society Commission on the Legislative Process entitled *Making the Law*. Standing committees remain the Government's preferred method of detailed and systematic scrutiny of bills in the House of Commons: special standing committees, which combine features of select and standing committees, continue to be very sparingly used.

The first main weakness of legislative scrutiny – the limited information available to Members – has been tackled in a number of ways. The Explanatory Memorandum that used to be published at the front of Bills and the Notes on Clauses formerly provided to standing committee members in the Commons have been superseded by Explanatory Notes published separately but accompanying all government Bills. Regulatory Impact Assessments, which shed further light on the anticipated effects of a Bill on the private and voluntary sectors and on the costs falling on the public, are also available.[8] And a memorandum explaining the purpose and justification for provisions for delegated legislative powers must be sent to the Delegated Powers and Regulatory Reform Committee of the House of Lords by the time the bill enters that House.

The select committees in both Houses are now far more involved than in the past in seeking and analysing information about Bills before Parliament. The Joint Committee on Human Rights examines all Government Bills to establish whether significant questions of human rights appear to be raised by any of their provisions, a process which has informed and sometimes influenced debate in both Houses. The work of the Delegated Powers and Regulatory Reform Committee and the Constitution Committee in the House of Lords are described below. Departmental select committees in the House of Commons have also begun in recent years to examine bills more frequently than in the past.

The other main development in advancing the rationalist approach to legislative scrutiny has been the introduction, and subsequent universalisation, of 'programming' in the Commons. Programming, in essence, establishes a timetable to a bill's progress immediately after second reading. In particular, it establishes an 'out date' for the conclusion of its consideration in standing committee. Within this fixed period, there is provision for the fine-tuning of the timetable by the setting of 'internal knives', which require all the proceedings necessary to complete consideration of particular parts of a bill to be concluded at some fixed point. Although this has largely been a post-97 phenomenon, it has long antecedents.

The regular timetabling of bills, to avoid the arbitrary effects of the guillotine, was first seriously proposed by the Commons Procedure Committee in 1985. They were picked up and developed by the Jopling Committee of 1992, as part of a package of reforms for rationalising the sitting hours of the House. On neither occasion did the proposals make any headway. The Procedure Committee continued to plug away at the idea from 1992 to 1997, the first report from the Modernisation Committee of 1997 proposed that the idea be experimented with, and the Official Opposition consented. The report was adopted unanimously. Since then, programming has passed through distinct stages: while in 1998 the opposition were prepared to consent to even the devolution Bills being programmed, the consensus broke down as the Government sought to widen its application. By 2004, the process had been refined and was applied routinely to virtually every government bill, but the Opposition invariably divided the House on the matter, and so far as the motions remained debatable, they were subject to ritual denunciation. The Lords have not yet found it necessary to adopt any formal approach to timetabling, relying on their tradition of self-regulation.

Three other aspects of the modernisation agenda deserve mention. The first is the use of 'carry-over' as a regular proceeding. In current parliamentary practice (by convention rather than statute) a bill 'dies' if it has not obtained the royal assent by the end of the session in which it was introduced. It must therefore complete its second reading, committee, report stage and third reading in both Houses, as well as subsequent exchanges between the two Houses, within a period book-ended by a Queen's Speech and a Prorogation. This convention inhibits the planning of a steady legislative load across the parliamentary terms. By the end of 2004, following some experimentation, both Houses had agreed that in specific circumstances motions allowing bills to be restarted in a second session at the point they had reached in the previous session could become a regular feature of proceedings. The agreement of the Lords to this applying to bills which started there was conditional.

Second, the Modernisation Committee envisaged experimentation with a wider range of types of committee in the Commons to conduct the committee stage examination, including special standing committees (a sort of hybrid of select and standing committee procedure) and on occasions select committees (a procedure currently confined almost exclusively to the quinquennial Armed Forces Bills). Nothing has come of this recommendation.

Thirdly, the modernisation Committee exhorted, rather imprecisely, the development of better 'post-legislative scrutiny' by Parliament, recognising the inability of both Houses, and the House of Commons in particular, to undertake systematic and sustained scrutiny of legislation in its policy, administrative and budgetary contexts. The only parliamentary body to come forward with a coherent proposal on how to conduct such scrutiny, or even a useful definition of what it might involve, has been the Lords Constitution Committee in its November 2004 report on *Parliament and the Legislative Process*.[9]

A great impediment to such post-legislative work is that the duty to scrutinise bills and draft bills is diffused between many committees in both Houses. The main burden of scrutiny often falls on committees with no prolonged existence – such as *ad hoc* joint committees established to examine draft bills and standing committees on bills in the House of Commons. The collective knowledge built up within Parliament about the aims and details of a particular bill is thus dissipated even before a bill reaches the statute book. A perhaps greater impediment is the nature of much legislation itself. In many of the areas where legislation is most controversial and most central to policy development – health, social security, taxation, criminal justice, and asylum and immigration, for example – the statute book rarely stays static long enough to be put under the microscope. Bright ideas, new initiatives, and the demands for something to be done mean individual measures in such areas are only rarely coherent packages; they repeatedly amend and extend previous Acts long before it would be possible to make any evidence-based assessment of the effects of earlier legislation on the problems they were supposed to solve.

The upshot is that there remains a paradox in recent developments in Parliament's work in relation to primary legislation. It has raised its game in an area where many others can also contribute – collecting and analysing information and opinions about legislation and prospective legislation – but appears to have gone backwards in its area of unique competence – formal amendment and authorisation of legislation. The developments in what might be termed 'para-scrutiny',

examination of bills and draft bills by select committees, has run in
parallel with the essentially unreformed standing committee system
and a continued adherence to the adversarial model of debate, rather
than inquiry.

Notes

1   (1611) 12 Co. Rep. 72
2   (1765) 19 St Tr 1030
3   See for instance Hansard Society Commission on Parliamentary Scrutiny,
    The Challenge for Parliament. Making Government Accountable. London: Vacher
    Dodd Publishing Ltd., 2001.
4   S. A. Walkland, *The Legislative Process in Great Britain*, Allen & Unwin, 1968,
    p. 71. See also, G. Drewry, 'Legislation', in S. A. Walkland and M. Ryle, eds.
    The Commons Today (1981), pp. 87–117.
5   First Report from the Select Committee on Modernisation of the House of
    Commons, *The Legislative Process*, HC 190, 1997–98, July 1997, para. 7.
6   B. Crick, *The Reform of Parliament* (1968 edition), p. 54; Fourth Report from
    the Procedure Committee, HC 303, 1964–65, pp. 133–134.
7   HC 539, 1966–67, para. 16; Crick, *op. cit.*, p. 86.
8   Second Report from the Select Committee on Modernisation of the House of
    Commons, *Explanatory Material for Bills*, HC 389, 1997–98, December 1997.
9   Fourteenth Report of the Constitution Committee, *Parliament and the Legislative
    Process*, HL 173, 2003–04, November 2004.

12
Modes of Scrutiny

Dawn Oliver, Paul Evans, Philip Norton and Colin Lee

Draft bills: Pre-legislative scrutiny

Arguably, from the perspective of the 'collaborative' model of Parliament's role in making the law, the most fruitful aspect of modernisation in the legislative field has been the growth of pre-legislative scrutiny, whether undertaken by *ad hoc*, usually Joint Select Committees or by existing select committees, most commonly departmental select committees in the House of Commons. Pre-legislative scrutiny has been championed by almost every advocate of rationalisation of the legislative process, from both outside and within Westminster. In February 2004 the Deputy Leader of the House of Commons stated that it was the Government's intention to adopt 'the presumption that bills will be published in draft for pre-legislative scrutiny unless there are good reasons for not doing so...'.[1] This conclusion was endorsed by the Constitution Committee of the House of Lords in 2004.[2]

Forty years ago the notion of draft bills being published for comment before being formally introduced into Parliament was not in the air. The major cultural change was heralded by the first report of the newly-formed Modernisation Committee following the 1997 general election.[3] In May 2002 the Commons agreed a resolution setting out the core tasks to be carried out by its select committees. One of these was 'to conduct scrutiny of any published draft bill within the committee's responsibilities'. Unusually, the House then put some money where its mouth was: a Scrutiny Unit was established to provide resources and support for select committees undertaking pre-legislative scrutiny. Between the 1997–98 and 2003–04 parliamentary Sessions a total of 42 draft bills were published. Of these, no fewer than 29 have been considered by a parliamentary committee: seventeen by departmental select committees, eight by joint Committees, two by temporary committees in the Commons or Lords, and two by other existing committees.[4]

Why should 'pre-legislative' scrutiny be better than traditional peri-legislative scrutiny? There are several arguments advanced in its favour, but in essence many of these boil down to a conviction that the lower level of commitment to a chosen course signalled by the publication of the draft bill as opposed to the adoption of a bill proper allows the government to accept change without losing face. The Modernisation Committee was frank about this in its first report –

> There is almost universal agreement that pre-legislative scrutiny is right in principle, subject to the circumstances and nature of the legislation. It provides an opportunity for the House as a whole, for individual backbenchers, and for the Opposition to have a real input into the form of the actual legislation which subsequently emerges, not least because Ministers are likely to be far more receptive to suggestions for change before the Bill is actually published.[5]

This suggests a commitment to a *collaborative* process between Parliament and the Executive in the making of legislation. It is a touchstone of the modernisers that Parliament should consider the principles underlying a bill in a relatively dispassionate atmosphere, make an evidence-based assessment of the practical and technical issues which might arise from its proposed provisions, and give space for a reasoned response from Ministers. Some years earlier the Hansard Society's Commission report, *Making the Law*, had asserted that –

> ... Parliament could play a greater part by pre-legislative inquiry in the preparation of legislation ... There are occasions, and topics, on which some broader political input at the stage when legislation is being considered and prepared could be helpful for all those concerned. For example, parliamentary debate or inquiry could promote more public discussion on the policy options, could encourage consultation or could help smooth the passage of the legislation through Parliament.[6]

This quotation illustrates a fundamental tension at play in almost all discussions of the rationalisation of the legislative process, including the emphasis now placed on pre-legislative scrutiny in arguments for reform. There appears to be an emerging consensus that pre-legislative scrutiny is not only a good idea, but that it is also effective in practice. But should Parliament be being recruited to 'encourage consultation' or 'help smooth the passage' of any bill? Or is it Parliament's role to make legislation as difficult as possible for the government? Nonetheless, the growth of pre-legislative scrutiny in recent sessions has been indicative of a genuine commitment to the experiment.

Those who champion pre-legislative scrutiny argue that publication of bills in draft offers the potential for *dialogue* between Parliament and Government (although such conversation can be initiated only by the government inasmuch as the choice of bills for pre-legislative scrutiny is made by it). Pre-legislative scrutiny can also help to provide a mechanism for collaboration or dialogue between the legislature and interested parties and the electorate more generally.

Traditionalists may find difficult to accept the notion of a corporate endeavour between Parliament and Government, but they are in a minority: the developing self-perception of MPs appears to tend strongly (in theory) to the collaborative model, which also brings in the new organs of 'civil society'. The Modernisation Committee's 1997 report argued that pre-legislative scrutiny 'opens Parliament up to those outside affected by legislation'. It can certainly stimulate and inform public and media debate on a subject. It can provide a mechanism for pressure and lobby groups to campaign on an issue. Commenting on the 2004 reports of the Joint Committee on the Draft Gambling Bill, The Guardian argued –

> Too many laws which have gone through Parliament in recent years have been badly drafted and hastily adopted. [Pre-legislative scrutiny has ensured] a much more serious public debate on gambling has been generated than would have been the case under the traditional flawed system. And all this without a major legislative vote being taken. This is good for Parliament, good for law making and good for politics. The process should be extended to all Government bills as a matter of routine.[7]

The figures for submission of evidence to the pre-legislative scrutiny committees suggests that, in this respect at least, such scrutiny has encouraged greater collaboration between Parliament and the wider public who are affected by the laws it makes. It has also provoked new levels of intra-parliamentary dialogue: the Draft Civil Contingencies Bill was the subject of reports by no fewer than five committees.[8]

A reading of the reports indicates that written and oral evidence taken was influential on the recommendations of the committees in many cases. The introduction of draft bills may not have affected the amount of lobbying that actually occurs – what it has done is to bring that process far more out into the open and place Parliament at its centre.

The more fundamental question is whether pre-legislative scrutiny has improved the quality of the legislation which receives the royal assent. As the Modernisation Committee put it, the success of pre-legislative scrutiny was to be measured by its outputs –

> ... Above all, it should lead to better legislation and less likelihood of subsequent amending legislation.[9]

The experience of pre-legislative scrutiny by committees reveals that the dialogue between Parliament and Government – or at least the exchange between committee and ministers in the form of the committee's report and the Government's response – has resulted in some substantial changes to the bills subsequently brought before Parliament. To take two particular examples of draft bills scrutinised by Joint Committees: the Draft Communications Bill and the Draft Civil Contingencies Bill. In its response to the 148 recommendations made by the Joint Committee on the former Bill, the Government responded by saying that it had accepted 120 of them. In its response to the latter, the Government acknowledged that '[t]o a large extent, we have accepted in full, or in part, most of the recommendations'. [10]

The perceived value of parliamentary involvement at this stage was well expressed by Dr Lewis Moonie, who chaired the Joint Committee on the Draft Civil Contingencies Bill, echoing the ambitions of the authors of *Making the Law*: 'Scrutiny at this stage can resolve potential points of conflict, remove contradictions or impracticable suggestions, and speed up the passage of legislation through both Houses'.[11] It may not only help speed up passage of legislation, it also has another advantage, which is to inform the debates on the legislation once before Parliament. The work undertaken by a pre-legislative committee can add considerably to the scrutiny at committee and report stages. This was apparent, for example, with the Communications Bill. As the Constitution Committee noted in its report on *Parliament and the Legislative Process:* 'The work of the [pre-legislative] committees is thus not something conducted in isolation of either House, but contributes to Members' understanding of the issues surrounding the bills. This enhances the quality of the scrutiny during the legislative process itself'.[12] Pre-legislative scrutiny thus not only introduces a dialogue between Parliament and government at a formative stage of the legislative process, it may also help maintain it during a bill's passage.

While the evidence suggests that good use is made of pre-legislative reports by members of Commons standing committees and other participants in debates in both Houses, there is some danger that the formal division of the two stages (pre- and peri-legislative scrutiny) will inhibit the most effective use of cross-fertilisation from the pre-legislative phase to the actual making of the law. The standing committee and report stages in the Commons (and increasingly their equivalent stages in the Lords) are conducted along traditional adversarial lines.

Pre-legislative scrutiny is advisory only – this is both the source of its strength (allowing change without loss of face or the unpredictability of proceedings on the floor of either House) and its weakness. Unlike standing committees, which have powers to alter the bill, select committees looking at a draft bill make recommendations which might be framed in general or more specific terms. To some extent this can be seen as a bargain in which formal power is traded for greater flexibility. The downside is that it relieves the pressure on legislators to look at the words on the page – pre-legislative scrutiny has not in general been anything like 'line-by-line' examination of draft bills. The tendency so far seems for the pre-legislative committees to take more interest in broad concepts and assessments of potential effectiveness than in detailed matters of drafting. This means that it is more than ever important to link the pre-legislative and peri-legislative phases of scrutiny.

If there is one persuasive objection to the broadening of the pre-legislative project it is this danger of further dilution of the specialised focus of Parliament on a well-understood (if inadequately discharged) task – line by line scrutiny through the process of debate, amendment and decision. A number of proposals[13] have been advanced to try and address this gap – where most are likely to founder is on the commitment of MPs and Peers to using pre-legislative scrutiny genuinely to inform the later stages, rather than as an excuse to allow those later stages to become even more formulaic.

The evidence suggests that, so far as better engaging a wider range of organisations and individuals with the process of making the law is concerned, pre-legislative scrutiny can already be counted a success. It is impossible yet to hazard even a tentative answer as to whether the other objective of pre-legislative scrutiny – better law – has been achieved. There is simply too little evidence to go on, and the majority of bills subject to the process have yet to be put into effect.

Finally, it must be doubtful if there is a preponderant opinion within Whitehall that pre-legislative scrutiny has made the job of government easier. Neither side of the dialogue can be said yet to have fully embraced a culture in which reasoned disagreement can be separated from opportunistic point-scoring.

Rational scrutiny: a chimera?

The question arises then whether Parliament is the right body to conduct rational scrutiny of bills or draft bills. The answer depends in part on which House is engaged in scrutiny. Given the influence of party and politics on its activities it will often be unrealistic to expect the House of Commons to engage in scrutiny that can readily be presented as 'rational' to the outside world of business, specialist NGOs, professional lobby groups and other organs of civil society. The House of Lords has a better track record than the House of Commons, but here there are problems of legitimacy deriving largely from mixed and inconsistent understandings of what the function of the House of Lords is, and the reality that, despite its high self-regard, its deliberations are a mix of party politicking and more objective scrutiny.

The ideal description of a forum for rational scrutiny would be one that is independent of party politics, and operates according to explicit criteria as to scrutiny – for instance, workability, good technical drafting, compatibility with the UK's international commitments and with the Human Rights Act, with other principles that need to be articulated authoritatively such as those in the Ministerial code, the civil service code, and others such as the rule of law, non-discrimination, non-retroactivity and so on. A major task would be to produce statements of these principles. The body that applied these principles in legislative scrutiny needs to include people with expertise in the particular subject matter of the bill, and in international law, human rights law and so on. It could consist of a range of part time members, with expertise across a wide range of subject matter, including lawyers, and a legally qualified president of senior judicial or equivalent status. It would need a secretariat of experts and possible recourse to specialist expertise on particular bills. Its advice should be influential and would be likely to result in amendments, without the loss of face that party political defeat entails. If the advice of this body were rejected and the measure passed, then unless the courts were to find it incompatible with, for instance, the ECHR or European law, it would be a legally valid measure though tainted with the finding of this new body.

This description of a platonic ideal is often applied by its champions to the procedures of the House of Lords. The House of Lords can be argued to add value to the legislative processes of the Commons in three ways, one relating to structure, one to procedure, and the other to composition.

The first is through the systematic application of general principles, as described above. Each bill brought before the House is considered by two committees of the House, in addition to the Joint Committee on Human Rights. The Delegated Powers and Regulatory Reform Committee, to which reference has already been made, examines the powers delegated by the bill and considers whether delegation is appropriate and the parliamentary scrutiny stipulated appropriate for the particular provision. The recommendations of the Committee are usually accepted by the Government. The Constitution Committee considers whether a bill has constitutional implications and submits each to what it terms the two Ps test: whether it affects a principal part of the constitution and raises an important issue of principle. If it meets the test, the committee reports on the bill. In the 2003–04 session, for example, it reported on nine bills (and also on an Act) in addition to writing to Ministers about particular provisions of other bills; changes were made in the light of the questions raised by the committee.[14]

The second way in which the House of Lords adds value in the legislative process is by virtue of the permissive procedures of the House. Though characterised by some as being archaic, they permit sustained scrutiny driven by the preoccupations of its individual members rather than those of the government. Amendments are debated for as long as peers wish to discuss them; there is no provision for preventing particular amendments, or parts of a bill, being considered.

The third way in which value is added derives from the expertise or experience of the members. Although bills go through the same stages as in the Commons, those engaging in the scrutiny of the provisions differ in terms of background and interests.

Whereas the Commons is increasingly populated by career politicians – whose skills and knowledge derive principally from the political arena – the Lords relies primarily on part-time members who are able to, or who must, hold jobs outside the House (though it also contains a substantial proportion of career politicians who have come from the Commons on retirement).[15] The basis of membership of the House (appointment for life) provides a form of protection for the independence of members, and the experience and expertise of members enables the House to take a different perspective to that taken of the Commons.

The Lords, then, not only can provide the means for Government to amend its own bills, having had second thoughts, but also adds value of its own by amending Bills and sometimes by inducing the Government to have its second thoughts. The House serves as a chamber in which in an average parliamentary session two-thousand amendments or more (sometimes considerably more) are secured to bills; in the 1999–2000 Session, the number was 4,761. The overwhelming majority of amendments are government amendments and are accepted by the House of Commons.

Notes

1 HC Deb 24 February 2004, vol. 418, col. 19.
2 Fourteenth Report of the Constitution Committee, *Parliament and the Legislative Process*, HL 173, 2003–04, November 2004.
3 First Report of the Modernisation Committee, *The Legislative Process*, HC 190, 1997–98, July 1997.
4 A. Kennon 'Pre-legislative scrutiny of draft bills' [2004] *Public Law*, 478.
5 First Report of the Modernisation Committee, *The Legislative Process*, HC 190, 1997–98, July 1997.
6 Hansard Society, 1992.
7 *The Guardian*, 8 April 2004.
8 Including the Joint Committee on the draft Civil Contingencies Bill (reports at 2002–03 HL 157, HC 705 and 2003–04 HL 184, HC 1074); see A. Kennon [2004] *Public Law* at p. 487.
9 First Report of the Modernisation Committee, *The Legislative Process*, HC 190, 1997–98, July 1997.
10 Cabinet Office 2004: 3.
11 Constitution Committee, *Parliament and the Legislative Process*, HL Paper 173–I, 2003–04, para. 25.
12 Constitution Committee, supra., para. 24.
13 See for instance Constitution Committee, HL Paper 173–I, 2004, chapter 3.
14 Constitution Committee, *Annual Report*, 2003–04, November 2004.
15 See above, pp. 41–44, 54–55.

13
Untouched by Reform – Private Members Bills and Delegated Legislation

Dawn Oliver, David Miers and Paul Evans

Private Members' Bills

Private Members' Bills (PMBs) are an area of the legislative process which remains almost entirely untouched by reform. Forty years ago was perhaps the golden age of the PMB. They were used to allow the House of Commons to put 'conscience' issues on the parliamentary agenda, and led to famous legal changes heralding the 'social revolution' of the 1960s: for example, abolition of the death penalty (1965), homosexual law reform and the legalisation of abortion (1967), and the abolition of theatre censorship and divorce reform (1968). Since then the tradition of using PMBs has withered. 'Matters of conscience' such as Sunday trading, the equalisation of the age of consent for heterosexual and homosexual acts, and changes to the law on abortion have been effected through government bills.

The zenith of PMBs in recent times was in the dying months of the second Major administration: in the 1996–97 Session over 26% of the bills which received the royal assent were PMBs. In the last session of the first Blair administration (2000–01) they hit their nadir: exactly none received the royal assent.

Under the current system of dealing with PMBs twenty MPs are selected by ballot to have the first claim on the time set aside on thirteen Fridays a session for the consideration of PMBs. The first bill up on a Friday has a chance of getting a second reading in the face of opposition because the closure can be claimed. If 100 Members vote in favour of putting the question and are in the majority, then a second reading can almost certainly be secured, but the hurdle of keeping 100 supporters at Westminster on a Friday is a high one. Proceedings in Standing Committee C are often perfunctory: custom and practice allows the sponsoring Member to pack the committee. It is the report stage that is fatal, even to a well-supported bill which commands support from across the political spectrum. It requires little ingenuity to devise a sufficient number of amendments to ensure the bill is talked-out. Other PMBs (ten minute rule Bills and 'presentation' bills) are extremely unlikely to make any progress at all.

The supporters of Private Members' Bills champion them as a means for backbench MPs to exercise some control over the parliamentary agenda. However, the attrition rate is huge and, in any event, a significant proportion of bills getting through in private Members' time is made up of thinly disguised government bills, handed out to willing backbenchers who have won a slot in the ballot.

PMBs can achieve a number of aims which cannot sensibly be measured by success rates in getting royal assent. These include giving publicity to an issue aimed at eliciting legislation from the government. Legislation outlawing mobile phone use by drivers started life as a PMB. The embarrassment caused by a botched attempt by the government to use procedural ruses to frustrate a PMB on disability discrimination in 1995 led to such adverse publicity (including a ministerial resignation) that the Conservative government was cornered into an undertaking to introduce its own legislation – which resulted in the Disability Discrimination Act 1996.

By and large though, the system is extravagantly and egregiously wasteful both of resources and the reputation of Parliament. Seen from the backbench Members' perspective the problems include: the lack of certainty that the bill will be able to progress even if it commands majority support; the existence of what is effectively a single veto allowing bills to be blocked, particularly at report stage, by opposition from a single Member; the ghettoising of PMBs to Fridays, a non-day for most MPs who have many pressing needs to be elsewhere, so that assent to or dissent from a bill in principle cannot be measured; a perception that, as usual, the usual channels control every detail of parliamentary procedure; and the absence of any mechanism to separate gesture bills with no hope or intention of success from those seriously intended, so that they all go down together.

The authors of a 1985 article concluded that the failure of bills which apparently command overwhelming support at second reading led to –

> ... not merely ... dissatisfaction with the ... procedure, which few understood, but to a more general disillusionment with the legislative process.[1]

The squandering of time, talent, effort and money on a process that pretends to offer hope of change but turns out to be a theatrical sham, often descending into farce, is corrosive of public trust in the democratic process.

Government resources are also wasted. Each PMB must be studied and circulated within Whitehall. The expensive time of parliamentary counsel may be put into work on PMBs which ultimately fail. A lot of energy in the Whips' Office and other branches of the usual channels must go into managing bills on the floor and in committee.

Reform could focus on dealing with some of these impediments, or it could be used to remove this final residue of the power of Parliament to initiate legislation and hand over the expression of backbench opinion to the host of alternative vehicles which have been developed in the last forty years (select committees, Westminster Hall, the media). The status quo is not really an option – the present system serves only to make Parliament look ridiculous.

The obvious solutions which are aimed at increasing effectiveness must be first to borrow from the wider procedural reforms which have been applied to government bills; second to exploit existing and new channels for the advancement of some of the aims of PMBs which go wider than securing legislation; and third to provide mechanisms for the wresting of some control back from the usual channels to Parliament as a corporate body. Many such reforms are likely to confront backbenchers with the unpalatable task of discriminating between the deserving and undeserving amongst their colleagues. This would not necessarily be a bad thing.

A starting point in reform might be the proposition that the promoters of ballot bills should have a reasonable chance to test whether they command support of a majority in the House. One possibility would be to borrow from programming and guarantee each a specified maximum amount of time for debate at second reading, after which an automatic closure would occur. Mischievous or unworkable bills should be rejected at an early stage, even if they were high up the ballot. This would have the benign effect of allowing other bills further down to progress, although it would not eliminate the perverse incentive to debate a bill higher up the list solely in order to block one lower down.

The stage at which PMBs are likely to fail is the report stage (and, rarely, consideration of Lords Amendments). There are two alternative approaches to this. The first would be to have a programming committee established for PMBs. An alternative would be for the report stage on PMBs to be taken in a standing committee. Third readings might follow the same form as proposed for second readings above, with an automatic closure after a specified maximum time (debates might extend over more than one sitting).

Another quid pro quo for reform may have to be a reduction in the number of bills introduced. Their high-profile time on the floor might be taken with, for example, a slot for the proposer (and an opponent) of an EDM to state their case. An alternative would be the introduction of a new procedure – short debates, starred questions or motions to take note of or adopt reports from select committees.

The House collectively might show some of the commitment to backbench legislation that it has accorded to backbench scrutiny. It could allocate resources to provide at least a modicum of drafting expertise to private Members, to level up, if only incrementally, the playing field on which they must take on the might of government. Alternative routes for backbenchers to explore serious legislative proposals could include the opportunity to introduce draft PMBs, and have some of them seriously considered in a select committee forum.

There may never have been a golden age of Private Members' legislation. But the ritualistic residue that the present system represents is a symbol of the extent to which Parliament's right to initiate legislation has been ceded to Government. There is little alternative to reform other than to let the whole idea of backbench legislation die.

Delegated legislation

Up to this point we have focussed on primary legislation, which is of course the supreme form of parliamentary law making. But Parliament makes much more law than the 45 or so Acts of Parliament that it enacts in a normal year. In addition, some 3,500 general statutory instruments (SIs) a year are laid before Parliament, which, though less glamorous than Acts of Parliament, and typically receiving much less media attention than they do, affect our daily lives with as much legal force as does the primary legislation under which they are made. As an example of delegated legislation, statutory instruments may be well below most members of the public's legal horizon, but, to adapt some comments made over 30 years ago,[2] they affect the daily life of the ordinary citizen from cradle to grave. The food we eat, the education we receive, the social security benefits that we receive, the employment we pursue, the public and private transport in which we ride, and the environment in which we live are all regulated according to the terms of one statutory instrument or another. In its content, delegated legislation can indeed be very detailed, and for that reason apparently of little interest. But it is law, and for that reason alone warrants attention.

However, delegated (or secondary) legislation has been largely untouched by reform. Made by Ministers with only sketchy involvement by Parliament, it has continued to grow in volume and complexity over the last forty years. This Cinderella legislation is incoherently organised, superficially scrutinised, poorly debated, and inadequately monitored. The vast majority of SIs laid before Parliament (around 90%) are subject to a 'negative procedure'. This provides that a Member of either House can table a motion within 40 sitting days, seeking the annulment of the instrument. The 1946 Statutory Instruments Act which governs the procedure implies that any such motion will be debated and voted on. In practice (at least in the Commons), most such motions suffer the fate of all other early day motions and are given no time for debate. The vast majority of these SIs become law without any parliamentary opinion on them being formally expressed. More rigorous scrutiny of SIs is provided for by the 'affirmative procedure'. Under this, a proposed SI must be laid before each house in draft, and cannot become law until each house has voted to approve it.

Concerns about the legitimacy of delegated legislation and the adequacy of its parliamentary scrutiny have been around for a long time. Significant historical reforms include the establishment in 1944 of the Select Committee on Statutory Rules and Orders, the Statutory Instruments Act of 1946, the establishment in 1972 of a Joint Committee of the two Houses to consider SIs (the JCSI), the creation in the 1970s of a system of standing committees to debate them in the Commons, and the decision in the 1990s to use these as the default mechanism for examination of delegated legislation.

The end result of all these inquiries and reports is a situation which few find satisfactory. The Commons Procedure Committee's report of 1996 summed up the problem in the following terms –

> The volume of delegated legislation has undoubtedly grown in recent years ... There is in our view too great a readiness in parliament to delegate wide legislative powers to ministers, and no lack of enthusiasm on their part to take such powers.[3]

There is a dilemma. Parliament has an essential democratic role in ensuring that departments are making the law well, but at the same time it needs to avoid being swamped by detail. In 1975, the Renton Committee proposed that, 'Only details [of legislation] which may require comparatively frequent modification should be delegated',[4] whereas 20 years later the Hansard Society Commission on *Making the Law* recommended that, in order to focus Parliament's limited legislative time on key issues of principle, 'most detail should be left to delegated legislation'. But they added the vital proviso that this should only happen if: 'much more satisfactory procedures are adopted by parliament for the scrutiny of delegated legislation'.[5] Most examinations of the issue have come to the conclusion that, so far as delegated legislation is concerned, the right balance has not yet been struck between efficiency and accountability.

Most SIs are considered by the JCSI to determine whether they are intra vires the powers given to Ministers under the parent act and whether they are unclear or defectively drafted. This Committee has no power to consider the 'merits' of an instrument. Although in principle no instrument should be passed by either house before the JCSI has completed its scrutiny, this convention is regularly ignored in the Commons. Concern over the quality of parliamentary scrutiny of SIs has been intensified by the perception that some acts of Parliament are being passed as 'framework legislation', where the details which remain to be filled in by orders and regulations are the substantive portion of the operative part of the legislation. The House of Lords responded to these concerns by establishing, in 1992, its Delegated Powers Committee. The Committee's terms of reference were –

> ... to report whether the provisions of any bill inappropriately delegate legislative power, or whether they subject the exercise of legislative power to an inappropriate level of parliamentary scrutiny.

In 1994 the Committee was also given responsibility for examining deregulation orders, subsequently (from 2001) regulatory reform orders (see below), and is now known as the Delegated Powers and Regulatory Reform Committee. The Committee polices the allocation of powers to these various types of delegation before legislation is actually passed – in effect the DPRRC tries to regulate the use of delegated powers at the input stage and the JCSI at the output stage.

The Jopling reforms

Since the reforms initiated by the report of the Jopling Committee,[6] the vast majority of affirmative procedure SIs are not debated on the floor of the House of Commons but in a standing committee. In the case of a substantial proportion of affirmative procedure instruments no-one has anything to say about them, while in the case of a substantial number of negative procedure instruments (which can often concern far more controversial matters) it is impossible for those who object to them to secure any debate at all. Once an instrument has been debated in one of these committees it is reported to the House and then voted on without any further debate. Since the establishment of the JCSI the number of instruments it considers has risen from about 1200 a year to over 1500. The proportion of these that are subject to affirmative resolution procedure has risen slightly from around 11% to around 13%.

The essential problems with this system of parliamentary scrutiny were identified by the Procedure Committee[7] as follows:

- a frequent lack of apparent proportionality between the type of parliamentary procedure which applies to an SI and its political or legal significance;
- the inability of parliament to amend SIs, or even formally to express a reasoned opinion on their merits or defects;
- the procedurally ineffective nature of the decisions made by standing committees on delegated legislation, which is a powerful disincentive to government, opposition or backbenchers taking them seriously;
- the lack of systematic parliamentary scrutiny of SIs for their political or legal significance, with the risk that, except by happenstance, major legislative changes could pass through parliament entirely unnoticed;
- that control of the parliamentary procedures which do exist lies almost entirely in the hands of the government.

More reform of delegated legislation?

A number of remedies were proposed by the Procedure Committee in its 1996 report. The first was the establishment in the Commons of a 'sifting committee' to examine all SIs laid before the House to determine whether they raised significant legal or political questions. It, rather than the government, would then decide which required debate.

The Procedure Committee also proposed beefing-up the standing committees on delegated legislation, extending the time available for debate and altering the procedures to require ministers to make an explanatory statement on which they could be questioned by the committee and allowing the committees to debate substantive and amendable motions. While stopping short of recommending that the House should be able to amend an instrument directly, they proposed that such motions could be amended to express reasoned dissent from the detailed provisions of an instrument.

The Procedure Committee's 1996 recommendations received widespread support but, contrary to expectations, in 1997 the new Modernisation Committee did not take up the recommendations but passed the subject back to the new Procedure Committee for further consideration. The Royal Commission on House of Lords reform (the Wakeham Commission), however, did take up the 1996 recommendations.

The Wakeham Commission proposed[8] that the House's power to unmake delegated legislation – one of the few unilateral powers it possesses – be replaced by a power of delay (or 'suspensory veto'), thereby freeing the Lords to be more direct and robust in their approach to the scrutiny of delegated legislation. The Commission also proposed that the 'sifting committee' recommended by the Procedure Committee of the Commons in 1996 should be a joint committee of the two Houses.

In the House of Commons, the new Procedure Committee reported in March 2000 and endorsed, almost without qualification, the recommendations of its predecessor's 1996 report. It concluded its report with the words –

> The proposals have now been endorsed by the Procedure Committee under both a Conservative and a Labour administration, as well as by the Royal Commission on House of Lords Reform and by the Chairmen's Panel in the House of Commons. We believe they represent a significant contribution to the process of modernising parliament, and we press the government to accept them as a matter of urgency.[9]

Towards merits scrutiny of delegated legislation in the House of Lords

In the event, it was the semi-reformed Lords that moved first, establishing a Committee on the 'merits' of statutory instruments. Despite the urgings of the Commons Procedure Committee to make this a joint endeavour, the government declined to enable the two Houses even to discuss the proposal. The Lords Committee was appointed in December 2003 with a remit to examine the merits of any statutory instrument subject to either the affirmative or negative procedure. It has power to draw the 'special attention of the House' to any instrument which it considers:

a) has important legal or political implications;
b) inappropriate because of changed circumstances since the passage of the Act of Parliament that established the power to make the instrument;
c) inappropriately implements European Union legislation;
d) imperfectly achieves its policy objectives.

To aid it in its work, the Committee now requires Explanatory Memoranda to be made available in relation to each SI which are supposed to be designed to enable the Committee to assess instruments against the above criteria.

'Super-affirmatives' and the Deregulation Order model

The only major development in the field of delegated legislation in the last forty years has been the invention of the super-affirmative process. The 1996 Procedure Committee report[10] proposed the creation of a category of 'super-affirmatives', where the extent of delegated powers was so wide that an SI deserved detailed examination more akin to that given to a Bill. The model they used for this was the then newly-introduced 'deregulation' procedure established under the 1994 Deregulation and Contracting Out Act. Deregulation orders could be used to repeal or amend primary legislation (so long as it is designed to 'remove a burden and maintain any necessary protection') even where there had been no provision in the parent Act for this to be done by secondary legislation. The Act laid down an extensive consultation procedure before a Minister could lay a deregulation order before Parliament, close to the United States 'notice and comment' requirements.

The Regulatory Reform Act 2001 significantly widened the scope of the deregulation process to allow whole areas of legislation to be reconstructed by means of the super-affirmative process. The Human Rights Act 1998 also provided for a form of super-affirmative procedure to be applied to 'remedial orders' made under section 10 of the Act, which provided for a fast-track mechanism to change the law in the event of a finding of incompatibility by Strasbourg or a UK court. Like regulatory reform orders, these can amend primary legislation even where the Act so amended made no provision for it to be altered by means of secondary legislation. A similar procedure was also applied to certain categories of legislation made under the Northern Ireland Act 1998.

The super-affirmative system prefigured to some extent the development of draft bills, and it could even be argued that it has some advantages over that procedure in putting the consultation processes on a statutory footing, and formalising the involvement of Parliament in the consultation phase.

The key defining feature of the super-affirmative process is that it is used in effect to make primary legislation – something that would once have been held to be a constitutional outrage. In practice, its use has been relatively uncontroversial, and arguably the process involves a more effective type of scrutiny than the traditional stages of taking a Bill through the two Houses.

The super-affirmative procedure is also successful in engaging consultation with affected parties, in the committees' focus on different aspects of the criteria, and in their examination of departmental justifications against those criteria. The care and attention given to scrutiny is a model. But resources (the other side of volume and detail) preclude this kind of engagement for all but a minority of measures. The underlying problems are simply the numbers and the detail of SIs. Successful scrutiny of any kind requires management according to some reasonably clear criteria. There have been efforts to generate such criteria, principally through the work of the Lords Committees, but the sheer volume makes the task of applying the criteria a daunting one. A merits committee is the only mechanism that could address this problem, assuming there was the political will to do so, but the process of selection from thousands of measures will always be problematic.

The failure to modernise delegated legislation

The Government's failure, save in relation to 'super-affirmatives', to implement reforms aimed at improving the processes relating to delegated legislation has continued to infuriate critics of the current system. The reasons are not hard to divine – secondary legislation is a tremendously convenient way of making the law, and greater scrutiny of it would be tremendously inconvenient. Since the Government controls almost all the available parliamentary time in the Commons the vast majority of negative procedure SIs will not be debated. As the Procedure Committee noted in 2000 –

> The reduction in the overall number of negatives debated, at a time when there has been no decrease in the numbers laid or it may confidently be assumed in the complexity or importance of the instruments themselves, strengthens the supposition that existing arrangements for triggering debate on negatives are less than adequate.[11]

Strengthening Parliament, the report of the Conservative Party Commission of 2000 claimed that the negative resolution procedure 'is close to preposterous. Major changes are needed to existing arrangements'. The Commons Liaison Committee declared that the scrutiny of delegated legislation generally was 'woefully inadequate'.[12] The *Parliament First* group of MPs argued that 'changes to the way Parliament deals with secondary legislation should be brought forward as a matter of urgency. More detail should be provided within primary legislation and more care taken to provide the best possible legislation through the normal routes'.[13]

The opposition and backbenchers are unable (and mostly unwilling) to secure proper scrutiny of delegated legislation – and the procedures of the Commons are designed to make political effort seem futile. The Lords has a distinctive approach to the handling of delegated legislation, and on paper seems to take it more seriously. But the outcome of its efforts are not obviously very strikingly positive.

These shortcomings have been addressed by recommendations from successive committees and commissions, but with only very limited progress. The House of Lords Delegated Powers Committee, which examines proposed delegation of powers to Ministers in Bills, has not been able to develop a coherent body of 'jurisprudence' on what types of law should and should not be made in these ways – not least because the options available are so limited. The Joint Committee on Statutory Instruments is routinely ignored in the Commons, and is unable to tackle the key issues of accountability within its terms of reference. The new 'merits committee' of the Lords has the potential to make a real impact on this aspect of the legislative process, but the government's refusal (and the Commons supine acceptance of the decision) to establish it as a joint committee will severely curtail its possible impact.

Given that Parliament makes more law than it can effectively handle, leading to over-legislation, over-regulation, redundancy and superfluity in the statute book, and downright bad law, the way in which it handles delegated legislation (particularly in the Commons) at present can be regarded only as one more example of Parliament's abdication of its responsibilities and the Government's readiness to evade scrutiny. Approached more creatively, the proper use of delegated legislation could be seen as part of a radical reform of the law-making process. But, on past experience, this opportunity is bound to be missed.

Notes

1   *British Private Members' Balloted Bills: A Lottery with Few Winners, Small Prizes, but High Administrative Costs*, D. Marsh and M. Read, Essex Papers in Politics and Government, University of Essex, 1985.
2   *The Preparation of Legislation*, 1975, Cmnd 6053, para. 7.3 (the Renton Report). See also, E. Page, *Governing by Numbers*, Hart Publishing, 2001.
3   Procedure Committee, *Delegated Legislation*, HC 152, 1995–96.
4   Cmnd 6053, 1975.
5   Hansard Society for Parliamentary Government, *Making the Law: the Report of The Hansard Society Commission on The Legislative Process*. London: Hansard Society, 1992, paragraph 267.
6   Select Committee on Sittings of the House, HC 22, 1991–92.
7   Procedure Committee, *Delegated Legislation*, HC 152, 1995–96.
8   *A House for the Future*, Cm 4534, January 2000, chapter 7.
9   Procedure Committee, *Delegated Legislation*, HC 48, 1999–2000.
10 Procedure Committee, *Delegated Legislation*, HC 152, 1995–96.
11 Procedure Committee, *Delegated Legislation*, HC 48, 1999–2000.
12 Liaison Committee, *Shifting the Balance: Select Committees and the Executive*, HC 300, 1999–2000.
13 *Parliament's Last Chance*, 2003.

14
Less is More?

Dawn Oliver, David Miers and Paul Evans

Despite the lip-service paid, the objective of rational, measured and full consideration of proposed legislation is not one that all participants in the process of making the law share. The motto of 'legislate in haste, repeal at leisure' is one which post-war governments of all complexions have adopted. But to both the technocrat and the democrat the present approach of Parliament to the task of legislating is one which evokes a strong sense of disappointment and pessimism about the possibility of radical reform.

The first and most obvious conclusion to be drawn from any analysis of the present system is that there is simply too much legislation (both primary and secondary) for Parliament to handle effectively, even if it had the collective will to do so. A starting point for meaningful change would be for governments to give far more attention to making things work, rather than incessantly redesigning them. Parliament could move this aim forward both by better scrutiny of service delivery (through its select committees) and through a more rigorous approach to examining the consequences of the laws it makes.

A second conclusion that we must draw is that the duplication of legislative procedures by the two Houses appears a cumbersome way of bringing the special skills of each to bear on legislation. If the Lords is the place in which proposed laws can be measured against agreed standards, there seems little point in undertaking this work exclusively through the laborious process of debate, division and amendment followed by a rather amateurish poker game with the Commons played against a clock marking a wholly artificial deadline determined by an obscure constitutional convention. The champions of the Lords' special value might recognise that its unique qualities could be brought to bear on the process in a far less confrontational style.

The Commons needs to apply its own democratic scrutiny with more forensic selectivity. That goal should not be seen as the property of one party, or as having benefits only for the Government of the day. Its achievement is deserving of support by all serious parliamentarians. There are patches that could be usefully applied to the current system, but no amount of tinkering will work unless there is goodwill from the Opposition and the Government to make the system work. Somehow the House needs to have the confidence and the commitment to ensure that the gain of greater certainty about the Government's legislative timetable should be balanced against the opportunity for less rushed, more thorough, and more effective scrutiny. Only by developing some corporate governance of its procedures, as it has been able to do in respect of its administration, will it be able to achieve this. The possibility of its doing so in the face of the Executive's vested interest in the *status quo* is remote.

For those MPs (a theoretical majority) who appear to wish to see the Commons recover some real influence over the legislative process, modernisation is seen as an essential part of achieving better scrutiny, better use of time, increased transparency and, ultimately, an improvement in the quality of legislation. To those who give priority to Parliament's role as an inhibitor of government, modernisation is caricatured as easing the burden on the Government's business managers rather than a means of securing better legislative scrutiny – an abuse of process in which the usual channels have as usual been complicit.

It would be possible to combine the aims of inhibition and collaboration in a creative way – principally by using the investigative or forensic approach to making the law (draft bills, pre-legislative scrutiny, measurement against objective standards, sifting) to focus the political attention of the House on what really matters.

The test of the success of the modernisation of the legislative process is whether it restores Parliament's active participation in the making of the law, and persuades the electorate that the law-making process is a common endeavour for the common good.

Part V
Guarding the Citizenry

15

Time for Coherence: Parliament and the Constitutional Watchdogs

Oonagh Gay

Introduction

Parliamentarians need as much help as they can get to scrutinise the work of the executive effectively. But MPs seem to be increasingly by-passed by a series of independent or semi-independent agencies with the task of regulating public policy objectives. Yet these bodies would actively welcome more interest in their work from Parliament.[1] How is this conundrum to be resolved? We need to return to the nineteenth century to find an answer. The concept of Officers of Parliament has much to offer, but needs modernising to make a more coherent framework for key constitutional watchdogs and Parliament. The pre-eminent Officer is the Comptroller and Auditor General (C and AG), whose modern powers date from 1866, but the characteristics of the post have been borrowed for other watchdogs, and more coherence is necessary after decades of inchoate growth.

This chapter concentrates on 'constitutional watchdogs' – used as shorthand for bodies with powers of persuasion and publicity to alter the actions of the executive in areas characterised as constitutional. This includes human rights, electoral matters, the redress of grievances and the voting of supply. The boundaries of the category are imprecise. Some watchdogs also have judicial powers or powers to enforce decisions. The wider regulatory sector has been examined by the Lords Constitution Committee, which has also recommended more formal and effective mechanisms to ensure effective scrutiny by Parliament.[2]

There are three watchdogs currently designated as Officers of the House of Commons. These are:

- Comptroller and Auditor General
- Parliamentary Ombudsman
- Parliamentary Commissioner for Standards

Each has different institutional designs and the Electoral Commission has markedly similar design features to the other three Officers, but lacks formal designation.

The term is used as a device to denote a special relationship with Parliament, emphasising independence from the executive. Formal mechanisms, such as restrictions on dismissal of Officers and direct appointment of staff as non civil servants uphold this distance. The concept is also in use in Canada and New Zealand, but with the term Officer of Parliament. Often by accident rather than design, other constitutional watchdogs do not possess institutional safeguards and do not have a special involvement with Westminster. This lessens their effectiveness.

Independent 'experts' became necessary when concepts of honour proved insufficient to maintain public faith in the political system. Many watchdogs have their origin in mismanagement by government, necessitating the creation of independent officials. The involvement of unelected officials in supervising elected politicians can damage democracy, if independence is the dominant characteristic. Some form of accountability is desirable, even if this amounts only to transparency. Direct accountability to parliament, by-passing ministers, can enhance that transparency by establishing a formal channel of communication with elected representatives of the people.

But dependence on government should not be replaced by dependence on parliament – particularly since parliament is not as such directly accountable to anyone. This could even be more harmful to an Officer's overall independence. Institutional mechanisms should protect watchdogs from arbitrary dismissal and ensure adequate budgets and independent staff. The parliamentary connection should enable key aspects of independence, such as appointment, financing and reporting, to be more open and transparent than if these were matters for government. Westminster has a long way to go to achieve this.

The origin of the term

The terms 'Officers of Parliament' and 'Officers of the House' appear very rarely in statute and have never been subject to judicial interpretation. Originally, they were confined to senior officials of each House. Successive editions of Erskine May give the fullest description of the applicability of the term, but it was not until the 15th edition (1950) that the term was applied to the Comptroller and Auditor General (C and AG). Recent editions refer to 'statutory' officers – the C and AG, and the

Parliamentary Commissioner for Administration. The Parliamentary Standards Commissioner is treated as a senior Commons official.

The Speaker's salary is a direct charge on the Consolidated Fund following the precedent of the judiciary under the *Act of Settlement 1701*. The independence of the Speaker's office was adapted as a model for constitutional officers, such as the C and AG, who began to be described colloquially as an Officer of the House from the nineteenth century onwards. The main practical effect of Officer status is to confer parliamentary privilege, protecting exchanges of information between Officer and committee or reports to the House from legal challenge or requests under the *Freedom of Information Act 2000*. The value of the term for watchdogs is that it denotes both independence and accountability.

The comparative context – New Zealand and Canada

Canada has five constitutional watchdogs accorded the status of Officers of Parliament.[3] Federal Canadian Officers are appointed by the Governor in Council, following parliamentary resolutions approving government nominations and have the right to report directly to Parliament. But most do not have the type of budgetary independence from the executive possessed by the UK's C and AG and Electoral Commission. The resignation of the Privacy Commissioner in June 2003 following criticism from a parliamentary committee led to debate about mechanisms of accountability of Officers to Parliament. A number of Canadian provincial assemblies appoint their Officers using a selection committee of Members and have full control over their budgets. This can lead to strain when the prevailing administration does not feel attuned to the policies of each Officers – in British Columbia for example an incoming administration cut budgets by 20-30% in one year, demanding back – office savings.

The New Zealand Parliament's Officers of Parliament Committee[4] is chaired by the Speaker and has other senior members, including whips from major parties. Its functions are to recommend a budget, to make audit arrangements, to consider the creation of new Offices and to develop codes of practice applicable to Officers. The Finance and Expenditure Committee developed guiding principles for the creation of new Officers which noted that:

2. An Officer of Parliament must only be discharging functions which the House of Representatives itself, if it so wished, might carry out

The justification was that watchdogs with judicial powers would not be appropriate, since the House did not have judicial powers itself. There are difficulties with including non-constitutional subjects – Children and Young Person's Commissioner in Scotland – Police Complaints Commissioner in British Columbia – within the subset of Officers of Parliament, because there needs to be an underlying rationale to prevent proliferation which would devalue the concept.

Core characteristics of the Officer of Parliament model – the C and AG

Drawing mainly on the institutional design of the C and AG, which sets the standard in terms of accountability and independence, the essential characteristics can be seen as:

* parliamentary involvement in appointment and dismissal
* a statutory committee which is responsible for budget approval and oversight, and
* a separate select committee to which the Officer is bound to report
* staff independent of the civil service.

How were these characteristics developed? In the 1970s the constitutional position of the C and AG came under scrutiny, resulting in the *National Audit Act* 1983, a product of backbench initiative. Section 1 gives the C and AG operational independence. His salary is met directly from the Consolidated Fund standing services, thus bypassing the annual supply procedure whereby Parliament approves government estimates. This mirrors arrangements for the Speaker's salary. The costs of the National Audit Office (NAO) are met by funds voted by Parliament and the estimates are laid by the Public Accounts Commission, a statutory parliamentary committee established by the 1983 Act. The Commission examines the budget and expenditure of the NAO and appoints its auditor. Its membership is the Chairman of the Public Accounts Committee (PAC), the Leader of the House of Commons and seven other backbenchers.

There is considerable overlap in personnel between members of the Commission and the PAC, but the value of a separate Commission is seen as offering a buffer between Officer and select committee, so that personal antagonisms do not influence the budgetary process. The PAC chair is, by convention, an Opposition backbencher, indicating a bipartisan nature to the process and an important backbench role in the actual appointment, if not the recruitment process.

The 1983 Act requires the Prime Minister to propose a name, having consulted the Chair of the PAC. So far, candidates have been suggested by the civil service, whose interest lies in an office-holder sufficiently trust-worthy to be allowed access to all types of documents and accounts. The C and AG holds office during good behaviour and can only be dismissed following resolutions of both Houses. There is no set retirement age. This is clearly based on similar procedures for the pro-tection of judges. Since 1983 NAO staff are no longer civil servants, but employed directly by the C and AG.

The Parliamentary Ombudsman

An explicit analogy was made in the debates creating the office of Parliamentary Commissioner for Administration (PCA).[4] But because the institutional design of the Ombudsman has not changed since its foundation in 1967, the office lacks an equivalent to the Public Accounts Commission, and is funded *via* a depart-mental vote from the Cabinet Office. So it does not meet all four of the characteristics outlined above. The Ombudsman is appointed by the Crown on letters patent and can only be dismissed by an address of both Houses. But there have been developments in secur-ing more parliamentary involvement in the appointment process. The selection of Sir Michael Buckley in 1997 was the first time the PCA had been appointed following open advertisement and discus-sions with the Leader of the Opposition and the Chairman of the Select Committee. The recruitment process was handled by the Cabinet Office.

A permanent select committee for the PCA was established soon after the Office was set up, but the Ombudsman was not required to submit his reports to them and the resulting relationship had no statutory basis. There was no consultation with the Ombudsman's office when the PCA select committee was merged with the Public Service Select Committee after the 1997 general election. The select committee was modelled on the PAC, but the debates in 1967 did not fully appreciate the differences as the PAC produces several reports annually and has a very close relationship with the C and AG. The Ombudsman's staff remain civil servants, although there is a separate career structure. This makes it feasible to consider granting them equivalent status to NAO staff.

The Parliamentary Commissioner for Standards (PCS)

The status of this post has been unclear since its inception in 1995 following recommendations by the Committee on Standards in Public Life (CSPL). Selection is by the House of Commons Commission. Its characteristics are closer to a senior staff member than an independent watchdog. The first PCS, Sir Gordon Downey, was chosen partly because, like the first Ombudsman, he was a former C and AG and therefore familiar with the House and personally prestigious enough to establish the importance of the post. The PCS reports to the Standards and Privileges Select Committee. Due to public concerns about sleaze, Sir Gordon's conclusions were almost all accepted by the Committee, but it began to reject some conclusions of his successor, Elizabeth Filkin, and the Commission failed to re-appoint her. This was the trigger for another enquiry into parliamentary standards of conduct by the CSPL, chaired by Sir Nigel Wicks.[5]

Wicks concluded that there was insufficient operational independence: there were no powers to call for witnesses and papers separate from those of the Standards and Privileges Committee, there was a short three year term, and ambiguity about the possibility of renewal, Mrs Filkin had had difficulties over obtaining further resources following staff inspections and her statements to the press had resulted in concern expressed by the Speaker. Finally, the salary of the PCS came from the House of Commons' Vote rather than the Consolidated Fund.

The CSPL's main recommendations were rejected, with the Parliamentary authorities arguing that statute was necessary to create such an independent post.[6] Given the slim prospects of legislation, changes were made in July 2003 to standing orders, giving the Commissioner a five-year term and preventing dismissal unless the Standards and Privileges Committee reported (with reasons) unfitness for office or a failure to carry out functions. This Committee no longer has a government majority, and is now chaired by an Opposition speaker (selection remains with the whips). The Commissioner still lacks powers to make his own appointments and does not meet the criteria outlined above for independence.

The Electoral Commission – officers in waiting

The Electoral Commission's design displays the four characteristics although its members lack the title of Officer, either in statute or by convention. The Commission has important regulatory roles in checking expenditure returns from political parties. Since politicians exercise a supervisory role, there are particular sensitivities for the Commission. Its genesis was the CSPL's fifth report on reform of party funding, which contained detailed proposals for an independent commission, translated into the *Political Parties, Elections and Referendums Act 2000 (PPERA)*.

The Speaker's Committee – explicitly modelled on the Public Accounts Commission – provides oversight of the Commission's budget and strategic plans. It contains two ministers, for elections and local government. The rest are backbenchers, including the chairman of the Department for Constitutional Affairs select committee. The Commission employs its own staff. The Electoral Commission lacks a dedicated select committee due to split responsibility for electoral matters between the ODPM and the Department for Constitutional Affairs. Although independent, its advice is not always accepted by Government which insisted on using two additional regions for postal voting in the European elections of June 2004.[7] This raises profound questions about the value of independent agencies with an advisory role.

Other constitutional watchdogs – a patchwork of design features

Some, but not all, of these four characteristics are found in the structure of other constitutional watchdogs established in the last thirty years. A rough division can be made between those established by statute and those under the prerogative. The former betray more evidence of deliberate constitutional design than the latter, where the use of an 'off the peg' Non Departmental Public Body structure is widespread. Practice appears to depend on the most appropriate precedent discovered by the sponsoring department. It is a quintessentially British approach, which refuses to categorise by function or purpose. Statutory watchdogs include the Information Commissioner, the Audit Commission, the Health Service Ombudsman, the Local Government Ombudsman, the Standards Board for England, the Equal Opportunities Commission, the Commission for Racial Equality, and the Disability Rights Commission.

Key non-statutory bodies are: the CSPL, the Commissioner for Public Appointments, the NHS Appointments Commission, the Civil Service Commissioners, the National Statistics Commission, the Commission for Judicial Appointments and the House of Lords Appointments

Commission. These models exhibit bewildering variations in appointment and dismissal procedures, in budgetary freedom, and arrangements for reporting to parliament. Some Commissioners are paid even where the work is part-time only, but others receive expenses only. Smaller non-statutory bodies are staffed by civil servants, often on secondment, which gives some measure of operating independence.

Only a minority of constitutional watchdogs have formal reporting responsibilities, on a spectrum ranging from presentation of annual reports to Parliament to a structural (not necessarily statutory) relationship with a parliamentary committee. Non-statutory bodies issue annual reports to their sponsoring departments and the wider public, but extra-parliamentary accountability tends to be underdeveloped. Some smaller bodies have developed working relationships with a particular select committee, which may or may not involve regular appearances. The quality of the relationship varies and can be overly dependent on personal relations between chairman and head of the body.

New watchdogs – current proposals for reform

Parliament has begun to take an interest in the institutional design of both existing and new constitutional watchdogs. The Select Committee on Public Administration recommended in its report on Patronage that the Office of the Public Appointments Commissioner (OCPA) become an Officer of Parliament. Its comments are worth reproducing in full:

> 98.... The simple fact that the Commissioner and her Office are funded and serviced from Whitehall creates the impression that she works for and reports to ministers.
> 99. Just as independent assessors working in different departments should be truly independent of those departments, so too should the Office that assumes overall responsibility for the independence of the process in central government be independent of the executive. The Commissioner recognises that there are advantages in employing officials who are well versed in the ways of government departments, but she has long argued that OCPA should be funded and housed independently of the executive; and that she should have the power to appoint staff permanently. If the Commissioner's office is to be independent of the executive, it should be rooted in Parliament. The Commission should therefore be an officer of

Parliament, as one of the key constitutional watchdogs. The appointment should be approved by Parliament and it is to Parliament that the Commissioner should report.[8]

The Joint Committee on Human Rights also drew attention to the inadequacies of the NDPB model for constitutional watchdogs in successive reports on the case for a Human Rights Commission.[9] It concluded that the appropriate model of accountability was that based on the concept of an Officer of Parliament:

> 45. The new Commission will not be like the existing equality commissions. This proposal is not acceptable. The EOC told us that the proposals in the White Paper are 'not enough in themselves to ensure the necessary independence from government'. [55] The far more radical proposals we made in our report were broadly endorsed by the DRC. [56] The time has come for the Government to recognise that there is a class of public bodies which have a distinctive constitutional role, and that these need to be designed with this special status in mind. It is not sufficient to pick the NDPB model off the shelf and apply it to every new public institution.[10]

The proposed abolition of the office of Lord Chancellor and the creation of a Supreme Court has prompted a new interest within Government about constitutional design, but a lack of coherence over the solution. Proposals for a statutory Lords Appointments Commission followed those recommended by Lord Wakeham – based on the Electoral Commission precedent. But proposals for a new Judicial Appointments Commission in the *Constitutional Reform Bill* did not offer the same institutional independence.[11] Although there is a separate recommending body for appointments, the Commission is a NDPB with no independent budget or regular scrutiny by parliamentary committee.

Institutional independence is only part of the issue. The South African constitutional watchdogs have their independence guaranteed by the founding constitution. But their relationship with parliament has been slow to develop effectively. There are equivalent concerns at Westminster. Officers are meant to improve Parliament's surveillance capabilities. But Parliament does not necessarily use these sources of information effectively. The PCA has not undergone regular scrutiny since the merger of 'his' committee with the Public Service Committee in 1997. The former Information Commissioner complained that her

annual reports did not prompt a hearing by a parliamentary committee. This is the most difficult aspect of the Officer package to tackle, but
where it works, the most rewarding.

Scotland as comparator[12]

The Scottish Parliament offers an opportunity to observe how a more
coherent approach to watchdogs might operate in practice. Establishment by legislation has meant that more serious attention has been
given to issues of accountability and independence. Once again, the
Auditor General (AGS) has set the 'gold standard', both in the method
adopted to make appointments, which has much more serious parliamentary involvement, and in the creation of an equivalent to the
Public Accounts Commission, the Scottish Commission for Public
Audit.[13]

The Financial Issues Advisory Group (FIAG) – part of the preparation for devolution – proposed a selection procedure for the AG
involving an open recruitment exercise and a selection panel making
a recommendation to the full Parliament. The relevant procedural
requirements were included in the Parliament's initial SOs. These
provisions provided the template for later 'officers' – in 2001 the
SOs were extended to apply to all such appointments. These include
Scottish Public Services Ombudsman (and deputy Ombudsmen),
Scottish Information Commissioner, the Commissioner for Public
Appointments in Scotland, the Commissioner for Children and
Young People.

Following devolution, the Parliament began to take a more proactive and distinctive approach, even though the new posts have
been created both under Executive and Parliament initiative (including in the form of committee Bills). This reached the stage of being
described as 'an acceptable and workable model' in the Executive's
consultation on its proposed Scottish Human Rights Committee. The
main exception has been the Parliamentary Standards Commissioner.
As the Commons illustrates, this is an office difficult to define as a
constitutional watchdog rather than senior member of staff.

The template includes the use of an in-house selection panel,
chaired by the Presiding Officer, followed by a motion put to the
Parliament. Until the nomination of the Information Commissioner
on 12 December 2002, this process had proceeded smoothly. The
plenary debate revealed that that selection process had been riven by
party political considerations. The developing norm for dismissal pro-

cedures is for removal by the Crown, following a recommendation of the Parliament, supported by a specified majority. Once again, the initial requirement came from legislation at Westminster to protect the AGS – perhaps exhibiting that special British talent for perfecting everyone else's constitutional arrangements but their own.[14]

The workload is potentially considerable for the Parliament, both in terms of committee and SPCB time, and for administrative services such as legal, information, procurement and personnel, which individual Officers may not have sufficient staff or resources to provide 'in-house', though some may pool resources. The burden raises the questions about the extent to which it is practicable for the Parliament to be a substantial 'sponsoring body' for this growing cadre of public officers. This is being increasingly discussed within the Parliament and has wider relevance for Westminster.[15] The answer may lie in stricter limitation of the full Officer model to constitutional areas.

A design checklist

Given current interest in institutional design, how should the structure of constitutional watchdogs be overhauled? Officers need independence from the executive, involvement from Parliament and accountability to Parliament and the public for their effective operation. The following key principles should apply.

1. The constitutional design of the watchdog should reflect its independent nature

This requires formal parliamentary involvement in the institutional design, including a committee for oversight of the budget, expenditure and strategic plan. Appropriate models for major watchdogs with executive responsibilities are the Public Accounts Commission, the Speaker's Committee or the New Zealand Officers of Parliament Committee. A select committees or joint committees of both Houses may be more appropriate where the watchdog is small and has advisory responsibilities only. Strong backbench involvement in these committees is essential. There should be statutory guarantees of independence from parliament and the executive, such as contained in the *National Audit Act 1983*.

2. A watchdog should have independent funding arrangements

There are two mechanisms: the Consolidated Fund – to which are charged the budgets of the C and AG and the Electoral Commission rather then a departmental vote. This arrangement protects Commissioner(s) from cuts in the budgets of sponsoring departments. It is not sufficient for the watchdog salaries alone to be paid from the consolidated fund – this offers just symbolic, rather than real, financial independence. The alternative developed in Scotland and a number of Canadian provinces is funding from the Parliamentary budget requiring negotiation with the Executive.

The use of grant in aid or annual grant is preferable to budgets drawn from the departmental vote – appropriate only for very small advisory bodies relying on common departmental services. Where these models are used, there should be a statutory duty for a watchdog to publish its own assessment of its funding requirements. This transparency is likely to inhibit routine requests for budget cuts.

3. A watchdog should have independent staffing arrangements

Staff should be public, rather than civil, servants where the body in question is large enough to offer an appropriate career structure. Use of secondments from the civil service or other parts of the public sector may be unavoidable for small watchdogs, and offer important networks, but care should be taken over how the watchdog is perceived. The possibility of using parliamentary staff should be explored for smaller watchdogs, rather than relying solely on civil servants. Training staff in the 'culture' of the watchdog is important.

4. Parliamentary involvement in appointment should be essential, with the minimum a formal address or resolution by one or both Houses

Present options are:

- C and AG model. Name jointly proposed to Commons by (Opposition) Chairman of the relevant parliamentary committee and Prime Minister. Following address by Commons, appointed by Crown. Unanimous agreement is expected, but not required
- Electoral Commission model. Commissioners proposed to Commons after consultation with Speaker and registered political parties. Following address by Commons appointed by Crown. Unanimous agreement is expected, but not required
- Scottish Parliament model. Selection panel established Motion put to Parliament by Selection Panel, following agreement, a recommendation is made to the Queen to appoint. If there is a division on the

motion, more than 25 per cent of all Members must have consented for it to have validity.

Personal ministerial involvement should be reduced to the minimum, and for this reason the guidance used by the Civil Service Commissioners may be preferred – one name, to be accepted, or the competition re-run – rather than the OPCA Code offering the minister a shortlist. Commissions to appoint Commissions tend to be unwieldy and of course do not resolve the problem but simply transfer the process one step back. The model of appointment should include formal consultation with other parties to ensure maximum cross party agreement. Appointment following recommendation by a minister, as in the NDPB model does not signify sufficient constitutional independence from the executive. The application process can be out-sourced or conducted by civil servants or parliamentary staff, as long as it conforms to the OPCA and includes outside assessors.

Length of term

There are various models, ranging from for life until retirement, (C and AG) maximum ten years (Electoral Commission) five years (Information Commissioner) three years (CSPL). Five years should be a minimum to establish independence. Many constitutional watchdogs are uneasy about re-appointments, given that the responsibility for evaluation is in the hands of the executive. If possible re-appointments should be avoided for this reason, implying instead a longer term. It is unacceptable constitutionally for the performance of Commissioners to be assessed by civil servants on behalf of ministers. The Chair would expect to report on the performance of his individual members, but who will report on the Chair? A single long term of office provides the most suitable option for avoiding these concerns. Where a Commission rather than a single Commissioner is appointed, it is preferable not to appoint members with the same fixed term for all Commissioners, as renewal becomes difficult.

Payment

Full time Commissioners should be paid, and part-time appointees should receive expenses, unless responsible for major projects. Salary costs should be charged to the standing services element of the consolidated fund, to denote independence from the executive. Should the salary increase in line with a comparator, such as a High Court judge? This is common practice.

5. Watchdogs should be removable by the Crown only on an address from one or both Houses of Parliament

This provides protection from executive interference. The statute should specify reasons for dismissal, such as illness or bankruptcy. In practice, Parliament offers an early warning process if there are issues about individual performance, as the new arrangements for the dismissal process of the Standards Commissioner demonstrate. The Scottish Parliament requirement for a two third majority of all MSPs to vote in favour of a dismissal motion is a sensible precaution and ensures cross-party agreement.[16]

6. Reporting responsibilities to Parliament should be effective in nature

There are three main forms of accountability:

- Reporting to Parliament as a whole through an annual report, or a special report. For this responsibility to be effective, it is essential either to refer the report to a relevant committee or to schedule a debate, for example in Westminster Hall
- Reporting to a relevant select committee, on a regular basis
- Providing information in relation to a parliamentary question. A backbench member of the Public Accounts Commission and the Speaker's Committee answer questions in a regular slot. This avoids ministerial involvement and is the model also used for questions to the Church Commissioners. The NDPB model requires ministers to answer questions in Parliament and is therefore an insufficiently visible guarantee of independence.

The potential involvement of the House of Lords needs to be addressed, given the expertise of many of its members. In its current form, as a non-elected body with very limited powers to consider government expenditure it is neglected as part of the formal institutional design for constitutional watchdogs. In principle, however, its permanent committees, such as the Constitution Committee or the Joint Committee on Human Rights should have a formal role. Involvement may not be appropriate for established Officers where there are well-known formal relationships with the Commons, but newer bodies would benefit from expert scrutiny in the Lords, as a less partisan House. Canadian experience is particularly relevant, as their Officers generally have a formal relationship with both Houses.

7. Extra-parliamentary accountability mechanisms should apply

At the minimum, a watchdog, however small, should have an independent web presence not formally connected to a department. It should promote mechanisms to encourage dialogue with the public as citizens. Where a small watchdog is established as a NDPB, the sponsoring department will want some kind of accountability relationship, if only to ensure that public money is properly spent. But departments can be subject to machinery of government changes without notice, so inhibiting a long-term relationship.

From institutional design to effective relationship with Parliament

A consistent template is not enough. Watchdogs can offer MPs valuable information about the operation of government policies on the ground, and this resource needs more systematic attention. If Westminster is to be serious about its scrutiny role, it needs to reorganise its committee structure to facilitate the task. Its Officers could provide the resources to enhance the scrutiny work, but full parliamentary engagement is required to ensure that resources are directed where needed.

Officers need to develop effective dialogue with Parliament *via* select committees. Canadian examples demonstrate the importance of the auditor post in establishing a 'gold standard' for other Officers. The New Zealand Committee's responsibility for developing Codes of Practice on access to the Parliament's Officers should be emulated at Westminster, so that select committees can understand the potential and the limitations. Officers could be used far more effectively to enrich scrutiny work, which retains its haphazard nature, despite the use of NAO staff in the Scrutiny Unit within the Commons Committee Office and the establishment of core tasks for select committees. More involvement by permanent, impartial parliamentary staff appears inevitable to ensure that these core tasks are tackled at the appropriate depth.

The Liaison Committee should become the main driver of scrutiny in the Commons, ensuring that reports from major watchdogs receive immediate acknowledgement and appropriate attention. Information provided by watchdogs could then be systematically used by select committees. The role of both committee and watchdog staff in formulating the terms of relationship should be made more explicit. It is unlikely that other select committees would welcome the same amount of involvement in drafting their reports as the PAC receives from NAO staff, as there is danger of institutional 'capture'. However, there is considerable scope for closer working arrangements, so that committee and watchdog are more familiar with each other's role and functions. This would be a real 'result' from attention to the constitutional architecture advocated here.

Notes

1 *Parliament at the Apex: Parliamentary Scrutiny and Regulatory Bodies*, Hansard Society, 2003.
2 Sixth Report of the Constitution Committee, *The Regulatory State: Ensuring its Accountability* HL 68, 2003–4, May 2004.
3 The five Officers are: Auditor General, Chief Electoral Officer, Privacy Commissioner, Information Commissioner and Official Language Commissioner. See O. Gay and B. K. Winetrobe *Officers of Parliament: Developing the Role* (London: Constitution Unit, 2003).
4 New Zealand Parliament Finance and Expenditure Committee, *Officers of Parliament*, Wellington, New Zealand, 1989.
5 See Roy Gregory and Philip Giddings *The Ombudsman, the Citizen and Parliament*, Politico's, 2002.
6 Committee on Standards in Public Life, *Standards of Conduct in the House of Commons*, Eighth Report, Cm 5663, November 2002.
7 House of Commons Commission Report, HC 422, 2002–3. See Chapter 3 in O. Gay and P. Leopold *Conduct Unbecoming: The Regulation of Parliamentary Behaviour* (London: Politico's, 2004) for a full discussion.
8 See House of Commons Library Research Paper 04/57 *Referendums on Regional Assemblies* from the Commons website.
9 Public Administration Select Committee, Fourth Report, *Government by Appointment: Opening Up the Patronage State* HC 165, 2002–3, para. 99, July 2003.
10 Joint Committee on Human Rights, Sixth Report, *The Case for a Human Rights Commission* HL Paper 67/HC 489, 2002–3, March 2003; Eleventh Report, *Commission for Equality and Human Rights: Structure, Functions and Powers* HL 78/HC 536, 2003–04, May 2004.
11 Joint Committee on Human Rights, Sixteenth Report *Commission for Equality and Human Rights: The Government's White Paper* HL 156/HC 998, 2003–4, August 2004.
12 Department for Constitutional Affairs, *Constitutional Reform: a new way of appointing judges,* CP 10/03 (2003).
13 Part II of O. Gay and B. K. Winetrobe *Officers of Parliament: Developing the Role*, London: Constitution Unit, 2003.
14 *Public Finance & Accountability (Scotland) Act 2000.*
15 HL Deb Vol 592 c1718.
16 See, for example, the discussion at the Finance Committee's meeting of 8 October 2002 at cols 2211–2, on the SPCB's budget submission for 2003–04.
17 For some officials, dismissal is possible with a two-thirds vote of those MSPs present.

16
Judges, Lawyers and Parliament

Dawn Oliver and Paul Evans

Parliamentary sovereignty: A judicial invention

In his classic definition of Parliament's legislative sovereignty, Thomas Erskine May expressed the High Victorian view of the matter –

> The legislative authority of Parliament extends over the United Kingdom ... there are no other limits to its power of making laws ... than those which are incident to all sovereign authority – the willingness of the people to obey, or their power to resist ... it is bound by no fundamental charter or constitution; but has itself the sole constitutional right of establishing and altering the laws ...[1]

Even in the mid-nineteenth century this was a contestable if majestic definition of the role of Parliament (including the Queen in Parliament), but it is one which forty years ago still dominated in the minds of the legislators and, for the most part, the judges. But the doctrine of the sovereignty or legislative supremacy of the UK Parliament cannot be derived from *a priori* principles. It is the creation of the courts developing the common law.

This constitutional debate has tended to work through territorial metaphors, in which the arguments are about the precise boundaries of the dominions of the legislature and the courts. While in the past it was mostly the courts which theorised about and settled these determinations, in recent years Parliament has appeared to collaborate more actively in delineating the landscape of the supposed constitutional settlement, though its participation seems frequently to be either accidental or opportunistic, and is often apparent only in retrospect. On the courts' side of the border, in a period which has seen an exponential growth in judicial review and a significant reduction in what has been called the 'zone of immunity' around executive action,[2] these developments would often appear to be driven, at least in part, by what Lord Irvine, Lord Chancellor in waiting, characterised in 1996 as a recognition of a 'democratic deficit', or want of parliamentary control over the Executive.[3] To paraphrase another famous judge,[4] it seems that judicial assertiveness flows into the estuaries and runs up the rivers left empty by the ebbing tide of confidence in the democratic process as the prime means to seek redress of grievances or protection of the individual from the overbearing state. A number of factors combine to contribute to the sound of this melancholy, long withdrawing roar.[5]

But just as the sovereignty doctrine is for the most part a judicial invention, so its development is largely in the hands of the judiciary. The ways in which the courts explain their doctrine of parliamentary sovereignty is that it is their constitutional function to give effect to the will of Parliament, mainly on democratic grounds, since the House of Commons is elected and the courts are not. Other rationales for the courts' acceptance of Parliament's legislative supremacy include that, in a customary and unentrenched constitution such as that of the UK, it is essential that good relations and comity be maintained between the institutions of government. It would not be regarded as legitimate by Parliament or the Executive, or by sections of the population, if the courts were to refuse to give effect to Acts of Parliament. Conflict over such matters could lead to confrontations between Parliament and the courts, which the courts would not have the capacity to win and which would be contrary to the culture of mutual self-restraint which pervades our constitutional arrangements, whether expressed in laws (including the law and practice of Parliament) or conventions, codes, concordats or the many other 'soft law' documents which seek to regulate relations between Parliament, the executive and the courts. But, as in any argument, each side will appear selectively to invoke at different times axioms derived from irreconcilable premises depending on whether they are promoting deference or assertiveness on the part of one or other branch of the constitution.[6]

The orthodox expression of the doctrine is that the courts will give effect to a provision in an Act of the UK Parliament in preference to any other source of law (for instance the common law).[7] Where two Acts conflict, the courts will give effect to the more recent one, which is taken to repeal impliedly the inconsistent provision of an earlier Act in the same field or area to the extent of the inconsistency between the two.[8] In contrast to some other jurisdictions, international treaties cannot give rise to rights that are directly enforceable in the UK courts, unless they are incorporated into domestic law by Act of Parliament.[9]

However, the doctrine of parliamentary sovereignty has always been more complex and less pure than was often claimed as it was developed and articulated by the courts from the seventeenth to the nineteenth century. A number of relatively recent developments have brought out starkly some of the paradoxes and problems that are inherent in the doctrine. These are considered in the following sections of the chapter. They include developments in the principles of statutory interpretation, British membership of the European Union, the Human Rights Act 1998, parliamentary privilege, and a growing consciousness on the part of the courts of the existence of inconsistent democratic theories that run through our constitutional arrangements.

Statutory interpretation: Divining the intentions of Parliament?

It has been held to be an underlying principle of the common law doctrine of parliamentary sovereignty that the courts are to give effect to the intention of *Parliament* when applying its legislation. Whether in practice the courts give effect to the intention of Parliament or of the executive is far from clear. The case of *Pepper v. Hart*[10] involved a dispute between the Inland Revenue and a taxpayer in which the court was considering referring to parliamentary debates to assist in the interpretation of a statutory provision in order to discover Parliament's intention. The Clerk of the House of Commons raised with the Attorney General the question whether it would be a breach of parliamentary privilege for the courts to look at Hansard without the House having first granted leave for reference to be made on a petition. Why Parliament should oppose resort to Hansard, from which one might have expected Parliament's intention to be revealed, is not immediately obvious, though the underlying anxiety seems to have been about maintaining the boundary between the two branches of the constitution. The Attorney General (who was instructed for the Inland Revenue in the case) adopted and argued the point: it was in the interests of Government in that case that the courts should not look at Hansard, since a minister had expressly indicated that a person in the taxpayer's position would not be liable to be taxed. The Attorney-General's point was rejected by the House of Lords by a majority.[11] The majority in the Appellate Committee held that reference to Hansard would not amount to a 'questioning' of proceedings in Parliament contrary to Article IX of the Bill of Rights of 1689 or parliamentary privilege; however, it was legitimate for the courts to refer to Hansard only in very limited circumstances, namely where legislation was ambiguous or obscure or a literal interpretation led to absurdity, where the material relied upon consisted of statements made by a *minister* or other promoter of the Bill together with any other parliamentary material that it was necessary to refer to in order to understand such statements and their effect, and the statements relied upon were clear. Although on the face of it the decision may assist the courts in determining Parliament's intention, in practice the rules seem to give far more weight to the Executive's views of what its intentions were in proposing legislation than to the (admittedly unfathomable) question of what the intentions of Parliament were in assenting to the proposal.

This raises the question whether the courts should be trying to give effect to the *actual* intentions of Parliament, or to the words Parliament used, or to what Parliament's intention *ought* to have been (for instance in relation to compatibility with European law or human rights provisions or what the courts consider to be fairness). The curiosity is that in assigning intentionality to Parliament the courts appear to be exercising deference to the Executive.[12] And in the act of interpretation the courts appear to many parliamentarians to be asserting a degree of omniscience which is unwarranted – hence the dismay in some quarters at the decision in *Pepper v. Hart*. What Parliament means by its legislation, say these conservatives, is what Parliament says in its legislation, not what was said in the arguments and speculation which led up to it. *Pepper v. Hart* suggests the alarming idea that Parliament and the courts should talk to, and listen to, each other.

Membership of the European Union

Since the UK joined what were then known as the European Communities the courts have come to accept the primacy of European law over an incompatible provision of an Act of Parliament.[13] They have argued that they do this on the basis that the European Communities Act 1972, section 2, enables, indeed commands, them to disapply a provision of an Act that is incompatible with European law, even if the UK Act is more recent. In practice this has happened only in a limited number of cases, but these represent a radical change from the previous legal doctrine and, on the court's interpretation, a self-imposed (though theoretically rescindable) derogation by Parliament from its full exercise of sovereignty.

The courts have been subtle in the way in which they have sought to justify their acceptance of the primacy of European law. To the extent that such acceptance involves recognition of a limitation on the doctrine of implied repeal which has been regarded as a cornerstone of the doctrine of sovereignty, this has been explained, at least by one judge, as a development of *English* common law: Lord Justice Laws in the case of *Thoburn v. Sunderland City Council*[14] held that the common law had come to recognise that there are two classes of statutes, 'constitutional' and others. Constitutional statutes include Magna Carta, the Bill of Rights of 1689, the Act of Settlement, the Human Rights Act, the devolution legislation and so on – and most importantly in the *Thoburn* case, the European Communities Act 1972. While most statutes remain subject to the doctrine of implied repeal, 'constitutional statutes' could, according to Laws LJ, only be repealed by express provision in a later Act of Parliament. On this argument, when the courts give priority to European law, they are doing so because they are required to do so by English law, whether the common law or statute.

There remain unresolved issues as to other justifications for, and the democratic and other implications of, the willingness of the UK courts to accept the primacy and direct effect of European law. There is a functional justification for the position taken by the courts, in that the European Union cannot be effective unless all member states accept the doctrines of the primacy and direct effect of European law. The UK cannot logically complain when other member states breach European law if it does not itself conform to that law.

There is also a contractarian justification, which was articulated by Lord Bridge in the *Factortame (no. 2)*[15] case: the courts' recognition of the primacy of European law was justified on the basis that it was well known by the time that the UK joined the European Communities that all member states are required to give direct effect and primacy to European law. This was part of the deal that the country was doing in order to join the community, and section 2 of the European Communities Act 1972 made it plain that the UK courts should accept this position. This version of what happened in Parliament in 1972 is, of course, much contested in Parliament itself, not without some justification when Hansard is looked at.

The European Communities Act has also been interpreted as inviting the courts to look to European institutions directly and independently as a source of law, and as the permanence and authority of the EU has become apparent the courts have increasingly done so, in ways which might be seen to go beyond the sanction of section 2.

The legislative supremacy of Parliament may be considered to survive in relation to Europe notwithstanding the acceptance of the primacy of EU law, in two possible ways, neither of which has yet been tested in the courts. On one theory, if the UK Parliament were to pass legislation which was expressed to be contrary to EU law and in which it was made clear that it was Parliament's intention that the Act should prevail over the European rule, then our courts would give effect to the UK statute. Lord Justice Laws' comments in *Thoburn* seem to leave this possibility open. On another approach Parliamentary sovereignty survives in relation to Europe only in the sense that it is legally possible for the UK to end its membership of the EU, and for Parliament to repeal the European Communities Act 1972, in which case the supposed prelapsarian state of full scale legislative supremacy would be reinstated as a matter of common law. Neither of these scenarios carries much conviction as a real political possibility.

The Human Rights Act 1998

The risks to the constitutional settlement between the courts on the one hand and the (sovereign) legislature and executive on the other were often cited as the ground for resisting attempts to incorporate the rights guaranteed by the European Convention on Human Rights into domestic law. The new Labour government arrived in office in 1997, however, with an explicit manifesto commitment to do so.

The Human Rights Act 1998 represents an elegant attempt to balance the notion of entrenched rights with the doctrine of Parliament's legislative supremacy. By section 2 of that Act the courts are required to take into account the jurisprudence of the European Court of Human Rights when interpreting statutes. By section 3 they are required to interpret statutes 'so far as possible' compatibly with the Convention rights. This means that the process of interpreting statutes will involve an extra step. In any particular case, after interpreting the law according to the current principles of interpretation, the court will then have to ask whether the result produced is compatible with the Convention rights. If it is not, the court will have to try to re-interpret it in a compatible manner. In doing so, the desirability of achieving compatibility (section 3) will outweigh all the other principles of interpretation, in particular the traditional view of the courts, expressed for instance in *Pepper v. Hart*, discussed above, that their function is to give effect to the intentions of Parliament when passing the provision in question.

There are a range of interpretive techniques which the courts can avail themselves of in this process. In some cases provisions can be 'read down' where necessary to narrow the scope of apparently broadly-expressed powers so as to make them compatible with Convention rights, as in USA and Canadian constitutional jurisprudence. In other cases, courts are able to read words into or out of the legislation in order to make it comply, as they are already accustomed to doing in relation to subordinate legislation which would otherwise be incompatible with EU law.

In relation to post-Human Rights Act Acts of Parliament in respect of which the responsible Minister made a statement of compatibility on introducing the Bill, courts are likely to start from an assumption that the legislation must be interpreted compatibly with all Convention rights, in order to give effect to the executive's intentions to comply with Convention rights, evidenced by the ministerial statement of compatibility.[16] For this purpose, courts could regard themselves as having a wide scope for creative interpretation.

Where it proves impossible to achieve an interpretation which is compatible with Convention rights, most subordinate legislation becomes invalid and ineffective, but primary legislation remains valid and effective notwithstanding the incompatibility.

The court may then make a 'declaration of incompatibility' and section 10 then provides for a minister to remedy the incompatibility by means of a 'remedial order'. For the change to have effect Parliament must then approve the change in the law, after receiving the advice of its Joint Committee on Human Rights.

Although the Human Rights Act provides mechanisms allowing for both prospective and retrospective consideration by Parliament of the human rights implications of the legislation it is required to pass, it is not our purpose here to explore the operation of the Human Rights Act within Parliament, but to consider how the relationship between Parliament and the courts is affected by the Act. One effect has, most certainly, been to make Parliament more conscious of the judge looking over its shoulder as it goes through the legislative process, and to bring the language of rights more to the forefront of debate. It also has potentially radical implications for the way judges think about their relationship to the intentions of Parliament. The duty of the courts to give, so far as possible, a Convention compatible meaning to statutes could result in extremely strained interpretation which might well be directly in conflict with Parliament's intention, or the sponsoring minister's intention, when the Act was passed. That, the parliamentary sovereigntists feared, would open the way to judge-made legislation.

For instance, in the case of *R. v. A (no. 2)*[17] the courts were dealing with a provision which sought to prevent a defendant in a rape case from cross examining the victim about her past sexual conduct in various respects. The House of Lords were concerned that this would prevent the defendant from putting his defence effectively, and strained the meaning of the statutory provision by reading into it words that would permit cross examination if this were necessary for a fair trial, which is guaranteed by Article 6 of the European Convention on Human Rights. The court did not therefore have to make a declaration of incompatibility in relation to the statutory provision. Lord Steyn expressed the function of the court in such cases as follows:

> In accordance with the will of Parliament as reflected in section 3 it will sometimes be necessary to adopt an interpretation which linguistically may appear strained. The techniques to be used will not only involve the reading down of express language in a statute but also the implication of provisions. A declaration of incompatibility is a measure of last resort. It must be avoided unless it is plainly impossible to do so. If a *clear* limitation on Convention rights is stated *in terms*, such an impossibility will arise ...[18]

This approach was subsequently modified in later House of Lords decisions. For instance, in *Re S (Care order: Implementation of Care Plan)*[19] and *R (Anderson) v. Secretary of State for the Home Department*[20] the House of Lords held that the courts should not interpret a statute in such a way as to give it a meaning which departs from a fundamental feature of the Act: that would be legislation, not interpretation. In those two cases the court could not find a compatible interpretation without running counter to the fundamental features of the Acts in question and so made declarations of incompatibility. Thus the courts are now choosing not to put very strained interpretations on statutes for the sake of finding Convention compatible interpretations but instead are batting the ball back to the politicians – Parliament and the Executive – to deal with what the courts consider to be incompatibilities. They are maintaining a kind of separation of powers between themselves and politicians in this area, but it is a separation which must now involve conversation as well.

The most dramatic example of the role of the courts in returning human rights issues to be resolved by Parliament and the government and opening up a conversation is the Belmarsh prison case, *A (FC) v. Secretary of State for the Home Department.*[21] The Appellate Committee of the House of Lords decided, by a majority of eight to one, that the provisions of part 4 of the Anti-Terrorism, Crime and Security Act 2001, which permit the detention without charge or trial of foreign suspected terrorists who cannot be deported, were incompatible with Convention rights (rights under the relevant articles of the ECHR). The majority made declarations of incompatibility and quashed the Derogation Order under which the government claimed to be entitled under the ECHR to interfere with Convention rights. In effect the Law Lords were *advising* the government and Parliament of the incompatibility, the implication being that if and when the claimants in this case were to take the matter to the European Court of Human Rights it was most likely to find the UK government to be in breach of its obligations under the Convention. As of the date of writing (January 12, 2005) we do not yet know what the government response will be. But the speeches of the Law Lords open up wider debates than the technical issues to do with interpretation of the Convention, as a number of them put their decision in broadly normative constitutional terms. Lord Bingham accepted the importance of the separation of powers when it came to the delicate political question whether there was a public emergency threatening the life of the nation, one of the preconditions for a derogation, but found against the government on the basis that if (as the Act implied) it was not strictly necessary to detain British suspects, it could not be strictly necessary to detain foreign suspects simply because they were foreign. The provision was also discriminatory. Lord Bingham was relatively restrained in not going beyond the legal arguments necessary to found his decision, but he did adopt the view that it was wrong to stigmatise judicial decision making as undemocratic, since the courts had been charged by Parliament under the Human Rights Act with delineating the boundaries of a rights-based (as opposed to majoritarian) democracy.[22] A number of the other Law Lords however went further in criticising the legislation and thus government and Parliament, stressing for instance that 'Parliament must be regarded as having attached insufficient weight to the human rights of non-nationals'[23]; 'Nothing could be more antithetical to the instincts and traditions of the people of the United Kingdom [than the power which the Home Secretary seeks to uphold]'[24]; 'Indefinite imprisonment in consequence of denunciation of grounds that are not disclosed and made by a person whose identity cannot be disclosed is the stuff of nightmares, associated ... with France before and during the Revolution, with Soviet Russia and the Stalinist era and now ... with the United Kingdom'.[25]

The courts have also begun to be explicit about the nature of the exercise they have to undertake, particularly but not only under the Human Rights Act, in deciding how to interpret statutes and in determining whether a decision of a minister which, on the face of it, appears to encroach on human rights might be justifiable on the basis that it was necessary in a democratic society for a range of reasons. The debate has been conceptualised as a question of 'deference', that is whether or when the courts should defer to the executive, conceding that it is for a minister to determine such balances, or when the courts may come to a different determination. This debate is not primarily about the relationship between Parliament and the courts but about relationships between ministers and the courts. But it surfaces in questions and debates in Parliament in the aftermath of cases where the courts have found that a minister has acted in a way that interferes with rights which was not justifiable, or on those rare occasions where the court has found that the law made by Parliament is incompatible with the Convention rights in its application.[26] Parliamentary rules prevent attacks on individual judges, but this has not prevented some ministers, notably Home Secretaries from time to time, from expressing their anger to and in Parliament at judicial decisions.

The debates in Parliament become more neuralgic where it appears that it is being required to legislate in ways which defer to the decisions of courts, especially those of the European Court of Human Rights. This strand of reaction can be found running through debates on recent legislation relating to gender change, civil partnerships and corporal punishment of children, as well as much of the legislation relating to asylum and immigration and counter-terrorism powers.

The Human Rights Act has also opened a novel area of judicial review. Section 6 of the Act obliges 'public authorities' to comply with the Convention rights in their actions. The activities of a vast range of public bodies are therefore now open to review on a wide range of grounds beyond the traditional considerations of vires, procedural propriety and rationality. Here again, it is essentially acts, omissions and policies of the executive branch of the state that fall under review, but the decisions of the courts in such cases can have wide-ranging policy implications. Intriguingly, the Joint Committee on Human Rights has taken on the courts directly in their application of section 6, which provides for its application to certain private bodies where they are 'discharging a public function'. In a report published in 2004 the Committee concluded that the courts had failed to interpret correctly the intentions of Parliament in making section 6(3)(b) of the Act, stating that –

> ... there is a fundamental problem not with the design of the law, but with its inconsistent and restrictive application by the courts.[27]

Parliamentary privilege and exclusive cognisance: How important?

Article IX of the Bill of Rights 1689 famously declares that –

> the freedom of speech and debates or proceedings in Parliament ought not to be impeached or questioned in any court or place out of Parliament

Pepper v. Hart could be seen as one way in which this prohibition has been nibbled-away at, to the advantage of the executive. But the most vexatious point has arisen because Article IX has been interpreted so as to prevent an action in defamation to be brought in relation to anything said or done in the course of parliamentary proceedings. This doctrine has placed an obstacle in the way of proposals to reform the law that currently immunises Members of Parliament against prosecutions for bribery or breaches of other parliamentary rules such as requirements to register interests.[28] While bribery of an MP and acceptance of a bribe by a MP would be regarded as a high crime and misdemeanour in the law and practice of Parliament (reflecting the ancient position of the two houses as courts of record, an obsolete approach in modern conditions) they are not prosecutable in the courts. In section 13 of the Defamation Act 1996 the two Houses cast aside part of this protection with hardly a word of protest in order to facilitate Neil Hamilton's pursuit of a defamation action against *The Guardian* relating to his financial dealings with Mohamed Al Fayed. The disastrous personal consequences for Hamilton of the failure of that action, and the enormous ramifications in terms of the internal procedures of the House of Commons for the regulation of the conduct of its own members, are well known. The results may be benign in some perspectives, but that such an enormous cultural change proceeded from such an unconsidered piece of legislation (the amendment was introduced at the very last stages in the House of Lords by Lord Hoffmann, a Law Lord, at the request of Lord Chancellor Mackay) should serve as a warning.

Another aspect of the relationship between Parliament and the courts is the courts' recognition of the exclusive cognisance of Parliament in relation to its proceedings (a privilege claimed by the Speaker at the start of each Parliament). Thus the courts will not entertain a complaint that either House did not follow its own standing orders and procedures in the legislative process, or in its exercise of jurisdiction over its own members.[29] So far as such procedures are concerned, the courts have not so far been invited to trespass on the realm of exclusive cognisance. But increasingly, the Houses have applied to themselves statute law (either directly or voluntarily) in areas such as health and safety, employment law and freedom of information, where before such application has been fiercely resisted. The motives for doing so are 'modern' – that each House should be seen to accept those duties and responsibilities it places on others. More widely, they can be seen as evidence that Parliament sees itself as something more of an equal partner under the law with the other branches of the constitution. But the effect may be, if only subtly, to diminish the sense of awe that parliamentary privilege might once have evoked. If that is the effect, then it is one which Parliament has wished on itself.

The future of parliamentary sovereignty

Has the balance between Parliament and the courts shifted towards the courts, then, in the last 40 years? And would this matter? There is always a paradox at work in this debate. Can a sovereign body, logically, give away some of its sovereignty and yet remain sovereign? Charles I thought not. In the case of the deferral to European law, and the incorporation of the ECHR, as well as the smaller concessions on its exclusive cognisance, Parliament has quite specifically ('deliberately' would not always be the *mot juste*) legislated away some of its sovereignty and expanded the power of the courts.

Moreover, Parliament's ability to exercise its legislative powers to the full (always bearing in mind Erskine May's warning of revolution) is subject to increasingly extensive political constraints, especially in relation to human rights and devolution (where the Sewel Convention and a number of Memorandums of Understanding and Concordats between the different levels of government regulate legislative activity, considered in chapter 18 of in this volume). In other words, the practical reality is, as it has always been to a greater or lesser extent, that Parliament's legislative supremacy is informally and formally constrained in a number of ways to do with political realities and pressures. Greater acknowledgement of these realities has begun to surface in the courts from time to time. The courts have been evolving the doctrine to meet modern circumstances and new conceptions of democratic legitimacy – Parliament has no clear vehicle for examining and resolving such questions. This consciousness of the political constraints that affect Parliament lay behind the comments of Laws LJ, for instance, in the *Thoburn* case about constitutional statutes, noted above. A related approach is reflected in some of the judgements of Lord Steyn. For instance in *R. v. Secretary of State for the Home Office, ex parte Simms,* he noted that –

> Parliament does not legislate in a vacuum ... Parliament legislates for a European liberal democracy based upon the principles and traditions of the common law ... and ... unless there is the clearest provision to the contrary Parliament must be presumed not to legislate contrary to the rule of law.[30]

What can we predict as to the future of parliamentary sovereignty so far as it is a judge-made doctrine? Elliott, in an important article,[31] speculates that the courts will develop their principles of statutory interpretation so as to accommodate factors such as the Sewel Convention and others, and constitutional principles reflected in 'constitutional' legislation, such as respect for the rule of law. The courts, he suggests, may in due course modify the scope of the substantive doctrine of parliamentary sovereignty in various ways, in response to these developments.

Alongside these developments in the relationship between the courts and Parliament, in recent years some influential judges have begun to question the merits of the majoritarian version of democracy that is commonly taken to justify parliamentary sovereignty – a debate which has tended to place in opposition ideas of democratic collectivism (based on conceptions of parliamentary sovereignty) and liberal constitutionalism (argued from the common law and the sovereignty of the individual, the rule of law and the entrenchment of human rights). This has particularly been the case in some high profile extra-judicial lectures, in which indications have been given that in the most unlikely event of Parliament passing an Act that contained provisions that were contrary to the rule of law or very undemocratic the courts would be justified in refusing to give effect to them.[32]

By raising the legal and political status of human rights, the Human Rights Act has stimulated discussion of the place of rights in a democracy. A shift in democratic theorising away from majoritarianism and towards constitutionalism may be taking place in some quarters, notably the legal establishment. Over the last decade or so a category of common law fundamental rights or principles in addition to Convention rights, has been identified by the courts[33] which they will protect by developing principles of statutory interpretation requiring explicit authorisation of breaches of those principles. This shift is reflected in a comment by Laws LJ.[34] He suggested that the British system was 'at an intermediate stage between parliamentary sovereignty and constitutional supremacy', the word 'constitutional' imparting the idea that certain fundamental rights and values are implicit in our constitutional arrangements, and the courts are entitled to protect them, even in the face of contrary statutory provisions.

Another possibility might be the development of a jurisdiction at common law for the courts to declare that a statutory provision is contrary to constitutional fundamentals, thus alerting government and Parliament, and commentators, to the position while nevertheless giving effect to the offending provision. But it would be open to a minister to do nothing in response to such a declaration, and there is no general statutory power to introduce 'remedial orders' of the kind authorised by the Human Rights Act 1998. Whether any of the parliamentary committees operating in the area of constitutional matters, such as the JCHR, the House of Commons Constitutional Affairs Committee or the House of Lords Constitution Committee would take up such a challenge, or do so effectively, it is impossible to predict.

Does Parliament need independent legal advice on constitutional issues?

The instruments that Parliament has at its disposal to address itself, whether positively or negatively (should it have a collective will to do so – which is unlikely since Parliament is not a collective) to the drift in judicial thinking to constitutionalism are limited. As we have noted in considering the *Pepper v. Hart* case, in the past the Attorney General has acted as legal adviser to, and (in litigation) counsel for, the two Houses. He has been regarded as, among other things, guardian of the privileges of Parliament, an odd position since the interests of Parliament and the government of which he is a member will commonly conflict – as they may have done in *Pepper v. Hart*.

The two Houses appear still to be very focused on the Attorney General as a source of legal advice. In the debates on the legality of the invasion of Iraq, in 2003, members of the House of Commons pressed for the disclosure of the Attorney General's advice to the government. The Government claimed legal privilege and refused to disclose it. The two Houses did not seek, and appeared unable in any practical way to seek, their own advice on the legality of military action. In another, less momentous, example the government produced the Attorney General to give advice to the House of Lords on the legal effect of proposed amendments to the law relating to the corporal punishment of children.[35] This was presented as if legally indisputable, given in support of the government's position in a highly-charged political atmosphere. The Attorney General's legal conclusions were subsequently disputed by the Joint Committee on Human Rights.[36] One inference to be drawn from this may be that the two Houses have no collective interest in obtaining independent legal advice, since the parties in Parliament will have conflicting interests in the substance of the advice obtained and its implications for the government. But if that is so, then Parliament will be hobbled in the dialogue with the courts over the developing constitution.

Two parliamentary committees, the Joint Committee on Human Rights and the Constitution Committee of the House of Lords, do have specialist legal advisers, as well as containing eminent lawyers in their membership. Those committees have legal advice available to them, which they make available to both Houses in their reports. Indeed, Lord Lester and David Pannick suggest that the Joint Committee on Human Rights has taken on a role as legal adviser to Parliament on matters within its remit, and has been effective in doing so.[37] The Lords Constitution Committee scrutinises Bills for their constitutional implications, but in that field there is no definitive list of constitutional norms and principles, and ministers are under no explicit duties to respect any constitutional principles that do exist. Nor is there any general obligation on ministers to present a memorandum about constitutional implications of Bills either to the Cabinet Legislative Programme Committee or to the Constitution Committee of the House of Lords.[38] But the work of these committees does at least suggest that Parliament is beginning to recognise that its legislative activity must increasingly be seen as taking place in a constitutional space in which dialogue and negotiation are inevitable.

Towards a constitutional, rights-based system?

How the courts and Parliament itself might shift yet further away from using the doctrine of supposed parliamentary sovereignty as the sole justificatory principle towards a constitutional, rights-based system is an open question. Tucked away in an obscure report from the Joint Committee on Human Rights is a little nugget of constitutional development. The report was discussing, *inter alia*, the Civil Contingencies Bill. Like several other committees of both Houses, the JCHR took grave exception to the provisions proposed in the draft of this Bill which could have put emergency regulations outside the ambit of the courts to strike down on grounds of incompatibility with Convention rights. (While the courts cannot strike down primary legislation on grounds of incompatibility they can rule that secondary legislation is ultra vires if it is incompatible. The draft civil contingencies Bill proposed to designate emergency regulations as 'primary legislation' for the purposes of the Human Rights Act, thus circumventing this possibility of judicial intervention.) The Government retreated, apologetically, from this stance in the Bill as introduced, but the JCHR still had concerns. It commented –

> We note the Government's recognition of those judicial authorities which hold that there are some statutes of such constitutional significance that Parliament cannot be taken to have intended that they can be amended or repealed unless Parliament has expressly stated that intention. This is obviously potentially important for the effective protection of human rights. We hope that it will be possible in due course to identify the statutes or statutory provisions which should be regarded as having constitutional status for this purpose.[39]

The Committee was referring to a letter it received from Douglas Alexander MP, Chancellor of the Duchy of Lancaster, responding to questions it had raised about the Bill. The letter was printed as an appendix to the report. The relevant passage states –

> ... one can expect the users of the legislation (and the courts) to interpret the scope of the power in light of the class of action which Parliament must have contemplated when conferring the power. There is nothing on the face of the Civil Contingencies Bill which requires emergency regulations to modify or disapply the Human

Rights Act ... there is nothing to indicate that Parliament intended to permit modification or disapplication of the Human Rights Act ... It is also important to interpret the power in light of the status that has been accorded to the Human Rights Act by recent judicial pronouncements. In *Thoburn v. Sunderland City Council* (2002 4 All ER 156), Lord Justice Laws identified a class of 'constitutional' enactments which, by reason of their importance, are to be regarded as having a particular strength which puts them, for example, beyond the reach of the traditional doctrine of implied repeal. This includes the Human Rights Act. It is clear from Lord Justice Laws' judgment that the courts will require clear language from Parliament before they will acknowledge that Parliament intends to amend an enactment such as the Human Rights Act. The Government considers that the courts will expect Parliament to use equally clear language before delegating the power to amend substantively the Human Rights Act to the Executive. The Bill contains no such language.

This rather pleasing circuit of confirmation – from judgment of the court, through approving citation by the executive, to delighted acknowledgement by a committee of both Houses – may indicate that the three branches of public power have begun to reach a quiet consensus on a fundamental constitutional principle.[40]

Notes

1 Thomas Erskine May, *Treatise on the Law, Privileges, Proceedings and Usage of Parliament*, 1st edition, London, 1844, p. 29.
2 L. Friedman, *Total Justice*, Russell Sage Foundation, 1985.
3 Lord Irvine of Lairg, QC, 'Judges and Decision Makers: The Theory and Practice of Wednesbury Review' [1996] *Public Law*, 59–78.
4 Lord Denning in *Bulmer v. Bollinger* [1974] Ch. 401.
5 c.f. Matthew Arnold, *Dover Beach*.
6 See e.g. Murray Hunt, 'Sovereignty's blight: Why public law needs the concept of "Due Deference"' in N. Bamforth and P. Leyland (eds), *Public Law in a Multi-Layered Constitution*, Hart Publishing, 2003.
7 *Edinburgh and Dalkeith Railway v. Wauchope* (1842) 8 Cl and F 710.
8 *Ellen Street Estates v. Minister of Health* [1934] KB 590.
9 *Civilian War Claimants v. The King* [1932] AC 14.
10 [1993] AC 593.
11 Lord Mackay, the Lord Chancellor whose Department had an interest in the case, and one other Law Lord dissented.
12 Although deference is in practice to the executive it is worth noting that much of the justification for it relates to the role of Parliament. See Lord Woolf in *R. v. Lambert* [2002] AC 545: 'Legislation is passed by a democratically elected parliament and therefore the courts ... are entitled to and

should, as a matter of constitutional principle, pay a degree of deference to the view of Parliament as to what is in the interest of the public generally when upholding the rights of the individual under the Convention'. The degree of deference paid also depends on (amongst other things) proximity to Parliament, and the degree of democratic accountability of the decision maker, with the highest degree of deference likely to be paid to Parliament: *R (on the application of Prolife Alliance) b. BBC* [2003] 2 WLR 1403, HL; *International Transport GmbH Roth v. Secretary of State for the Home Department* [2002] EWCA 158.

13   *R. v. Secretary of State for Transport, ex parte Factortame (no. 2)* [1991] AC 603.
14   [2002] 3 WLR 247.
15   At p. 643.
16   Although s.19 will lead to a presumption of compatibility (adding force to s.3) it may be worth noting Lord Hope in *R. v. A.* [2002] 1 AC 46, at para. 69, that s.19 statements 'are no more than expressions of opinion by the minister. They are not binding on the court, nor do they have any persuasive authority'.
17   [2002] 1 AC 46, esp. para. 46, per Lord Steyn.
18   *Ibid.* at para 44.
19   [2002] AC 291.
20   [2002] UKHL 46.
21   [2004] UKHL 56.
22   Para. 42.
23   Per Lord Nicholls, para. 81.
24   Per Lord Hoffmann, para. 86.
25   Per Lord Scott, para. 155.
26   For example in relation to section 55 of the Asylum and Immigration Act 2000.
27   Seventh Report from the Joint Committee on Human Rights, Session 2003–04, HL 39, HC 382, *The Meaning of Public Authority under the Human Rights Act*, Summary.
28   This may be contrasted with the position in the Scottish Parliament, where not only bribery but also failure to register interests may be criminal offences.
29   *Edinburgh and Dalkeith Railway v. Wauchope* (1842) 8 Cl and F 710; *Pickin v. British Railways Board* [1974] AC 765.
30   [1998] AC 539, at p. 575.
31   M. Elliott 'Parliamentary sovereignty and the new constitutional order: legislative freedom, political reality and convention' (2002) 22 *Legal Studies* 340.
32   See Lord Woolf 'Droit public – English style' [1995] *Public Law* 57; Sir John Laws 'Law and Democracy' [1995] *Public Law* 72.
33   See for instance *R. v. Secretary of State for the Home Office, ex parte Leech (no. 2)* [1994] QB 198 (right of a prisoner to communicate in confidence with his lawyer); *R. v. The Lord Chancellor, ex parte Witham* [1998] QB 575 (right of access to the courts for those unable to pay court fees); *R (Anufrieva) v. Secretary of State for the Home Department* [2003] 3 WLR 252 (right to be notified of a decision that affects a person's status is a precondition to the decision taking legal effect – in this case a decision to refuse a claim for asylum).

34 In the case of *International Transport GmbH Roth v. Secretary of State for the Home Department* [2002] EWCA 158, at para. 71.
35 HL Deb, 5 July 2004, col. 563.
36 Nineteenth Report form the Joint Committee on Human Rights, Session 2003–04, *The Children Bill*, paras 164 ff.
37 See generally Lord Lester of Herne Hill and David Pannick (eds), *Human Rights Law and Practice* (2nd ed. 2004) ch. 8; see also David Feldman, 'Parliamentary Scrutiny of Legislation and Human Rights' [2002] *Public Law* 313, and 'The Impact of Human Rights on the Legislative Process' (2004) 25 *Statute Law Review* 91.
38 There is an obligation under the government's *Guide to Legislative Procedures* on ministers to provide a memorandum for the Cabinet Legislative Programme Committee on the compatibility of Bills with Convention rights, but this is not disclosed to the Joint Committee on Human Rights. There is also an obligation on government to provide the Delegated Powers and Regulatory Reform Committee of the House of Lords with a memorandum and justification for the delegation of powers.
39 Fourth Report from the Joint Committee on Human Rights, Session 2003–04, *Scrutiny of Bills: Second Progress Report*, para. 1.22.
40 The Minutes of the Committee's report reveal that the only Conservative MP on the Committee dissented on the inclusion of the approving sentences.

Part VI
The World Beyond Westminster

17

To War or Not to War: That is the Question

Philip Giddings *

The decision to go to war is arguably the most significant decision a state can make. Who decides that question says much about the distribution of power within a political system. In some cases, for example, the United States of America, it is a decision regulated by the Constitution and by legislation.[1] In the United Kingdom, 'the decision to use military force is, and remains, a decision within the Royal Prerogative and as such does not, as a matter of law or constitutionality, require the prior approval of Parliament'.[2]

But lack of prior parliamentary authority for a declaration of war may be much less significant than it appears. With the creation of the UN wars in the traditional sense became illegal. Article 51 of the Charter permits military action in self-defence, subject to certain conditions, and other types of action can be taken in furtherance of UN resolutions. Thus, in the armed conflicts in which UK forces have been engaged since 1945, there has been no declaration of war: Korea, Malaya, Cyprus, Suez,[3] the Gulf, the Balkans, Iraq.

The real issue now is not who declares war but who authorises the deployment of British forces in actual or potential armed conflict. Her Majesty's Ministers exercising the prerogative powers of the Crown may be the formal legal authority but there is more to be said than that. Nowadays political authority requires parliamentary backing for such ministerial decisions. This is an instance in which parliamentary involvement is growing – and rightly so.

In this chapter we examine the most recent instance of Parliament grappling with this question in March 2003. We consider its significance for the role of Parliament in such decisions; its aftermath; and what the implications might be for Parliament's future ability to act as 'the cockpit of the nation' in such instances.

Parliament decides to fight

The decision that British forces should join their US counterparts in invading Iraq in the Spring of 2003 was one of the most controversial parliamentary decisions of recent years. The allegation that 'Parliament was misled' about the case for using armed force against Saddam Hussein has remained at the forefront of public and parliamentary controversy month after month. Inquiry has followed inquiry but the charge has not been laid to rest, to the evident discomfiture of Prime Minister Blair.

It has become commonplace to lament that the House of Commons is no longer the 'cockpit' of the Britain's national political life. Decisions are made in Whitehall and debated in press conferences and TV studios. Parliament's role, as either intermediary or forum, has been eclipsed – or so it is often argued. Yet, on 18 March 2003, with the prospect of British soldiers fighting and risking their lives, the picture changed. The Commons benches were packed; key speeches and votes were eagerly awaited. The media actually wanted to report the parliamentary action.

Undoubtedly one factor contributing to media interest was that the debate brought to a head the deep divisions within the Government and the Parliamentary Labour Party over the Prime Minister's support for American policy. On the previous day the Leader of the House, Robin Cook, two junior ministers and several parliamentary under-secretaries, had resigned from the government because they were not willing to support the Prime Minister's policy. With this highly charged background, the debate was fully attended, widely broadcast and reported in the UK and around the world.

The outcome of the debate was closely contested. The Government won the Commons' endorsement for its approach, including the decision to employ 'all necessary means' to disarm Iraq, by 412 votes to 149, with the Liberal Democrats abstaining. An amendment stating that 'the case for war against Iraq has not yet been established' was defeated by 396 votes to 217. Although these were decisive majorities, the crucial political issue for the Government was whether it could carry its own MPs. In the British parliamentary system a ministry which lacks majority support on its own side of the House is in a perilous position – hence the Government deployed what the BBC described as 'a whipping operation unlike any previously seen'.[4]

In the event 139 Labour MPs voted for the amendment, and were joined by 53 Liberal Democrats, 15 Conservatives and 11 MPs from the smaller parties. Around 20 Labour MPs abstained. If the 'payroll' vote of ministers, whips and parliamentary private secretaries is subtracted, then Labour Members divided almost equally on the amendment. According to media reports at the time,[5] as many as 20 Labour MPs may have changed the way they intended to vote while the debate was proceeding. Had there been more cabinet resignations (Clare Short had been widely expected to resign, but did not) voting on the amendment may have produced a different result.

The significance of the debate

Two factors gave particular significance to the debate of March 2003:

- The global scale of the likely consequences – significant casualties and unpredictable diplomatic, military, political and economic consequences
- The decision to send forces was a national one which transcended party lines – there were sceptics and critics within the governing majority as well as on the opposition benches; and alliances spanning the chamber

Global consequences: 'On this decision hangs the fate of many things'

The 18 March debate had been clearly marked out in advance as one of momentous decision. For some months previously the question of whether and how the House of Commons would be able to have its say on war in Iraq had been aired in the House itself and in the media. The Prime Minister told select committee chairmen in January that, what-ever the niceties of the constitutional position and the royal pre-rogative, 'the reality is that Governments are in the end accountable to Parliament, ... and they are accountable for any war that they engage in, as they are for anything else'.[6] In the Lords in February the Attorney General (Lord Goldsmith), having rehearsed the conventional position, went on to state that the prime minister had made clear that there would be a vote in the House of Commons and 'having the support of Parliament in going to war is a matter of political practice'.[7]

The question was how that support might be expressed. Past practice was by means of a procedural motion ('that this House does now adjourn') rather than a substantive motion addressing the govern-ment's policy and intentions. This had been the case, for example,

with the Falklands War in 1982.[8] Similarly, with Kuwait in 1990:
between Iraq's invasion and the onset of Allied action there were five
Prime Ministerial statements on the crisis (and two others following
European Council meetings at which the situation was discussed)
and three debates, all on the procedural motion to adjourn; debate on
a substantive motion expressing 'full support for British forces in the
Gulf' came four days after the Allied action had begun.[9]

The March 2003 vote on a substantive motion *before* hostilities
began therefore broke new ground. The Foreign Secretary, Jack Straw
pointed out that 'never before, prior to military action, has the House
been asked on a substantive motion for its explicit support for the use
of our armed forces. The House sought that, but, more important, it is
constitutionally proper in a modern democracy'.[10] In this Mr Straw was
echoing the Prime Minister's remarks when opening the debate.[11]

Mr Blair had also drawn attention to the global implications of the
decision:

> [It] will ... determine more than the fate of the Iraqi regime and
> more than the future of the Iraqi people ... It will determine the way
> in which Britain and the world confront the central security threat
> of the twenty-first century, the development of the United Nations,
> the relationship between Europe and the United States, the relations
> within the European Union and the way in which the United States
> engages with the rest of the world. So it could hardly be more
> important. It will determine the pattern of international politics for
> the next generation.[12]

Although the motion referred euphemistically to employing 'all necessary means' to disarm Iraq, no-one was in any doubt what was meant:
British forces going to war, with its attendant consequences, including
the likelihood of significant casualties. Although everyone was also
aware that in this crisis the United Kingdom was acting in close collaboration with the United States, it was clear that the decision to send
in *British* forces was a British prerogative to be decided at Westminster.
Some NATO allies, including France and Germany, opted to stay on
the side-lines.[13] The European Union, grappling with its embryonic
common foreign and security policy, was split on the issue. Britain had
to make its own decision, mindful of its likely impact on other states,
particularly in the Middle East, where it was seen as another instance
of American political and economic imperialism. As with Afghanistan,
so with Iraq, the consequences could not be confined to the theatre of
war; they were global.

National unity?

When a nation goes to war it should be united, so that the whole national effort can be devoted to defeating the common enemy and no energies or resources are diverted to internal dissension. One feature of this approach is that at Westminster, when matters of war, peace and national security are being discussed, party point scoring is usually suspended and a more generous attitude adopted towards opponents. On the other hand, the prospect of war may also lead to the formation of political 'coalitions' across party lines. In March 2003 the Leader of the Opposition was firmly behind the Government.[14] Another senior Conservative spoke of the Prime Minister's 'brilliant, articulate and powerful case for the motion ... The overwhelming majority of people in this country ... will be persuaded by the transparent and powerful way in which he presented the argument ...'.[15] This support from the Opposition front bench and the great majority of Conservative backbenchers was to prove very important to Tony Blair in the months to come, allowing him to represent the decision as one made by a cross-party consensus in Parliament as a whole.

It was not, however, a consensus which everyone joined. While cabinet and shadow cabinet stood together, the cross-party spirit was consciously rejected by the Liberal Democrats, who wanted a more specific UN security council resolution before supporting military action. Although this position was widely supported outside the House, it earned the Liberal Democrats much obloquy from Labour and Conservative loyalists.

Also dissenting from the Government/Official Opposition line were a small group of Conservatives and some Labour rebels, including former Foreign Secretary and Leader of the House Robin Cook who made a powerful critique of the Government's position in his resignation statement the day before the debate.[16] Leading Conservative dissidents included former Cabinet members Kenneth Clarke, John Gummer and Douglas Hogg who argued in the debate that the moral case for war was unconvincing.[17] Mr Clarke and Mr Hogg had signalled their opposition to the Government's policy line in earlier debates and were to continue to be critical afterwards.

The aftermath

Calls for an inquiry into the Iraq war of 2003 began almost as soon as the regime of Saddam Hussein had fallen. The main reason was the dawning realisation that the Prime Minister, and many other participants in the debate, had been arguing from a false premise, namely that the Iraqi regime actually possessed weapons of mass destruction which posed an immediate threat to world peace. The Prime Minister had said in the debate:

> Iraq continues to deny that it has any weapons of mass destruction, although no serious intelligence service anywhere in the world believes it

And:

> It is true that Iraq is not the only country with weapons of mass destruction, but ... back away from this confrontation now, and future conflicts will be infinitely worse.[18]

The Conservative leader, Iain Duncan Smith, was equally convinced:

> The threat that his arsenal poses to British citizens at home and abroad cannot simply be contained. Whether in the hands of his regime or in the hands of the terrorists to whom he would give his weapons, they pose a clear danger to British citizens.[19]

Yet after Iraq had been invaded and Saddam Hussein's regime toppled, when the whole country had been scoured for evidence by the Iraq Survey Group and others, no weapons in the prohibited categories were found. Lord Butler's report on WMD intelligence concluded: 'prior to the war, the Iraqi regime ... did not ... have significant – if any – stocks of chemical or biological weapons in a state fit for deployment, or developed plans for using them'.[20]

There is no doubt that Saddam Hussein possessed and used chemical weapons in the 1980s, and that he had tried to develop both nuclear and biological weapons as well. However, the post-invasion findings appeared to show that the international effort to disarm had been successful and that Iraq had disposed of such weapons as it had possessed in the prohibited categories and not manufactured more. The Prime Minister had referred to this possibility in his Commons speech of 18 March 2003, only to dismiss it as 'palpably absurd'.[21]

The belief that the Iraqi regime had chemical and biological weapons ready to use and might be close to acquiring a nuclear bomb was clearly a most persuasive argument in favour of the decision to go to war, cited repeatedly in the debate of 18 March. The subsequent failure to find evidence to back this claim was bound to raise questions about the quality of the intelligence available to the US and British governments, and their interpretation and use of this information to make the public case. No less than four inquiries have taken place in the UK: by the Commons Foreign Affairs Committee [FAC], the Intelligence and Security Committee [ISC], Lord Hutton and a committee of privy counsellors chaired by Lord Butler.[22]

War entails risks, both military and political. In his speech at the end of the 18 March debate, the Foreign Secretary referred to the ghost which haunted the banquet: 'Our forces will almost certainly be involved in military action. Some may be killed.'[23] Mr Hogg had earlier put it more graphically: 'If we go to war, the probability is that thousands and maybe tens of thousands of people will be killed or injured on all sides. That seems to me the principal question with which we should concern ourselves'.[24] Such an argument raised not only serious moral issues but also the question whether it was constitutionally proper to send British forces into a dangerous theatre of war without the legitimising ritual of a parliamentary vote. Mr Hogg concluded, 'I cannot find a sufficient moral case for condemning thousands or tens of thousands of people to death and injury. For that reason, because I think war lacks a moral basis, I shall vote for the amendment and against the Government motion'.[25]

The House of Commons passed the Prime Minister's motion on 18 March 2003 by a substantial majority. It thereby endorsed the Government's policy and legitimised the decision to commit British forces to fight in Iraq. But subsequently the validity of that endorsement has been challenged on the ground that it was based on mistaken information. Kenneth Clarke put the point very crisply six months later: 'I think that the decision to go war with Iraq was the worst military decision taken by this country since the Suez invasion ... a bogus reason was given to the House of Commons for embarking on the war in the first place'.[26] Douglas Hogg echoed it in January 2004: we went to war on a false prospectus.[27]

The 'false prospectus' charge was a serious one which struck at the heart of the view that the March 2003 vote legitimised the decision go to war. Much emphasis has therefore been placed, in the various official investigations of the decision to go to war, on whether or not ministers, and especially the Prime Minister who played a central role in the debate as well as in the Government's decision-making, misled Parliament. It is important for our purposes to distinguish between the *intention* to mislead, which focuses upon ministerial motivation; and whether Parliamentarians were *in fact* misled, i.e. based their decisions on information which was unreliable or false. The former charge generates much political excitement but it is the latter which most directly concerns the role of Parliament. Parliament depends upon the veracity of the information which is put before it, which is why in the Westminster culture lying to Parliament is the most heinous of all offences.

In the event the FAC and the ISC (both reflecting the government's majority in their membership) found errors and misunderstandings, but absolved ministers of the more serious charge of deception.[28] The FAC was concerned at the Government's lack of co-operation in making witnesses and material available, in marked contrast to who and what was made available to the ISC and the Hutton inquiries,[29] a point to which we will return. The ISC did not judge whether the decision to invade Iraq was correct but rather whether the available intelligence which informed the decision was adequate, properly assessed, and accurately reflected in Government's publications.[30]

The immediate reason for the Hutton inquiry was that the BBC had questioned the motives behind Joint Intelligence Committee (JIC) dossier of September 2002 and become embroiled in a conflict with 10 Downing Street which culminated in the suicide of the 'whistle-blower' Dr David Kelly. Lord Hutton stuck closely to his brief and had little to say about Parliament as such, except that, because the dossier was to be presented to Parliament and the public, it was not improper for the JIC to take into account suggestions as to drafting made by 10 Downing Street'.[31]

Lord Butler's committee of privy counsellors focused on the work of the intelligence services and Whitehall apparatus. In assessing the reasons for the confident, but ultimately misleading, statements about Iraq's weapons capability made to Parliament on 18 March 2003 and on other occasions, the committee noted that the broad conclusions of the UK intelligence community were widely-shared by other countries. Where doubts existed, they were about the extent to which the intelligence amounted to proof as opposed to balance of probability. However, because of a tendency to over-react to previous errors, there was 'a risk of over-cautious or worst case estimates, shorn of their caveats, becoming the "prevailing wisdom"'.[32]

That tendency became particularly significant because of the Government's desire to use intelligence in the public presentation of its policy, the prime example of which was the dossier of September

2002. The Butler Committee commented, 'The dossier was not intended to make the case for a particular course of action in relation to Iraq. It *was* intended by the Government to inform domestic and international understanding of the need for strong action (though not necessarily military action)'.[33] [emphasis original]

However, the privy counsellors found that, in translating material from JIC assessments into the dossiers 'warnings were lost about the limited intelligence base on which some aspects of these assessments were being made ... the language in the dossier may have left with readers the impression that there was fuller and firmer intelligence behind the judgement than was the case: our view, ... is that judgements in the dossier went to (although not beyond) the outer limits of the intelligence available. The Prime Minister's description, in his statement to the House of Commons ... of the picture painted by the intelligence services ... as "extensive, detailed and authoritative" may have reinforced this impression.'[34] Whilst recognising the Government's need to meet mounting public and Parliamentary demand for information, and acknowledging the 'real dilemma between giving the public an authoritative account of the intelligence picture and protecting the objectivity of the JIC', the committee concluded that it was 'a mistaken judgement' to make public the JIC authorship of the dossier'.[35]

In sum, then, it became clear after the invasion of Iraq that the evidence with regard to Iraq's WMD capability on which Members of Parliament made their judgement in the March 2003 debate was, at best, insecure and arguably positively misleading. Whether this undermines the legitimacy of the parliamentary decision depends upon one's view of the significance of the WMD strand in the overall argument about the justification for using military force against Iraq. Some were influenced by the need for regime change in Iraq, said to be the principal motivation for the American Government. Some argued that military force was necessary to establish the credibility of the United Nations in response to Saddam Hussein's repeated violation of Security Council resolutions. But many recognised that emotionally the most compelling argument was the perceived threat that Saddam, who had used these weapons in the war against Iran and against his own people, would use them again, possibly against British targets. The dossier and other material made available by the Government, and ministerial speeches expounding them, were designed to underline the credibility of that threat. Subsequent events showed that it was greatly over-stated.

Conclusions and the future

The attention given since March 2003 to the intelligence issue, the Kelly Affair and the protracted dispute between the BBC and No 10 Downing Street has obscured the underlying question of Parliament's role in the decision to go to war. Had the Government been prepared to share its doubts as well as its certainties with Parliament ahead of the war, the twin processes of making a sound decision and gaining enduring public legitimacy for it might have run more smoothly. As it was, the war proved to be deeply unpopular and severely damaged the standing of the Government and particularly of the Prime Minister. Yet the fact remains that in the period leading up to the invasion the Government did take Parliament more into its confidence than had ever been done before. The publication of intelligence material and the debate on a substantive motion prior to commencement of hostilities were unprecedented. Equally, the Government's reluctance to co-operate fully with the Commons Foreign Affairs Committee was not: in 1998 the FAC made two Special Reports raising concerns about access to classified material in connection with its inquiry into Sierra Leone.[36]

The first conclusion to be drawn from these events is whether a precedent has been set. If so, will the new precedent be confirmed and evolve into a convention? Or will governments take fright at the political damage which the Blair Government has suffered and adopt a much more restrictive stance in relation to parliament and public in future? The latter would be to mis-read what occurred in 2002–2004. The problems which afflicted the Government in this period were not the consequence of taking public and parliament into its confidence but of the way in which that was done. They reflected a Government which was uneasy about its ability to win the whole-hearted support of the public, and particularly its own party supporters, for the enterprise to which it became committed. To enhance the prospects of winning that support Ministers over-stated their case, with ensuing damage to that case and their own future credibility. A more open and balanced presentation of the issues would have been more, not less, effective in achieving the desired end of building support for the Government's line of policy.

Whether the 2003 precedent becomes a convention or not, it is certain to be cited when the House of Commons is next required to decide an issue of war. Along with the distant echoes of 1939, 1956 and 1982 we will surely hear many evoking the 'lessons' of March 2003. Members will know that, given what happened in 2003–04, their decisions are likely to be deeply scrutinised after the event and the credibility of the British parliamentary system once more put to the test. For one of the clearest lessons of March 2003 is the continuing desire for openness and accountability. This is more than the customary unwillingness in the media, civil society and the public at large to accept that government knows best. It is a deep and growing scepticism about the competence, motives, judgement, and even the integrity of those who have the power of decision, and an interest in keeping it. In this Parliament has a dual role: first, to reflect that desire for accountability by demanding appropriate responses from government and subjecting them to thorough analysis and challenge; and, second, to allow its own decision-making and processes to be questioned, challenged and tested in the same way. As the intermediary between people and government, parliament is the vital link in the chain of accountability, its own effectiveness in that role included.

In February 2004, answering Questions the day after the Foreign Secretary had announced the setting up of the Butler review, Mr Blair commented that 'whether war was just justified or not ... is in the end ... a decision that we have to take as politicians'.[37] The problem is, however, that politicians, in government and outside it, take decisions on the basis of the information and advice supplied to them. They have, of course, to make their own judgements, but they do so on the basis of what is put before them. In matters of war and peace, in which the security of nations and communities and the lives of many may be at stake, the responsibility of judgement is a heavy one. It is especially so when all the factors which have to be weighed cannot be shared because some of them directly affect the safety and security of individuals, in the defence, security and intelligence services and beyond. In particular, when judging the intentions of a potential enemy, and preparing possible responses, much information – and especially its sources – will be highly sensitive, possibly useful to a potential enemy. Sensitive information can only be made available on a highly restricted basis, hence the 'ring of secrecy' within which the ISC operates,[38] and the fact that, like the Committee, the Butler inquiry was conducted by privy counsellors. The challenge to Parliament – both Houses – is to ensure that the relatively recent mechanism of the ISC is developed so as to enhance the credibility of Parliament in holding to account this crucial area of decision-making.

Here we come to the issues raised by the Foreign Affairs Committee in their special report of March 2004. It was extraordinary that the FAC was treated by the Government less generously than the ISC and a non-statutory inquiry (Hutton). The FAC's report documents in detail the persons and papers to which it was refused access, but to which the ISC and the Hutton Inquiry were given access. It noted that 'the Government chose to co-operate with the inquiry carried out by the ISC/Lord Hutton's inquiry in ways in which it did not co-operate with a select committee of the House'.[39] The FAC concluded that continued refusal by Ministers in cases of this kind hampered the work which Parliament was asking the Committee to carry out. Its recommendations to remedy that were rejected by the Government.[40] The FAC has further recommended that the time has come to reconstitute the ISC as a select committee of Parliament, a proposal which the Foreign Secretary is on record as supporting.[41] The experience of 2002–03 demonstrates how necessary that is – but also that it will not remedy the fundamental problem, which is the Government's control over access to persons and papers which are essential to effective oversight and accountability in this area. That the issues of intelligence and security are so vital to the interests of the state makes it more, not less, necessary that effective oversight is provided, and seen to be provided. If Parliament is to play its proper role in the process by which the United Kingdom decides to go to war (or not), then it must have access to the information necessary to make a responsible decision. Without it not only will Ministers' decisions be unaccountable, so will those of Parliament itself.

As we have already noted, the momentous nature of debates like that of 18 March 2003 means that they are usually conducted in a different way from the crude adversarialism which is the popular picture of Westminster at work. The lines of division of opinion did not run along party lines and the tone of the debate reflected Members' realisation that deep issues of conscience as well as strongly contested issues of fact and judgement were engaged. Partly because of that, and no doubt also because of expectations of a significant rebellion on the government side, media attention and coverage was very high. It showed that the lines of division (not the same as proportions) in the Chamber closely reflected those outside. MPs were able to break out of party constraints. In this respect the Commons *were* connected and *were* reflecting the communities from which Members were drawn. On that occasion, unusually in the modern era, Parliament was indeed the 'cockpit of the nation', even if the government's hand was on the rudder and had control of the maps.

Notwithstanding the fact that Parliament proved unable to resolve the controversy over the intelligence material, the dispute between the BBC and No 10, or the huge debate about the acceptability of Anglo-US policy in the Middle East, the debate of March 2003 was a significant milestone. In matters of war, Westminster will not be the same again. Parliament – albeit courtesy of Her Majesty's Ministers – has established its role in the process by which the United Kingdom goes to war. Constitutionally, the prerogative lies with the Crown and its advisers; but, to quote the Attorney-General,[42] as 'a matter of political practice' the exercise of that prerogative must have the assent of Parliament. To war or not to war is a question Parliament must decide.

Notes

*   I am grateful for the considerable amount of information and material provided by Dr Richard Ware in preparation for writing this chapter – but I alone bear responsibility for its contents.
1   Article 1, Section 8 of the Constitution and the War Powers Resolution, 1973. See James M. McCormick, *American Foreign Policy and Processes*, F E Peacock Publishers, 1998, p. 327ff.
2   HL Deb, 19 February 2003, c1139.
3   Prime Minister Eden informed the House of Commons on 30 October 1956 that the British and French Governments had addressed 'notes' to Egypt and Israel which included the warning that if their requirements were not met within twelve hours British and French forces would intervene to ensure compliance and they subsequently did so. This could be considered tantamount to a declaration of war.
4   http://news.bbc.co.uk on 19 March 2003 at 11.04 GMT.
5   e.g. Michael White, www.guardian.uk, 19 March 2003.
6   Liaison Committee, 21 January 2003, HC 334-I, 2002–03, q125.
7   HL Deb, 19 February 2003, c1139.
8   HC Deb 3 April 1982, cc633–88.
9   HC Deb 21 January 1991, cc23ff.
10 *Ibid.*, c900.
11 *Ibid.*, c773.
12 HC Deb, 18 March 2003, c761.
13 Iraq lies outside the North Atlantic Treaty area.
14 HC Deb 25 November 2002, c774.
15 *Ibid.*, cc799–800.
16 HC Deb, 17 March 2003, cc726–728.
17 HC Deb, 18 March 2003, cc795–97.
18 HC Deb, 18 March 2003, cc763 & 767.
19 *Ibid.*, c776.
20 *Review of Intelligence on Weapons of Mass Destruction*, [Butler Report], HC 898, 2003–04, 14 July 2004, para. 397(d), p. 99.
21 HC Deb, 18 March 2003, c762.
22 Foreign Affairs Committee [FAC], *The Decision to go to War in Iraq*, HC 813, HC 1025 and HC 1044, 2002–03; Intelligence and Security Committee [ISC], Report on *Iraqi Weapons of Mass Destruction – Intelligence and*

Assessments, Cm 5972, September 2003; *Report of the Inquiry into the Circumstances Surrounding the Death of Dr David Kelly CMG*, [Hutton Report], HC 247, 2003–04, 28 January 2004; *Review of Intelligence on Weapons of Mass Destruction*, HC 898, 2003–04, July 2004.

23 *Ibid.*, c901.
24 *Ibid.*, c797.
25 *loc. cit.*
26 HC Deb, 22 October 2003, c692.
27 HC Deb, 19 January 2004, c1136.
28 FAC, HC 813, 7 July 2003, para. 188; ISC, especially Conclusions K, L, O, R and W.
29 FAC, First Special Report, 2003–04, HC 440, 18 March 2004.
30 ISC, para. 11 and Conclusion A.
31 Hutton Report, p. 320.
32 Butler Report, paras 457–458.
33 *Ibid.*, para. 462.
34 *Ibid.*, para. 464.
35 *Ibid.*, para. 466.
36 FAC, First Special Report, 1997–98, HC 760, *Sierra Leone: Exchange of Correspondence with the Foreign Secretary*; and Second Special Report, 1997–98, HC 852, *Sierra Leone: Further Exchange of Correspondence with the Foreign Secretary*.
37 HC Deb, 4 February 2004, c755.
38 The ISC is established under the Intelligence Services Act 1994. Its members, drawn from both Houses of Parliament, are appointed by and report to the Prime Minister, and are notified under the Official Secrets Act 1989. The Committee sees significant amounts of classified material and the Prime Minister, in consultation with the Committee, excludes any parts of a Report which would be prejudicial to the work of the intelligence and security Agencies. Up to May 2004 no material had been excluded without the Committee's consent. [ISC Annual Report, 2003–04, Cm 6240, June 2004, p. iv].
39 FAC, HC 440, 18 March 2004, paras 8 and 12.
40 *Ibid.*, paras 13–14.
41 *Ibid.*, paras 15–16; compare FAC, HC 813, July 2003, paras 158–65.
42 HL Deb, 19 February 2003, c1139.

18
Devolution: From One Parliament to Four[1]

Barry K. Winetrobe

Devolution and parliaments

With the exception of the half-century of Stormont devolution in the mid-twentieth century, the UK has operated for the last 200 years with just one parliament. Now, because of the policy of devolution instituted by the Labour Government, there are four 'parliaments'[2] within the state. Two are called 'assemblies' and one of those (the National Assembly for Wales) also comprises the 'executive' as well as the 'parliamentary' arms of governance,[3] but that does not detract from the fact that the number of parliamentary-type institutions has quadrupled in the last five years. If we add the Greater London Assembly – serving a population not all that much less than that of the three devolved nations combined – and the possibility[4] of one or more English regional assemblies in the near future, it is clear that the idea in the UK of a parliament is no longer a Westminster monopoly.

This may seem a little strange at a time when parliaments are regarded, both by the public and by academic commentators, as weak institutions, too often dominated by their executives, and populated by poor quality Members. The jeremiads about Westminster are as intense as they have been for the last fifty years; the assemblies in Wales and Northern Ireland are finding it hard to become firmly established in the hearts and minds of their citizens, and the parliament in Scotland has been subjected to fierce criticism, and not a little derision, since its creation.

So this proliferation of parliaments is taking place at a time when they are not popular. Of course, these parliaments are not free-standing institutions,[5] and some of the negative perception may be due to the performance of their governments, and of governance more generally.

In particular, much can be ascribed to the relative failure of 'policy delivery', something for which elected representative assemblies are not directly responsible.[6] Indeed, it could be suggested that the increase in layers or tiers of governance is due to the failures of the central institutions of the state in Westminster and Whitehall, and of perceived 'democratic deficits' during the period of apparently unsympathetic London rule in the late twentieth century. The designers of what became the Scottish Parliament explicitly sought to make their new parliament very different from Westminster, for practical as well as for symbolic reasons.

The unpopularity of 'parliaments in practice' has tended to obscure the more positive potentialities of the UK's new multi-layered governance, not least as a catalyst for change and reform within such institutions, and in their relations with their wider publics. The scope for comparative analysis by parliamentary practitioners and academic students has multiplied enormously in this country since the late 1990s. The devolved parliaments, especially the Parliament in Edinburgh, have been the subject of sustained interest worldwide.

For Westminster,[7] this has provided both a challenge and an opportunity. As the parliament of the British state, and one of great antiquity, experience and prestige, it is an obvious role model for the new institutions which bear many resemblances to it. Equally, it has the opportunity to learn from the procedural and practical innovations introduced by them to see what, if anything, would enhance its own performance.[8]

These two forms of interaction work best if Westminster engages with the devolved institutions. How should it relate to them, and how has it done so since their creation? Are they seen as upstarts and potential challengers; as 'children' that need to be looked after; or as fellow parliaments, albeit on a 'lower' level? Westminster's approach will be affected, to some degree, by the attitude to it of the three institutions. The 'anti-Westminster' rhetoric common at the conception of some of them would not have endeared them to the members and staff of the UK Parliament. Again, we cannot divorce the parliaments from their political majorities, which, to varying degrees, condition their attitudes and actions. Finally, we have to bear in mind the direct impact of devolution itself on the procedures and practices of Westminster, and its potential (positive and negative) for disturbing, perhaps even disrupting, its established ways.

The chapter examines these themes to see how devolution, at least in its initial phases, has affected the UK Parliament, and speculates how it may do so in the future. While all three devolved parliaments are examined, because of the unique circumstances in Belfast, the focus is largely on those in Cardiff and Edinburgh. This should not be taken to imply that the Northern Ireland Assembly has not sought to engage fully with its fellow institutions, including Westminster, during its rather staccato existence so far, nor that it will not continue to do so in the future. Indeed, with the Northern Irish tradition of parliaments very much in the Westminster procedural and cultural mould, its development may be of especial comparative value to the UK Parliament.

The Westminster reaction to devolution

The main response from Westminster was a 1999 report from the House of Commons Procedure Committee.[9] Other than this, there have been relatively few formal examinations within Westminster of the impact of a significant constitutional innovation. There was an initial burst of activity, including a thoughtful report from the Scottish Affairs Committee, published at the end of 1998.[10] Since then the two principal outputs, to which we shall return later, were a Report from the House of Lords which dealt with inter-parliamentary relations among other matters,[11] and a report from the Welsh Affairs Committee.[12]

The Procedure Committee report was very positive in its promotion of what it called 'amicable relations' and 'mutual respect' between Westminster and the new devolved institutions,[13] and set out some 'common principles' which underpinned its approach.[14] But it emphasised that it was reacting to an evolutionary process, and therefore proposed only a limited number of procedural changes at that stage.[15] These changes, widely regarded as minimalist, were watered down by the Government, and implemented in October 1999.[16] Thus the 1999 Procedure Committee report, and the changes which flowed from it, neatly encapsulated the guarded approach of the UK Parliament and Government to the onset of devolution. It was dealt with piecemeal, as just another piece of parliamentary reform or 'modernisation', to be handled in a pragmatic and gradualist way, avoiding the potential risks of a holistic approach to change.

Contrast this parliamentary response to the comprehensive arrangements for the conduct of inter-governmental relations through the *Memorandum of Understanding* and the complex network of multilateral and bi-lateral concordats and related guidance notes which have been produced.[17] Clearly getting the relations between governments right had a higher priority than those between parliaments.

Since this early foray into post-devolution procedural change, relatively little has changed at Westminster in formal or structural terms directly related to devolution. Such changes as have occurred were either reactions to relevant changes in the machinery of government (especially the major changes in June 2003 which subsumed the Scotland and Wales Offices, and the Lord Chancellor's Department, into the new Department for Constitutional Affairs), or to other constitutional changes, such as the House of Lords Constitution Committee and the Joint Committee on Human Rights. Some changes have, at the time of writing, yet to be fully implemented, such as the reduction in the number of Scottish MPs, made possible by the Scotland Act 1998. However, two recent reports provide encouraging signs of genuine interest at Westminster in adjusting positively to the new devolved environment.

The Lords Constitution Committee report of January 2003, examining inter-institutional devolution relations, is noteworthy here for the unusually clear articulation of a parliament-centred approach to this constitutional change.[18] In particular, it found 'the neglect of inter-parliamentary relations regrettable', especially in the potential for Westminster learning from the new devolved institutions.[19] It recommended, for example, more interchange between Members of the four parliaments, other than through the existing Belfast Agreement mechanisms; the holding of joint inquiries on matters of common interest, and, perhaps more problematic, for the three devolved presiding officers to be members of the House of Lords, as was the position (by chance) between 1999 and 2003.[20]

However, its most radical and challenging recommendation was in relation to Westminster law-making in devolved matters, as with the Sewel Convention, and primary legislation for Wales.[21] It deplored the fact that initiative and negotiation of this essentially inter-parliamentary matter was executive-dominated, very much in the UK tradition. It should be for the parliaments, not governments, to agree and operate such 'co-legislating'. This runs counter to the UK tradition of government initiative and control of the legislative process, and is probably too radical for early adoption,[22] but provides a new and positive way of looking at both inter-parliamentary and parliamentary-executive relations which could have more general application for wider parliamentary reform.

The Welsh Affairs Committee's report of 2003, reflecting what the Presiding Officer of the Assembly has described as the 'co-legislator' roles of Parliament and the Assembly,[23] was prepared to be a little more radical. It suggested joint meetings between committees of the two bodies, an annual joint debate between the whole Assembly and the Welsh Grand Committee, and perhaps most radical of all for Westminster, a method by which amendments to bills suggested by AMs could be printed with the Commons papers. The suggestions were considered by the Procedure Committee, who drew on the work of a group of officials from the Commons and the Assembly. One proposal has been implemented. A temporary standing order was passed in the Commons in June 2004 allowing Assembly Members to participate in proceedings of the Welsh Affairs Committee when considering draft Bills affecting Wales, and a mirror-image standing order was passed in Cardiff. This (described a little inelegantly as 'reciprocal enlargement') was the first time since the Joint Committee on Indian Constitutional Reform of 1932–4 that non-Members have been allowed to participate in Westminster proceedings. Following successful joint sessions, the Welsh Affairs Committee and Assembly Economic Development Committee both reported on the draft Transport (Wales) Bill in July 2004.[24]

More fundamental issues arising from devolution, such as those characterised as the 'West Lothian Question' or the 'English Question', have not been formally addressed, because of their essentially 'political' nature. Scotland will lose seats at Westminster in the 2005 general election. Though this was foreshadowed in 1998, it is no more palatable to incumbents. Thus in Wales after publication of the Richard report,[25] battle lines were drawn by Labour MPs, some of whom were anxious not to find their number similarly reduced if the Assembly were to have extended powers. It is in the present Government's interests to portray its devolution scheme as a 'settlement', so that any change is incremental and organic, rather than radical, and it hopes, rather optimistically, that changes such as the creation of English regional assemblies may defuse some of the more inherent problems of asymmetrical devolution.

Almost five years into devolution, it is difficult to argue with the conclusions of a study from those who have been continuously observing Westminster's reaction to devolution:[26]

> After one full term of the Scottish Parliament and National Assembly for Wales, the impact of devolution on Westminster remains minimal. Despite initial reforms, what enthusiasm there was for Parliamentary changes seems largely to have drained away, leaving Westminster looking much the same as it did before devolution.

Inter-parliamentary relations: learning from each other?[27]

If the procedural reform picture has been rather bleak, then perhaps, at a more informal and practical level, Westminster has shown that it has adjusted to the post-devolution world. Looking at it from the other direction, have the devolved parliaments been more receptive to Westminster and its ways?

As noted earlier, there was a sense, especially in Scotland, that any new parliament should be very different from Westminster, because the UK parliament was seen to epitomise much that was wrong procedurally and culturally. Yet in practice, Westminster was the obvious comparator for any new parliamentary institutions in the UK, for a number of reasons:

- its pre-eminent position in the 'Westminster Model' family of parliaments;
- the devolution legislation (including the equally important consequential subordinate legislation) enacted at Westminster inevitably drew on many familiar structures and practices;
- many of the members of the new devolved parliaments were (and some continued to be, through a temporary[28] 'dual mandate') members of one or other House of Parliament, or had worked at Westminster for MPs or parliamentary parties;
- some of the staff of the new parliaments had a Westminster background;[29]
- quite a few of the officials and others who devised the detailed procedures and practices of the new parliaments had some form of direct Westminster experience,[30] and
- for most of the media and public in the devolved nations of the UK, whatever they may have thought of the UK Parliament in practice, 'Westminster' and 'parliament' were virtually synonymous.

This last point is one which was often either overlooked or even explicitly denied by those involved in the creation of the new devolved parliaments. One illustration was the swift introduction in the Scottish Parliament of a devolved version of 'Prime Minister's Question Time', a procedure which, ironically, is said to epitomise what is bad about Westminster. At a more fundamental level, it may explain the general lack of acceptance (both internal and external) of the corporate structure of the National Assembly for Wales, and the widespread demands for it to be transformed into something more recognisably parliamentary. Though different in many ways from the Stormont Parliament of the mid-twentieth century, the Northern Ireland Assembly operates within that former parliament's neo-Westminster surroundings and uses much of its procedure and practice.

So, notwithstanding their different structures and powers, there is much potentially in common between the three devolved parliaments and the UK Parliament. All four can learn from each other both in a positive ('how to do things') and negative ('how not to do things') sense. They all do substantially similar things, even if they do them in different ways. They hold their governments to account; they make or scrutinise various forms of legislation, and their members represent their citizens. They have to interact with European institutions, albeit at different levels and for different reasons.[31] They have common issues and problems of internal governance and institutional arrangements, including their relationships with the media and the public; constructing new parliamentary buildings, and, highlighted during 2004, in the management of their internal security.

It must be borne in mind that this is not a simple bilateral relationship. What has evolved over the last four years and more is not a situation of 'the Mother of Parliaments' and her three immature infants. In many areas (especially at staff or committee levels, for example), the three institutions in Cardiff, Belfast and Edinburgh have worked together (bilaterally, trilaterally or with other parliaments – especially, and interestingly, the Dail) without the direct involvement of Westminster. Sometimes this has been because Westminster has had procedural difficulties with formal relations or joint activities, especially between committees.[32] At other times Westminster has preferred to look further afield for comparative lessons from the Commonwealth, Europe or the USA. This last attitude does seem to be diminishing, especially through the attitudes of some particular committees and Leaders of the Commons like Robin Cook and Peter Hain.

Devolution itself, and as part of the wider policy of constitutional change, remains a matter of continuing party political debate. The different electoral timetables for the Commons and for the devolved parliaments mean that one parliament's elections can take place in the others' mid-term period. The constitutional and parliamentary complexities and asymmetries created by devolution inevitably condition how Westminster and its constituent members and parties respond in particular circumstances. Devolution was primarily considered initially in terms of legislative competence and policy divergence, and the legislation and subsequent administrative guidance sought to cover all expected eventualities. What has proved to be more troublesome in practice, especially in the Scottish context, has been the relationship between elected members in the devolved parliaments and the House of Commons. This is an area where no formal guidance or rules were produced, and where conventions were expected to evolve within the hoped-for climate of mutual respect and amicable relations.

The future impact of devolution on Westminster

How Westminster responds to devolution in the future depends on two broad factors:

- changes in the devolution schemes and other forms of territorial governance, and
- development of the institutional and practical relationships between Westminster and the devolved parliaments.

As for the first factor, it is easy to see how any changes in constitutional arrangements affect Westminster's response. Alterations in ministerial responsibilities, such as those in June 2003 (and few expect there to be no such further changes in the medium term), will affect the relevant parliamentary committees which scrutinise aspects of devolution,[33] as well as other accountability mechanisms such as PQs. The creation of a UK Supreme Court, and related judicial reforms, may affect the composition of the House of Lords, in terms of representation of Law Lords from the devolved nations. Any more general reform of the second chamber will affect, and be affected by, devolution, perhaps in ways in which the component nations and regions of the UK are 'represented' in a reformed chamber.

Significant alterations in the three devolution 'settlements' will have direct impacts on Westminster. Most radically (other than a partial or total dissolution of the Union), a federal or 'devolution all round' solution would transform the role and function of the UK Parliament. At an individual level, the restoration of some form of devolution to Northern Ireland will have an obvious effect, and, even during periods of direct rule, there may be demands for greater transparency and accountability in the handling of Northern Ireland business, especially in its legislation. It is possible that there will continue to be adjustments in the present Scottish 'settlement', perhaps in the boundary between devolved and reserved matters; the extent of use of the Sewel Convention or in the electoral system for the Scottish Parliament.

The territory where change is both most likely and potentially most significant is Wales, because its particular form of devolution 'settlement' gives the UK Parliament a direct and central role far in excess of that in relation to Scotland or (other than in periods of direct rule) Northern Ireland. The Richard Commission's recommendations[34] were unexpectedly radical, calling unanimously for a legislative Assembly for Wales very much on the model of the Scottish Parliament (though, interestingly, without recommending the renaming of the Assembly as a 'Parliament'); speaking of the desirability of giving that Assembly tax-varying powers; proposing a division between the legislature and executive; and arguing for 80 Member Assembly elected by STV, rather than the present 60 Member Assembly elected by first-past-the-post and AMS. After internal debate in the Labour Party, the Assembly Government and Peter Hain in his convenient role as both the Secretary of State and Leader of the House seem to have agreed a way forward. This allowed the Assembly Government to secure an Assembly Resolution which

> calls on the First Minister to urge the Secretary of State for Wales to bring forward proposals to amend the Government of Wales Act for the following purposes:
> 1. to effect a formal separation between the executive and legislative branches of the Assembly;
> 2. to reform existing electoral arrangements in order to eliminate anomalies;
> 3. to enhance the legislative powers of the Assembly.[35]

There is an expectation that if Labour wins a 2005 General Election, a White Paper and then legislation will follow, allowing a new statute to come into force before the Assembly elections in May 2007. The details of the new legislative powers to be given to the Assembly have yet to emerge. It is clear, however, that there will be changes not only within the National Assembly but also in its relationship with Westminster. The granting of primary legislative power would profoundly alter Westminster's salience in 'domestic' Welsh affairs, and diminish the importance of the Secretary of State, as well as the Welsh MPs and Welsh Grand and Select Committees.

The second factor – how Westminster responds to devolution – is of equal significance. Devolution in practice would look very different if there were different parties in power in London and in one or more of the devolved territories.[36] Whether or not that occurs, it should be safe to predict that all four parliaments will deepen their relationships with each other, especially at the informal and practical levels, and perhaps even in some formal procedural ways. Will such convergence in parliamentary procedures and practices prompt Westminster to consider their possible adoption or adaptation for the UK Parliament? This would not be surprising, as much of the 'not like Westminster' rhetoric of the last twenty years, especially in Scotland, was less an indicator of radical or innovative ideas or lessons from parliaments abroad than an adoption (often unconsciously) of the 'parliamentary reform agenda' familiar at Westminster since the early 1960s.

So, how might these developments, based on lessons from the experience of the devolved parliaments, change the UK Parliament? We can make a few speculations, based on recent trends.

- *Arrangement of business:* this is a feature of the central relationship between parliament and executive. It is possible that the experience of the devolved parliaments, already regularly cited by reformers, may provide the necessary additional pressure for more inclusive and transparent forms of business management. Possibilities might include a business committee; direct plenary involvement in deciding the order and content of future business;[37] perhaps, symbolising a changing executive-parliamentary relationship, or even the demise of the role of 'Leader of the House' in its present form.
- *The Parliamentary calendar:* despite the impression of glacial change at Westminster, this actually is an area where there has been a virtual revolution over the last decade. Most, if not all of it, has been generated internally, rather than directly from comparisons with the devolved parliaments. Nevertheless, the emphasis that the devolved bodies give to a calendar based on 'normal office hours' and schedules that are designed to be more family/public/member-'friendly' may deter or counter contrary pressures at Westminster for the abandonment of some recent changes. Increasingly, plenary time is concentrated in the middle of sitting weeks, with Mondays and Fridays as 'constituency days'. The Commons has recently followed the devolved practice of setting out the broad shape of the annual calendar, including recess dates, in advance. Whether or not it follows the practice of prohibiting committees and the plenary sitting at the same time remains to be seen.
- *Committee system:* Westminster traditionalists often defend the separation of committees into select and standing, on the basis that a combination of these two modes could well inject a more partisan element into the essential collegiality of committee scrutiny inquiries.

Experience in the devolved parliaments has arguably demonstrated that these fears are exaggerated, and that the benefits of a unified subject committee system (especially with a reasonable continuity of membership) outweigh any such disadvantages. In particular it could make detailed legislative scrutiny a more meaningful process than usually occurs in standing committee.

- *Public engagement and openness:* This is the area where the contrast between the UK and devolved parliaments is most marked. In part this is due to the relative youth and lack of self-assuredness of the latter bodies, who do not have the stifling burden of centuries of tradition and practice. Nevertheless, it is clear that the culture and ethos of the devolved parliaments, and the extent of their ambition, vision and aspirations, are different from the standard approach at Westminster, which was tellingly characterised by the Leader of the House of Commons, Peter Hain, during business questions on 29 January 2004:[38]

> We do not treat visitors with the respect that they deserve. After all, most of them are citizens of this country and, in the case of school students, future citizens, so we ought to give them a proper welcome. They should be entitled to the kind of facilities that they would expect when visiting any other important building in the country.... It is also a question of the whole attitude of the House. We treat our visitors as strangers – the title we give them, in our anachronistic fashion – rather than as visitors, many of whom are electors. They are entitled to be here and they should not be seen as being here on sufferance.

A June 2004 Report from the Commons Modernisation Committee, which adopted these sentiments,[39] lavished praise on the Public Information and Education Service in Cardiff and similar services in Edinburgh.

If these trends continue, we may see a situation in the UK of what may be described as 'asymmetric convergence', with all four parliaments more closely resembling each other in their procedures, practices and ethos, notwithstanding their structural, constitutional and legal differences. We should certainly see closer inter-parliamentary cooperation, especially in formal business such as law-making and scrutiny.

Genuine parliament-centred reform will require something like the vision articulated in the 2003 Constitution Committee report of autonomous, proactive inter-parliamentary cooperation. This would mean a fundamental shift from the present model of executive and party domination of parliaments, a model, it must be remembered, on which the institutions and operations of the current devolution schemes are predicated. Much will depend on the attitude of Westminster itself, its members (individually and collectively, in their parties and otherwise) and the staff of both Houses.

If we can dare to be visionary, and imagine that truly indigenous 'reforming' pressures can outweigh the current dominance of the executive-led 'modernisation' agenda, that may produce changes for the UK Parliament that benefit the parliament and the people, rather than the government. The 50th anniversary of the SPG may yet see the emergence of a new 'post-Westminster model parliament' template, combining the best of all four of the UK's parliamentary institutions. That really would be 'parliamentary reform'!

Notes

1 I am very grateful to those colleagues whose valuable comments have greatly improved my original drafts, especially Paul Silk, Clerk of the National Assembly for Wales; Philip Giddings, editor of this volume, and Janet Seaton, Head of Research & Information, Scottish Parliament.

2 Hereafter, the term 'parliaments' is used generically, except when the context indicates otherwise.

3 Changes to this arrangement are currently being debated. See R. Rawlings, *Delineating Wales*, 2004.

4 Now more remote, following the result of the North East referendum in early November 2004.

5 As already noted the Assembly in Cardiff comprises both a parliament and an executive.

6 See chapter 1 of J. Griffith & M. Ryle, *Parliament: function, practice and procedures*, especially on the meaning of 'parliamentary government' and the notion of the UK Parliament as a debating forum rather than a governing body: 2nd ed., by R. Blackburn & A. Kennon, 2003.

7 Unless otherwise stated, this chapter will focus mainly on the House of Commons, as the House most comparable with the three devolved parliaments.

8 For a recent example, see House of Lords Constitution Committee, *Parliament and the legislative process*, HL 173, 2003–04, October 2004, and for an external comparative analysis on the same topic, A. Brazier (ed.), *Parliament, politics and law-making*, Hansard Society, Dec 2004, esp chap. 7.

9 *The procedural consequences of devolution*, HC 185, 1998–99, May 1999.

10 *The operation of multi-layer democracy*, 2nd report of 1997–98, HC 460, Dec 1998. See also an Opposition Day debate on 11 May 1999, HC Deb vol. 331 cc174–224.

11 Constitution Committee, *Devolution: Inter-Institutional Relations in the United Kingdom*, HL 28, 2002–03.

12 *The primary legislative process as it affects Wales*, 4th report of 2002–3, HC 79, March 2003.

13 The Scottish Affairs Committee report had also emphasised the need for 'goodwill' by all concerned in making the new devolved arrangements work. See, e.g. paras 34–5.

14 Report, para. 5.

15 It promised 'a full review of the procedural consequences of devolution in due course', Report, para. 1. This has yet to occur.

16 See the debate on 21 October 1999, HC Deb vol. 336 cc606ff, and the resulting procedural changes on 25 October, HC Deb vol. 336 cc761ff.

17 Department for Constitutional Affairs http://www.dca.gov.uk/constitution/devolution/index.htm.

18 *Devolution: inter-institutional relations in the United Kingdom*, 2nd Report of 2002–03, HL 28, January 2003.

19 Paras 137 and 144–8.

20 Paras 138–143.

21 Paras 119–125 (Wales) and especially 126–134 (Scotland).

22 The Government briskly rejected the proposal: Cm 5780, March 2003, esp paras 25–26.

23 Welsh Affairs Committee, Fourth Report of the Session 2002–3, *The Primary Legislative Process as it Affects Wales*, Evidence taken on 21 October 2002, Q2, HC 580, 2 April 2003.

24 Fourth Report from Welsh Affairs Committee, Session 2003–4 *Draft Transport (Wales) Bill* HC 759, and Economic Development and Transport Committee *Draft Transport (Wales) Bill – Final Report* http://www.wales.gov.uk/keypubassemecondevtran/content/reports-e.htm.

25 See below, page 285.

26 G. Lodge *et al.*, 'The impact of devolution on Westminster: if not now, when?' chap. 8 of A. Trench (ed.), *Has devolution made a difference; the state of the nations*, 2004, p. 193.

27 See, further, B. Winetrobe, 'Inter-Parliamentary relations in a devolved UK: an initial overview' Appendix 5.1 of House of Lords Constitution Committee, *Devolution: inter-institutional relations in the United Kingdom*, Second Report, HL 28, 2002–03, January 2003, pp. 59–69.

28 If the new SNP leader, Alex Salmond, returns to the Scottish Parliament at the 2007 election, and also serves out the Parliament as a Westminster MP should he be re-elected in the 2005 UK general election, his example could influence the dynamics of inter-parliamentary relations.

29 The most visible example is the Clerk of the National Assembly for Wales, Paul Silk, who was previously a senior Commons Clerk.

30 As demonstrated in the detailed evidence to the Fraser Inquiry into the Holyrood Building Project: www.holyroodinquiry.org.

31 This is an area where there has been much interaction, especially between their respective European scrutiny committees.

32 These potential difficulties were noted by the Procedure Committee in its 1999 report, e.g. paras 40–48.

33 Though it should be noted that the transition of the Select Committee on the Lord Chancellor's Department to the Select Committee on Constitutional Affairs (with devolution and other constitutional issues in its expanded remit) has not to led any change in its exclusively English membership.

34 *Report of a Commission on the Powers and Electoral Arrangements of the National Assembly for Wales*, TSO, 31 March 2004.

35 *Official Record of the Assembly*, 6 October 2004.
36 In this context, Northern Ireland is a special case, as its parties are not those which compete for office at the UK level, at least directly.
37 See the recent Constitution Committee report, fn 10, paras 116–123.
38 HC Deb vol. 417 cols 403–4.
39 *Connecting Parliament with the Public*, First Report, Session 2003–4, HC 368. As Leader of the House, Hain chairs the Committee. The extent of conservative/traditionalist counter-influences can be seen in the debate implementing the abolition of the term 'strangers' on 26 October 2004, HC Deb vol. 425 cols 1308ff.

19
Westminster in Europe

Philip Giddings

When the SPG was founded, the United Kingdom had made one, failed application to join what was then the Common Market. In the forty years since then the UK has struggled to develop its relationship with its European partners. 'Common Market' became 'European Economic Community' and ultimately 'European Union'. A primarily trading and economic bloc developed its social and political aspirations generating significant political tensions in the UK. The Six expanded by stages to become the Twenty-Five. Throughout the period 'Europe' has been a topic of high political controversy, within and between the governing parties. It is in that context that the Westminster Parliament has sought to adapt to the major constitutional change which was effected by British accession to the Treaty of Rome and the enactment of the European Communities Act 1972 and subsequent amendments to it.

Insofar as sovereignty can be taken to mean the ability to act independently or unilaterally, there is no escaping the fact that accession to the European Community has meant its diminution. That diminution is most evident in the impact upon what the Parliament at Westminster can and cannot do. That very formulation indicates a significant departure from the Diceyan view of parliamentary sovereignty. For as long as the United Kingdom adheres to her treaty obligations, there *are* limits to the legislative consequences which the Westminster Parliament can enact; there *are* laws which bind the citizens of the UK which are made by another legislature; and there *is* a court which can pronounce upon the legality of legislation which the Westminster Parliament has passed. Since 1972 the Westminster Parliament has had to accommodate itself to a new situation, one of *restricted* legislative competence. To accommodate Diceyan theory it can be argued that as these restrictions were self-imposed, they could be, as it were, self-removed. But the fact was, and is, that in practice the restrictions were real and required significant changes both to the ways in which Westminster went about its business and, arguably more important and certainly more difficult, to its perception of its power and status.

Over the years the SPG has taken a keen interest in Britain's European relations. The evolution of parliamentary procedure for dealing with European business since accession has been fully documented and analysed in two publications, *Westminster and Europe* (1996) and *Britain in the European Union* (2004).[1] The clear lesson from those accounts is, first, the obvious one that Westminster cannot regain by procedural devices what has been ceded by treaty; and second, the pivotal role of the 'parliamentary reserve', now embodied in formal resolutions by both Houses of the Westminster Parliament. It is this reserve, and the attendant scrutiny processes which it protects, which gives Westminster the possibility of influencing – indirectly – the evolution of European policy and legislation. 'Indirectly' because the policy-maker and legislator of the European Union is the Council of Ministers with the consent of the European Parliament. Westminster's influence is possible insofar as it is mediated by British Ministers and, to a (much) lesser extent, British MEPs. And in many cases British Ministers as well as British MEPs have to obtain the support of others to bring that influence to bear – except in the diminishing number of areas in which unanimity rather than qualified majority voting applies in the Council of Ministers.

Such influence as Westminster may have on Euro-legislation depends to a large extent upon the work of its scrutiny committees. These operate differently in the Lords from the Commons, perhaps reflecting the less partisan atmosphere of the former, at least pre-2001. But, as the Lords' arrangements have reflected more fully than the Commons, there is more to European business than legislation. Indeed, given the need to obtain the necessary majorities in the European process, by the time policy is expressed in legislative form it can be very difficult to change. This is the reason why the scrutiny committees have been so anxious to obtain early sight of documentation and work programmes. They need to involve themselves early enough to be able to affect the process of decision-making – before the proposals have become set too firm.

By 2004 there were three policy areas upon which parliamentary (and public) opinion is particularly sensitive: the single currency; immigration and asylum; and defence arrangements. Equally, perhaps more, sensitive is the troubled subject of the European Constitution, an issue upon which unanimity was finally achieved amongst the Member States in June of that year. The resulting Treaty Amendments needed ratification by the Member States, which in the case of the UK means parliamentary endorsement, a referendum and the passage of the necessary amendments to the European Community Acts. As previous rounds of treaty amendment showed, notably the Maastricht Treaty in 1993,[2] these can be significant hurdles.

The setting up of a Standing Committee first for the Convention for the Future of Europe and then for the Intergovernmental Conference reflected the concerns at Westminster about the Convention process and the texts which emerged from it. The revival of the Constitution under the Irish Presidency led to renewed controversy about whether any resulting treaty or constitutional text should be put to a referendum, well illustrated by the exchanges in the Commons when Mr Blair reported on the Brussels Summit.[3] In April 2004 Mr Blair finally conceded to the political and media pressure by announcing that after the treaty had been agreed at the European Council and debated in Parliament (Westminster) his Government would 'let the people have the final say'.[4]

There are thus two key dimensions to the Westminster-and-Europe syndrome. First, it is deeply controversial – controversial between the United Kingdom and its partner Member States; controversial between Government and Opposition; controversial within the major political parties as well as between them. Second, notwithstanding considerable procedural ingenuity in both Houses, much dedicated work particularly by the staff and members of the scrutiny committees, and column after column of reports and debates, questions and answers, the *Parliament* at Westminster has little influence – and the little that it has depends upon the negotiating leverage of the British Government in the Council of Ministers/European Council. To echo Bernard Crick's comment about Parliament in general,[5] it is influence, not power – and not much by way of influence either. The question for the future, therefore, is how that influence can be maximised – or whether it is destined to decline even further.

Five scenarios

Scenario one: status quo

We can identify five possible scenarios here. The first is the *status quo*. Westminster struggles on with the present set-up, adapting the committee structures, perhaps improving the supply of documentation and the quality of explanatory memoranda and responses from government departments, finding a little more time for debate on committee reports, but in real terms able to make no significant dent in its marginalised status. What happens at Westminster will be of interest to a few at Westminster, but not to many beyond.

This is arguably the most likely scenario, given the cautious incrementalism which has been the culture of the Westminster Parliament for so long. But it is not a particularly attractive scenario, even if it is the one which Government prefers, judging by the Leader of the House's memorandum to the Modernisation Committee in March 2004: 'We must make sure that the work that Parliament already does on European scrutiny is done to better effect'.[6] But the memorandum was a hotch-potch of sketchy ideas, ranging from a new Joint European Grand Committee (concerning which the Lords have considerable reservations[7]) to abolishing European Standing Committees and transferring their work to departmental select committees.[8] Yet it is already difficult to motivate MPs (unlike peers) to involve themselves in the detailed work of scrutiny of European business[9] and that problem is likely to worsen rather than improve, especially as the legislative process of the post-enlargement EU will be even more difficult to influence. The existing processes do provide something of a forum for NGOs to comment upon evolving EU policy and law-making – but they know only too well that Brussels and Strasbourg provide more effective points of leverage than Westminster. Resort to Westminster is something of a last desperate throw.

Scenario two: extended engagement

The second scenario is one of extended engagement: given its powerlessness as a national legislature, Westminster reaches out to join with other representative institutions to mobilise greater, and possibly more effective, pressure on European level decision-makers. Principal among these institutions are the European Parliament, the legislatures of the other Member States and the elected assemblies in the devolved regions of the United Kingdom. The question is how such extended engagement could be achieved, and whether if achieved it would deliver the objective of enhancing Westminster's influence.

The attraction of this scenario is that it engages with Parliament's traditional role of representation. Its drawback is that it can so easily be portrayed by ministers as an alternative European policy to that being pursued by the Government. In parliamentary government systems the executive and legislative branches are fused: parliament exercises its influence and control through ministers and ministers govern through parliament. They do not operate in competition with one another, nor even in parallel.

The idea of the Westminster Parliament *independently* seeking to influence and mobilise the parliaments of other member states on governmental as opposed to purely parliamentary issues does not fit with the fused constitutional model, it would be argued. Ministers and government whips will want this to be left to the Executive. On the other hand, if the provisions in the proposed Constitution for Europe came to fruition and were developed, there would be some opportunity for member state legislatures to concert their efforts, with or without the encouragement of their governments, in response to legislative and policy proposals from Brussels. The proposed constitutional treaty includes a 'yellow card' procedure by which national parliaments can signal to the Commission that a proposal is deemed to be in breach of subsidiarity. However, it is not proposed that the Commission would be under obliged to withdraw such a proposal – which raises the question how effective this provision would be in practice. In addition, the proposed constitutional treaty provides for the Council to meet in public when it deliberates and votes on draft legislative acts. This greater transparency would increase the opportunity for national parliaments to hold to account their ministerial representatives on the Council of Ministers. But the question still remains: even if achieved, would a concertation of national parliaments' efforts deliver an increase in their influence on Council decision-making? The only direct leverage available would be through mobilising a majority in the European Parliament to operate the co-decision mechanism.[10] The European Union Committee launched an inquiry into subsidiarity in October 2004, intending to explore how the draft Constitution's early warning mechanism for monitoring subsidiarity compliance would work in practice.[11]

Scenario three: radical engagement

The third scenario is of more radical engagement with the public, both British and European. It would mean accepting, indeed promoting advisory referenda so as to underpin the representative voice of parliament; using the web and other IT resources to enable much more direct input from the citizenry, both individuals and groups, to the parliamentary process; holding regional and local hearings on the effects of proposed European policies and legislation. Parliament would effectively be mobilising the public so that it could more effectively represent and advocate what the public wants – or does not want. The April 2004 decision to hold a referendum on the constitutional treaty as well as on the Euro may be a sign of this kind of development.

For some, the need for a more radical engagement – and also its likely complexity – was illustrated in the results of the elections in June 2004 to the European Parliament. These elections were held simultaneously with local government elections in England and Wales. The results showed the ability of the electorate to differentiate: the proportion of the vote received by the two main parties (Conservative and Labour) was significantly lower in the European than in the local government elections [27 + 22 = 49% in the European elections; 38 + 23 = 61% in local government elections]. In part this reflects the impact of the United Kingdom Independence Party, which in the European elections received 17% of the vote. In consequence more than one in six of this electorate (i.e. not including Scotland and Northern Ireland) will have an elected voice in the European Parliament, but not in the UK Parliament. This also applies to those who voted for the Green Party (6%), so, together with the UKIP voters, this amounts to about one-quarter of the electorate who voted in the European elections in England and Wales. Even allowing for some of the more Euro-sceptic Conservative MPs who could be taken to represent a position approximately equivalent to that of the UKIP, there remains a substantial gap. That gap is a serious challenge to Westminster's claim to represent the UK electorate on European issues. And it is made the more serious by the dis-proportionality of the first-past-the-post electoral system for Westminster which has yielded a parliament dominated by Labour's 62% of the seats but 41% of the vote.

Whatever one's views of the respective merits of the different electoral systems, there is a clear challenge here to Westminster parliamentarians (including members of the Upper House) to ensure that the *whole* electorate, indeed the whole community, is effectively represented. That is a noble aspiration, but the hard question is how. A major obstacle is the difficulty which parliament, as opposed to government, has in making a corporate policy decision. For example, the idea of holding local and regional hearings seems attractive: for it to happen, many different committees at Westminster would need to adopt it. And if the concept were to be more than window-dressing, the outcomes of the hearings would need to find a significant place in the proceedings of the two Houses. We already know that the agenda of the two chambers are over-loaded, and that it is difficult to find space for debates on, for example, select committee reports. Making room for the outcomes of 'external' hearings would certainly be an acid test of the seriousness with which Westminster – and Whitehall – viewed any such exercise.

Imaginative use of the internet is a possible alternative, though it has (at least) two difficulties. The first is whether it differentially advantages the better-resourced groups (which is, of course, an issue with interest group activity of all kinds). The second is how the material would be digested, evaluated and transmitted to a significant point of decision. The resource implications of a properly operated 'sieve' would be significant. But if Westminster takes seriously the need to maintain its representative role, then this may be the price it will have to pay – in order to avoid further marginalisation.

Scenario four: no majority

The fourth scenario is much more speculative. It anticipates the changes which would occur if there were a major re-configuration of British party politics, perhaps as a result of a split on Europe itself or, more likely, following a change in the UK electoral system, as a result of which a Government's in-built majority in the Commons, drawn from a single party, could no longer be assumed. Majorities would have to be constructed, perhaps on an issue by issue basis, a form of politics familiar in Continental Europe but strange to United Kingdom ears – though becoming less so with the experience of coalition administration in Scotland and Wales. In such a circumstance the price for constructing a majority might well be more substantial *parliamentary* participation in policy-making on Europe (and indeed other issues).

Unlike the third scenario this is not one which Westminster will necessarily choose – whether or not it happens will depend upon the electorate and, to a lesser extent, the parties. If an election fails to yield a single party majority, the House of Commons, and particularly the leadership of the major parties, will have to decide how to respond. Amongst parliamentary systems of government Britain has been unusual in having a system and culture so dominated by the two-party model – or, rather, by the single-party-government model. There are therefore plenty of precedents to follow in other systems in addition to those periods in the UK between the world wars when Labour was emerging as the principal challenger to the Conservatives. Moreover, since devolution Britain has had working examples of multi-party government – and assemblies committed to operating in a different way from the Westminster model.

So we know that parliamentary government can work effectively without a single-party majority. What we do not know is whether the agreements, understandings and conventions which would be needed to make it work would affect how European Union matters are dealt with at Westminster. If differences over Europe contribute to the re-configuration of electoral support or the party system, then how those differences are to be addressed can be expected to be part of the package of agreements or understandings which emerges. Experience elsewhere shows that arithmetic will be the principal determinant of the outcome. It is not likely to be fruitful to speculate beyond that.

Scenario five: mandates

The fifth and final scenario could be combined with any of the above apart from the first. It envisages a move towards the Danish approach, in which parliament mandates ministers on the positions they may adopt in European Union negotiations. The parliamentary reserve would be upgraded to become a parliamentary *mandate* and ministers' positions and activities in the Council of Ministers and related bodies are subjected to close and continuing scrutiny.

Such a move would be very unlikely to be attractive to any currently foreseeable Government at Westminster, and even less to their official advisers. But even supposing Westminster were to make such a move, the crucial question is how this would work, and what its impact would be at the European level. Would the effect be simply to marginalise the United Kingdom in negotiations because the undertakings of its ministers could not be fully relied upon or they had insufficient flexibility to make the necessary deals? The problem here is that adding strength to one particular linkage in a chain can have two contrasting effects: it may make the chain stronger – or it may break it. In the case of the linkage between national parliament and minister representing a member state at EU level, it may strengthen the ability of the national parliament to influence the outcome at EU level, or eliminate it. Which it would be would depend on the political circumstances of the case – and in particular whether there is support amongst other member states for the concerns which the 'mandating' legislature wishes to pursue. Here the lack of transparency in the work of the Council of Ministers is a significant obstacle. Members of member state legislatures, like their publics generally, can only rely on ministerial reports of the form and balance of argument within the Council, and those reports are likely to be partial in both senses.

The reality is that negotiations require some degree of flexibility. This is especially true of international diplomacy and even more so in the expanded European Union. Negotiators given no freedom of movement are likely to fail. In a system like the EU where QMV applies failure to obtain unanimity is not a bar to a decision which is binding on the member states. That is all the more significant as the provenance of QMV is further increased in the 2004 Constitutional Treaty. The more productive way to maximise the influence of a member state legislature is therefore likely to lie in building an effective and constructive relationship between the legislature, or more likely its key committees, and the ministers who represent the state in European ministerial councils. In short, a political rather than a legal-constitutional method is more likely to succeed.

Cautious incrementalism and the problem of motivation

Such a characterisation of the possible scenarios can easily suggest a sclerotic system, incapable of change or development. That would certainly be an exaggeration, as the history of the period since the UK joined the European Community demonstrates: the processes and procedures of both Houses have evolved in response to developments within the Community/Union. The obvious examples are the incorporation of the parliamentary reserve into resolutions of both Houses and the bringing within the scrutiny system of the two additional pillars created by the Maastricht Treaty. These developments were not immediate but did eventually take place.[12] Cautious incrementalism has been the culture of Westminster's approach, with the caution most marked in the House of Commons. But development has not ground to a complete halt. For example, the Foreign Secretary made some further proposals for development in February 2004,[13] including the idea of a committee with a remit to cover the whole of the EU's work, a successor committee to the Standing Committees on the Convention and IGC – which were themselves incremental developments.

The evident caution about developments of this kind is not only a reflection of the reluctance of the Executive to expose itself to further parliamentary scrutiny and the prospect of delay and possible embarrassment. It also reflects a serious problem of motivation amongst Members of Parliament which manifests itself in difficulties in finding sufficient members to 'staff' scrutiny committees and concerns about the participation of members in the work of those committees. For example, in June 1990 the then Leader of the House, Sir Geoffrey

Howe, reported that the reason for reducing the proposed number of European Standing Committees from five to three was strictly practical, because of the difficulty in finding members who would agree to serve on them.[14] The detailed work of scrutinising the volume of legislation and documentation which the EU produces is hard grind which is not attractive to the average backbencher. The Procedure Committee had earlier acknowledged the difficulties in getting Members to serve on the committees, because of the volume of work and the 'indigestible range of unconnected subjects' they had to consider.[15]

The issue was visited again after the change of government in 1997. The Modernisation Committee agreed that more standing committees were desirable and proposed five – but again it proved possible only to appoint three. In 2002 the European Scrutiny Committee returned to the subject, commenting on poor attendance and lack of attention to debates. Again it proposed five committees but this was rejected by the Government because it had proved impossible to achieve.[16] Robin Cook, then Leader of the House, commented in November 2002 that the problem was a lack of willing volunteers: ' ... if there were colleagues out there who wanted to play a part, whips would jump at the chance of putting them on in the knowledge that it is somebody who will turn up'.[17] His comments were echoed by his successor in a memorandum to the Modernisation Committee in March 2004: 'the sad fact is that European Scrutiny is something of a minority interest'.[18] This is in marked contrast to the House of Lords where over 70 peers are already involved in the work of the European Scrutiny Committee – and there is a queue to join.[19]

Such comments aptly illustrate the fact that the lack of interest of MPs in detailed scrutiny is a major obstacle to developing the Commons' scrutiny system. This takes us to the heart of the question of Parliament's future role in relation to European business: how to engage the interest of MPs. As Mr Cook put it, 'unless the members of the House themselves are exercised and interested in looking at the detail of European legislation, any mechanisms that you propose or I set up are not going to meet that problem. I do not have a simple solution as to what we do to attract that interest'.[20] This was already a substantial problem prior to enlargement and the extension of EU competencies in the Maastricht and Amsterdam Treaties. With enlargement and the possible adoption of a European Constitution the need for such engagement is further increased. Given the character of public opinion revealed by the 2004 European elections, and evident in previous European and national elections and opinion surveys such as

Eurobarometer,[21] the challenge is a huge one, with which the Commons Modernisation Committee was grappling as this chapter was being written.

The marginalisation of National Parliaments

If MPs, and peers, are to be encouraged to invest their time and energies in scrutinising European legislation and policy documents, it will be necessary to demonstrate that such investment will be have a pay-back. The core issue here is the perceived marginalisation of national parliaments, itself an issue in the debate about the European Constitution. There are (at least) two dimensions to this.

The first is the use of the referendum. On both the Euro and the European Constitution the United Kingdom will have a referendum. Although formally the final decision on both will lie with Parliament and Government, politically the decisive voice will be that of the people, or of those people who exercise their vote. Some will see this as a further diminution of Parliament's authority, a further move away from the classical doctrine of parliamentary sovereignty. But it can also be seen as a clear opportunity for Parliament to exercise a key role in the process by which the voters come to their decision.

Both issues – the Euro and the constitution – are complex. On both issues the two main parties are divided, so the easy recourse for the puzzled voter of using 'party preference' as the surrogate for making a personal assessment is not available (though no doubt on both questions both parties will come to a majority position). Parliament can therefore provide the forum within which the arguments on the issues (and in both cases there are many issues to be disentangled) can be made – and challenged. If fully exploited the Parliamentary forum, notwithstanding the pressures on Westminster timetable, can provide a fuller and richer exploration of the issues than any discussion on *Newsnight*, *Today*, or *Panorama*, or a multitude of features in newspapers, however distinguished.

Austin Mitchell, MP, once compared Commons' debates on the European Union with meetings of the Sealed Knot society.[22] The implication was that few outside Westminster (and not many within) were interested. The challenge to a Parliament facing the prospect of marginalisation is to make its proceedings and debates relevant and interesting to the voters who are being called upon to decide these questions in a referendum. Good debate, like court-room drama, can provide good theatre.

The second dimension of the marginalisation issue is how Westminster can maximise its ability to exercise those opportunities which the EU's decision-making processes provide to affect legislation and policy formation. Such opportunities are admittedly limited, but the debates in the Convention for Europe and about the Constitution itself show that there is a tide (its strength is problematic) flowing to increase them. The first obstacle here is to overcome denial: the need to recognise that these are legislative and policy questions which cannot be decided by Westminster/Whitehall alone. Engagement with others is necessary in order to bring effective influence to bear in Brussels and Strasbourg. This means taking positive steps to work with other national and regional legislatures, the European Parliament and its committees, as well as engaging with the Commission, as the Lords Committee is beginning to do.[23] It means building on the 'antenna' in Brussels so that communication becomes two-way: not just Westminster parliamentarians trying to keep themselves informed about what is happening (which is of course the vital first step to effective influence) but also linking with others in order to affect outcomes. In effect it means that the Westminster Parliament would act as an interest group within the European policy forum – a significant change in self-perception for British parliamentarians. Mr Hain's memorandum for the Modernisation Committee in March 2004 showed some signs that the Government is beginning to grasp this point.[24]

If that change in perception occurs, and there is a willingness to adopt a proactive strategy to influence European Union decisions, then the resource obstacles will have to be addressed: not only will additional staff be needed but also Westminster parliamentarians themselves, especially MPs, will have to commit more of their own time and energies to the task. As we have seen, in the Commons this level of commitment has not been forthcoming in the past. To this extent the marginalisation of Westminster is the product of parliamentarians' own decisions about their priorities. The key question remains whether British parliamentarians consider that influencing European Union decisions is of sufficient importance for them to rank above their other personal political objectives, even at the risk of alienating their own party managers. That risk, and the unwillingness of most parliamentarians to incur it, has been the principal block to so much change at Westminster. The future for Westminster depends on whether that blockage remains.

Notes

1 Philip Giddings and Gavin Drewry, *Westminster and Europe; the Impact of the European Union on the Westminster Parliament*, Macmillan, 1996; Philip Giddings and Gavin Drewry (eds), *Britain in the European Union: Law, Policy and Parliament*, Palgrave, 2004.

2 For details see Philip Giddings and Gavin Drewry, *Westminster and Europe; the Impact of the European Union on the Westminster Parliament*, Macmillan, 1996, chapter 11.

3 HC Deb, 29 March 2004, c1259.

4 HC Deb, 20 April 2004, c157.

5 Bernard Crick, *The Reform of Parliament*, Weidenfeld & Nicolson, 1964, p. 77.

6 HC 508, 2003–04, 31 March 2004, para. 3.

7 HL 186, 2003–04, 26 October 2004, para. 144 and Appendix 7.

8 The Modernisation Committee had not concluded its enquiry at the time this chapter was written.

9 See below, page 223 [section on *Cautious Incrementalism*.]

10 For a succinct account see Helen Wallace and William Wallace (eds), *Policy-Making in the European Union*, OUP, 2000, p. 22.

11 HL 186, 2003–04, Thirty Second Report, November 2004, Appendix 4.

12 For details see Philip Giddings and Gavin Drewry, *Westminster and Europe; the Impact of the European Union on the Westminster Parliament*, Macmillan, 1996, pp. 58–66; Philip Giddings and Gavin Drewry (eds), *Britain in the European Union: Law, Policy and Parliament*, Palgrave, 2004, pp. 65–74.

13 HC Deb, 11 February 2004, c1415ff.

14 HC Deb, 28 June 1990, c528.

15 Third Report of the Procedure Committee, *European Business*, HC 77, 1996–97, paras 33–34.

16 Thirtieth Report of the European Scrutiny Committee, *European Scrutiny in the Commons*, HC 152–xxx, 2001–02, paras 67–74 and *Government Observations*, HC 1256, para. 27.

17 Oral Evidence to the European Scrutiny Committee, 5 November 2002, HC 1298, 2001–02, Q18.

18 HC 508, 2003–04, 31 March 2004, para. 2.

19 European Union Committee, *Annual Report 2004*, HL 186, 2003–04, Appendix 6.

20 *Ibid.*, Q3.

21 See Eurobarometer 61, Spring 2004, available on the EU internet site, www.europa.eu.int.

22 HC Deb, 23 November 2000, c501.

23 See the Committees *Annual Report 2004*, HL 186, 2003–04, paras 124–1134.

24 HC 508, 2003–04, 31 March 2004, paras 32–34.

Part VII
Parliament and Media

20

The Challenge of Adaptation

Ralph Negrine and Colin Seymour-Ure

The relationship between Parliament and the media is little different now from nearly half a century ago. Today, as then, its dominant feature is tension. This derives largely from the ambivalence of parliamentarians: they both recognise and dislike their dependence on the media for publicity, without which the effective representation and scrutiny of government are impossible. Some tension derives, too, from the dependence of the media on Parliament: the press has historic roots in party politics, while broadcasters have a 'public service' obligation to report Parliament. Parliament and media certainly retain mutual interests. But these are overlapping rather than identical. The balance of advantage is summed up in the truism that although the media can get on without politics, politics cannot get on without the media – and it is this last fact which is the main problem for Parliament.

Over the last fifty years the dominance of media has grown ever stronger. The forces of tension between Parliament and media have pulled almost entirely the media's way. The main change has been that Parliament has come to accept that it must work with the media less grudgingly than in the past, if it is to re-establish a claim to be the 'grand inquest of the nation'. Having seen that title pass to such media formats as *Newsnight*, the *Today* programme and even the occasional *Sun* exclusive, parliamentarians realise that their institution will risk atrophy, if they fail to claim the title back. Governments will continue to 'presidentialise', and to exert even greater control over the generation and execution of policy, in combination with interest groups and at parliament's expense, while the conduct of vigorous and influential debate will take place beyond the precincts of Westminster.

The general contention of this chapter, therefore, is that Parliament should always be predisposed to adapt to changes in media technology and practice. The more successfully it does so, the more effectively it will be able to use media in order to fulfil its various functions. Parliament shares a major interest with media, for example, in holding governments to account. Newspapers tend to put this goal ahead of party loyalty, even when they are in general sympathy with a government. Media love 'exposure', and so the accountability not just of governments but of persons and organisations with great power of any kind in society is also a concern shared with Parliament. Pick almost any function of Parliament, and it will be improved by effective media treatment: the big set-piece occasions in the Chamber (the epitome of the 'grand inquest'); the detailed work of legislative scrutiny and committee inquiry; the general goals of reflecting and setting national political priorities.

It would obviously be wrong to give the impression that Parliament has not adapted to changes in media at all. The problem, usually, has been dilatoriness – most conspicuously about permitting televised debates. Here, the Commons dithered for some thirty years, before letting in the cameras in 1989 (see next chapter). Albeit slowly, Parliament has adapted quite efficiently to the basic needs of the media in the twenty-first century. There is, for example, ample broadcast coverage of Parliament on the dedicated *Parliamentary Channel*, and Parliament's website (www.parliament.uk), whatever its limitations, offers unprecedented coverage. The restrictions that so curtailed parliamentary and political coverage in the past – the 14 Day rule, the secretive and restrictive Lobby rules, the lack of a right to film in the palace – have all been swept away.[1] Although debates in the Chamber get less detailed coverage than ever, the system of specialist and departmental committees has made up some of the lost ground, since coverage of committee proceedings and reports has steadily grown along with their industriousness and authority.

In this important respect, then, Parliament as a source of news and information is by no stretch of the imagination 'closed off' to the media. On the whole, however, these developments have not enabled media to find a satisfactory way to portray Parliament 'in the round'. Media still limit their coverage to those occasions when Parliament and politics satisfy general, everyday values of 'newsworthiness'. Such an approach inevitably downgrades those aspects of parliamentary business that the media deem worthy – but not *news*worthy. As Simon Jenkins, when editor of *The Times*, argued in support of his decision to abandon the paper's parliamentary page: 'We are not there to provide a public service for a particular profession or, for that matter, for a particular chamber. ... Newspapers are about providing people with news.'[2]

The critical issue for Parliament in the twenty-first century is how to re-establish itself as the leading forum of political discourse at a time when not only its own position but also the place of politics more broadly in civil society has been eroded. Little wonder, then, that in 2003–4 the Commons' Modernisation Committee drew attention to these issues in its aptly named report, *Connecting Parliament with the Public*.[3] But if Parliament is going to meet the challenge, it will have to halt, and ideally reverse, a number of trends that have gradually moved it away from the centre of political life.

These trends include the growing power of the executive in general and a progressive growth of public relations and news management activities, especially after the election of the Blair government in 1997. Both have increased the importance of the executive as a source of news, whilst simultaneously decreasing the importance of Parliament. It is worth noting that, as a consequence, Downing Street's website (http://www.number-10.gov.uk/output/Page1.asp) rivals, and probably supersedes, Parliament's own website as a *source* of news and information about the prime minister – including such items as his speeches, press conferences, lobby briefings and live webcasts of Question Time – and his government.

For the 'new-style' prime minister, as Richard Rose put it, 'the box that counts is the television set rather than the despatch box.... What is said on television matches or surpasses in importance what is said in Westminster'. As Rose also argued, the more Blair embraced the media, 'the less he communicates or feels the need to communicate with MPs at Westminster'.[4] If the prime minister and the government slight Parliament in this way, is it surprising if the media downgrade Parliament as a source of news and information?

In these developments there is more at stake than Parliament's media coverage in itself. The trends towards the presidentialisation of power and the emergence of a 'public relations state' licensed practices that led to a crescendo of hostility in the Blair government's second term. They provoked what a government inquiry called 'a three-way breakdown in trust between government and politicians, the media and general public'.[5] What is at stake, according to this argument, is public confidence in the very worth of political life. But, in truth, the causes of the 'breakdown' were arguably much more complex. Was public 'disengagement' with politics a manifestation of wider changes in society that undermined ideological certainties? Did these reflect a more individualistic and consumer-oriented view of politics? And what part did media play in such changes? As societies grew increasingly complex was there ever likely to be agreement about appropriate levels of trust?

Simply to ask those questions shows how far Parliament's treatment in the media is the outcome of many competing influences – commercial, political, social, technological. Some of them – discussed in the next section – involve the changing media landscape. Others, concerned with the government's attempts to manage its media relations most effectively, in and out of Parliament, are explored in the section following.

Old media, new media

If Parliament is to re-occupy the foreground of political life, it must do so in a media landscape that is vastly different from a mere fifty years ago. The number of national daily newspapers (depending on the definition) has varied slightly around ten, but total circulation is in long-run decline, particularly amongst the tabloids, whose circulation has fallen by just over 30% since 1980.[6] In contrast, the last half-century has seen not only the near universality of television but also the multiplication of services. More than half of households with television in Britain today have access to well over one hundred services, some licence-funded, others commercially (by advertising, subscription or sponsorship). This abundance is in itself less significant than the consequent fragmentation of the formerly national (or nationwide) television audience. Fragmentation has challenged the dominance of the familiar national broadcasters (BBC, ITV); it has created a more competitive marketplace for viewers; and it has introduced 'niche' channels for everything from news to pornography.

Perhaps even more significantly, abundance, competition and fragmentation have led to a general concern about the availability of news and current affairs programming. Steven Barnett and Emily Seymour have shown that there has not only been a change of emphasis in such programmes towards 'domestic, consumer and ratings-friendly subjects', but that this has been at the cost of 'more complex political and economic issues.'[7] With comparable concerns about 'dumbing-down' and 'tabloidisation' becoming commonplace, it is obvious that the genres which seem to have been adversely affected by these trends include precisely the kinds of programme in which Parliament and politics are likely to feature.

Those changes – with the occasional accusation of politically motivated reporting – invite the obvious conclusion that, in simple terms, the health of the democratic system is at risk. The market in communications and the availability of choice might encourage people to behave, so to speak, as consumers rather than citizens, choosing to disregard

Parliament, politics and policy. The fragility of the idea that the media will create 'an informed citizenry' is exposed. While media abundance means that those who do wish to engage with politics can sate themselves, those who do not have never been offered so many beguiling alternatives. Consumer and citizen may sometimes coincide, to witness 'the big stories'; but at other times their interests will diverge. Even when we do all become aware of such stories (during an election campaign, for example), our depth of knowledge will greatly vary.

The emergence of the internet since the 1990s (discussed further in the next chapter) has paradoxically exacerbated the problem. Although one can access Parliament and politics *via* the web more directly than ever before, the web may remain a method used mainly by a minority. Moreover, its very existence has provided a new excuse for the traditional mass media to curtail their detailed parliamentary coverage.

All these changes make it difficult to discuss the topic of 'Parliament and the media' as if it was composed of two homogeneous sets of institutions. On the one hand, we need to be conscious of the different interests represented in Parliament – party, constituency, government (and its advisers). On the other hand, we must not ignore the gulf that separates the dedicated TV channels and websites from the traditional, general-interest mass media of BBC and ITV and the national press, either tabloid or 'compact' (formerly broadsheet). What parliamentarians may want will very likely differ from what governments want; while the different media, for their part, will want varying types of news and amounts of 'serious' information.

Parliament, then, has to find ways of making the media see parliamentary affairs as more than a saga of conflict, splits and disagreements, underpinned by the odd soundbite, and to do so when the language of conflict is ingrained in journalistic custom. Even more exasperating for parliamentarians must be the journalistic suspicion and forensic dissection of motives, which characterise so much of their reporting. While politicians want the 'substance' of politics discussed, media prefer personalities and 'process'. Both preferences draw attention away from Westminster towards Whitehall and Downing Street. Media coverage of Parliament is thus partly conditioned by the way governments have sought to manage the flow and content of political news.

Media and government relations

Any government's media management necessarily pays due attention to Parliament, since so much of a government's programme surfaces there and is processed through it. Starting with the Thatcher decade, and partly in response to media developments, Downing Street news operations became both more high pressured and more high profile. Two names personified the changes and the issues: Bernard Ingham and Alastair Campbell. Both were the subject of biographies while in office, and they featured prominently in any account of the media and Parliament/government relationship of the period under review.[8]

Bernard Ingham, Margaret Thatcher's press secretary from 1979–1990, was the political ('lobby') journalist's *bete noir* in the 1980s. He was 'the source close to the Prime Minister' who skilfully used the lobby to do his mistress' bidding, to bully journalists, and to knife ministerial colleagues in a fashion that occasioned both admiration and hostility. The admiration came from his mistress and those who learnt to appreciate his skill at manipulating the press; the hostility, from newspapers which resented that skill, and from constitutionalists who accused him of behaving like a minister not a civil servant. Though only three newspapers withdrew from the routine daily lobby briefings in protest (and then only for a short while), this was indicative of the animosity building up in the media-government relationship.

Campbell – eventually styled Tony Blair's 'Director of Communications and Strategy' – took further in 1997–2004 the techniques which Ingham had developed. Overtly a partisan appointee, his closeness to Blair and his supervision of the Whitehall information machine in addition to the Number 10 press office, gave him unprecedented authority. This, and his combative style, meant that over the years he, rather than his master, too often became 'the story'. In addition, Blair permitted the appointment of partisan ministerial 'special advisers' in the Departments; and Downing Street acquired new units (notably a Strategic Communications Unit), to manage the government's public communications effort. All this amounted to a greater capacity than any previous government possessed, to try and control, both at large and in detail, the portrayal of the government's work.

There is nothing new in a government trying to be portrayed as (perhaps foolishly) it would wish. In the 1960s, Harold Wilson took more trouble than his post-1945 predecessors, within the media context of the times. As far back as the early 1950s, the Conservative party, with strong informal links to advertising and public relations, was alert to the potential of television. By Mrs Thatcher's time, professionals such as Harvey Thomas designed the annual party conference staging, and Gordon Reece coached the prime minister in voice technique.

Labour's commitment to techniques of public relations and political marketing reached a crucial stage in the mid-1980s. Key appointments, such as Peter Mandelson as the party's Director of Communications (1985) and the pollster Philip Gould as a consultant, helped reshape – and later rebrand – Labour as New Labour. The process can be seen as a party tuning itself to voters' wishes and – crucially – intent on fighting electoral battles on its own terms, not on terms set by a partisan press and entertainment-saturated TV. After the defeat of Neil Kinnock in the 1992 general election, the process continued, culminating in the electoral triumph of 1997.

Once in power, Blair's New Labour government was determined to keep the initiative (much helped by a weak Opposition). The greater the professionalism and the more robust the effort to control the news agenda, the greater was the antagonism of the media. This was ironic, in that Blair made several moves to open the channels of communication. Downing Street press secretaries no longer remained anonymous. Their twice-daily briefings to the lobby journalists were opened to others and reported on the internet. Blair himself began to hold regular monthly press conferences in 2002.

The result, nonetheless, was encapsulated in the media's hostility to 'spin' and 'spin doctors'. This exemplified a corrosive level of mistrust in government, which seeped out to politics more generally and was reflected in the low standing of politicians in opinion surveys. Such periods of animosity are not unprecedented: the Suez Crisis of 1956, for instance; Wilson's various rows with media in the 1960s and 1970s, and Thatcher's in her later years. Whether temporary or not, the hostility made the focus of media upon government and politics outside Westminster stronger than ever.

Parliament and the media: the future

Short run factors aside, that consideration of media relations with government, distinct from relations with Parliament more narrowly defined, simply reflects the fact that the government is drawn from Parliament, and that Parliament is but one of the forums in which ministers seek to reach the public. Media coverage has always been a mixture of both government and Parliament. Across the last century, under the impetus of two world wars and the welfare state, the role of government grew – and with it the media's interest. Tony Blair's personal contribution was to use techniques – new to a prime minister – which appeared to marginalise Parliament more than any prime minister before him. His monthly press conferences were admirable in principle: but they simply drew him away from the Chamber. They were a kind of alternative and less hazardous 'Prime Minister's Questions', with journalists taking the place of backbenchers and the Opposition. His appearances before the Liaison Committee (the Chairs of the Departmental Select Committees) were parliamentary occasions, but they were extremely rare (more or less annual) and were trivial as a method of accountability.

There is no structural reason why the balance of media attention between Downing Street and Westminster should continue to change in the one direction. In speculating about the future, the first point to make, therefore, is that media interest could shift back Parliament's way – certainly on a short-term scale. Tony Blair benefited from exceptional majorities. Less well endowed successors might have to court their majorities. Media interest in Parliament was much keener during the periods of wafer-thin majorities for Attlee in 1950–51, Wilson in 1964–66, Wilson/Callaghan in 1974–79 and Major in 1992–97.

A more difficult issue is the change in broader public attitudes to politics and parliamentarians. During the last decades of the twentieth century Parliament became demystified and MPs lost esteem. Many of the possible causes involved media, directly or indirectly. The common humanity of politicians was bared by the intrusion of television. John Major's term was marked by a barrage of stories about 'sleaze' – a mixture of financial and sexual indiscretions by politicians. These continued under Blair, but media aggression turned towards the excesses of 'spin'. Again, both the Major and Blair governments suffered unedifying exposure through public inquiries, too: Major, in the Scott inquiry into the sale of arms to Iraq (1996), and Blair in the Butler and Hutton inquiries into the events connected with the Iraq war of 2003 (both in 2004).

Although many such problems were strictly of government, not of Parliament, Parliament shared the consequences. In all of them, media were very active. They were good examples of the common phenomenon of a political crisis having a media subplot, wherein the role of media in provoking the crisis becomes part of the crisis itself. This loss of esteem could prove to be a short-term development, but it seems unlikely. The aggressiveness of media towards government has stronger roots. It is in part a result, probably, of the growth of media as a public policy field since the 1980s. News organisations are conscious, as never before, of the power of government to interfere with them.

The aggressiveness is probably linked, too, with the changing nature of parties and the party system. Newspaper readers are no longer committed to parties, as they were during the era of mass membership and distinct ideologies. Readers get most of their news from non-partisan broadcast media or the boot fairs of the internet. Editorially, and through their ownership, newspapers revert to traditional partisanship mainly during general election campaigns. Beyond that, they are (from the politicians' point of view) fickle: mistrust of the powerful is their guiding principle. None of this is likely to change. Indeed it is likely to be further entrenched, as print and electronic media melt into each other and newspapers lose clear editorial identity. The future of political opinion lies in the clamour of columnists, not in a single editorial voice.

Whichever way media develop, Parliament should continue to make itself as media-friendly as possible. Ideas such as those of the Modernisation Committee should be taken further. Let the Chancellor of the Exchequer see it as a matter of course, that he should deliver his Budget speech as a PowerPoint presentation. At the same time, however, we should recognise that parliamentarians carry out their roles in a far wider range of places than they used to, and that media are accessible to most of them. The Palace of Westminster itself now extends beyond its compact historic precinct. 'Media coverage of Parliament' now includes the buildings of Portcullis House, Norman Shaw and Millbank, and open air spaces in between (such as College Green). People routinely write of 'the Westminster village', a term which did not exist a few years ago. The best example of the changing link between purpose and place is the gloriously redundant Westminster Hall – glorious architecturally and redundant politically.

The point about these places is that the types of communication attractive to media vary between them.[9] The Chamber is general, populist, argumentative, talking largely in non-technical language, responding fairly quickly to topical issues, reflecting and helping to set the political agenda. The extreme case is Prime Minister's Questions, when to a significant extent the Members talk past the opposite benches to the outside world. To optimise media attention, therefore, the Chamber must talk the vernacular.

The most important contrast to the Chamber is the select committee system. Select committees have a different rhythm (different, too, from the twenty-four-hour news cycle of the press). They are subject to somewhat different rules of behaviour – in vocabulary and turn-taking, for instance. Such varied non-Members as civil servants, soldiers, academics, scientists and economists take part, each accustomed to their own codes of speech, dress and behaviour. Committees and the Chamber cannot and should not expect media coverage on the same basis as each other.

It is tempting to assume the parliamentary future lies more with committees than with the Chamber. But although the major national media – big papers and big TV channels – have woken up to the importance of committees, relative to the Chamber, they are becoming less interested, not more, in reporting the kind of specialised detail typical of committee work. We should therefore expect an increasingly *indirect* character in the coverage of Parliament. That is, not only is 'parliamentary business' decreasingly conducted in a single place, but its coverage will become less than ever the material of the old broadsheet 'parliamentary pages'. In the food chain of parliamentary news, stories will filter into general media – the daily press and broadcast bulletins – *via* specialist media, which have picked them up from the huge output of reports, evidence, debates and written answers emerging from the Chamber, Westminster Hall and the various flocks of committees. Already far more news than we realise, probably, originates in Parliament – but does not reach us directly as 'parliamentary news', rather than, say, in the financial or foreign pages.

One type of contributor to, and beneficiary of, the growth of select committees since the 1980s has been the pressure group. The rise of pressure groups went hand in hand with the decline of mass political parties, not least as engines of policy development. Just as newspapers had a symbiotic relationship with parties, when both types of organisation were growing in the late nineteenth century (papers often having organisational and ownership links with parties), so have papers and broadcasters fastened onto pressure groups in recent times. Obvious sources of media interest have included environmentalists, pro and anti European Union groups, gay and feminist groups, animal rights, health, education – a vast array of issues and activists which, up to half a century ago, sought advancement chiefly within the party system. Parliament concerns them to a varying degree; but, for some, select committee inquiries are one method of seeking publicity and political leverage.

Media interest in Parliament, in conclusion, is a product of Parliament's place both in a changing political world and a changing media world. Connections between these worlds have become progressively closer, as electronic media – at very much the same time as the Study of Parliament Group was founded – began to invade or usurp the principal political forums of the previous hundred years. Parliament has seen power trickle away from the Chamber: to its own committees, to deliberately devolved institutions in Scotland, Wales and Northern Ireland; to Brussels and the European Parliament; and to extra-parliamentary groups. All these are potential competitors with Parliament for media space, and they make less likely than ever a 'rounded view' of Parliament's work. How Parliament fares is only in part under its own control, as it competes also with the myriad sources of non-political news and entertainment. One factor influencing the outcome will be the 'new media', and to these the next chapter turns.

Notes

1 On those and comparable changes in media relations with Parliament, see for example Colin Seymour-Ure, *The British Press and Broadcasting*, Blackwell, 1996.
2 Simon Jenkins, quoted in the Committee on Standards in Public Life (Chair: Lord Nolan), *First Report*, vol. 2: *Transcripts of Oral Evidence*, Cm 2850-II), HMSO 1995, p. 7.
3 Select Committee on Modernisation of the House of Commons, First Report, HC 368 2003–04, *Connecting Parliament with the Public*, June 2004.
4 Richard Rose, *The Prime Minister in a Shrinking World*, Cambridge: Polity, 2001, p. 6, 24.
5 Bob Phillis (Chairman), *An Independent Review of Government Communications*, Cabinet Office, January 2004.
6 Roy Greenslade, 'National Newspaper Circulation', *Media Guardian*, 13 December 2004, p. 9.
7 Stephen Barnett and Emily Seymour, *A Shrinking Iceberg Travelling South ...: Changing Trends in British Television*, University of Westminster, 1999.
8 On Ingham, see Robert Harris, *Good and Faithful Servant*, Faber, 1991 and Bernard Ingham, *Kill the Messenger*, HarperCollins, 1991. On Campbell, see Peter Oborne, *Alastair Campbell: New Labour and the Rise of the Media Class*, Aurum Press, 1999. The rise of the Downing Street Press Office is traced in Colin Seymour-Ure, *Prime Ministers and the Media*, Blackwell, 2003.
9 Seymour-Ure, *Prime Ministers and the Media*, ch. 4.

21
New Media and Parliamentary Democracy

Stephen Coleman

Parliament inhabits the public imagination as much as the gothic citadel which is its physical embodiment. More than simply a physical place or a constitutional body, Parliament is an iconic symbol of democracy. We visit Parliament and bring to it affective and ritualistic expectations. We are visited by Parliament in our homes, *via* TV screens and websites, and through such mediation we witness a disembodied spectre of democratic theatre. Big Ben, as the emblematic image of parliamentary authority, is the most commonly purchased image by tourists to Britain.

The ways in which the images and messages of Parliament are mediated for public consumption play an important part in determining how Parliament is perceived and imagined. This chapter explores three images of Parliament: as an elitist club, speaking for but rarely with or even to the public; as a spectacle for mediated consumption *via* a range of media; and as an interactive space, not simply open to the public, but in an ongoing and meaningful conversation with the represented public. These three images might be categorised as past, present and future – but such rigid temporal distinctions should be adopted with caution, for in reality, even in its most elitist past Parliament had some interaction with the public (*via* petitions, for example) and even in the current age of televised Parliament, residual elitism constrains access to much of what goes on.

Parliament as an inaccessible club

Traditionally, Parliament was regarded as an exclusive space, not to be entered by or reported to the public. A tract of 1571 stated that 'every person of the Parliament ought to keep secret and not to disclose the secrets and things done and spoken in Parliament House to any other person, unless he be one of the same House, upon pain of being sequestered out of the House, or otherwise punished as by order of the House shall be appointed.' (*Order and Usage howe to keepe a Parliament,* 1571) Until the late nineteenth century it was illegal for visitors to write notes on parliamentary proceedings, so reporters had to rely upon heroic feats of memory. In 1884 a parliamentary press lobby was established. This comprised – and still does – a select group of approved journalistic scribes permitted access to the Members' lobby and other private parts of Parliament, in order to collect information about the background and implications of debates.

When broadcasting emerged, the general view of Parliament was that microphones and cameras would be an intrusion into a hallowed space. As early as 1923 John Reith, the Director General of the embryonic BBC, sought permission to broadcast the King's Speech at the State Opening of Parliament, but this was refused. In the same year Ben Tillett MP pressed the Prime Minister to agree to the broadcasting of parliamentary debates, but Bonar Law considered this to be 'undesirable'. In 1944 Leo Amery, the Secretary of State for India, tried to convince a committee of the War Cabinet that broadcasting the proceedings of Parliament would enhance its place in national life, but the committee concluded that 'the proceedings of Parliament were too technical to be understood by the ordinary listener who would be liable to get a quite false impression of the business transacted.'

In 1958 TV cameras were for the first time allowed in to the House of Lords, to record the State Opening of Parliament, and the following year the left-wing MP and former Minister, Aneurin Bevan, called for 'a serious investigation ... into the technical possibilities of televising parliamentary proceedings.' But it was not until 1975 that the House of Commons finally agreed to an experiment in public sound broadcasting. Initial assessments of the effect of letting the public hear the proceedings of their elected representatives were negative. William Price, the Government Minister who led the broadcasting negotiations on behalf of the Government, observed that 'We have on our hands a public relations disaster. We are in real danger of making a monumental laughing stock of ourselves. The great majority of listeners have been appalled at the noise – the bellowing, the abuse, the baying, the hee-hawing and the rest. People simply do not understand that the House of Commons is an excitable, emotional and noisy place.' Nonetheless, sound broadcasting of the Commons was made permanent in 1978.

In 1985 the House of Lords allowed TV cameras to enter for an experimental period. The following year this became a permanent arrangement. There has been television coverage of the Commons since 1989, at first giving rise to some optimism that if citizens could see Parliament in action they would come to understand and even like what went on there. One MP, Austin Mitchell, argued that 'Parliament is at last reaching the people, however imperfectly. As a result it can begin to move back to the centre of national interest. It belongs to the people. They must have access to it, even if they do not use that right obsessively.' A quarter of a century later, assumptions about the relationship between television coverage and public connection to Parliament are much more subdued. MPs complain that there is too little broadcast coverage of Parliament and what is broadcast tends to be either theatrical (such as the rowdiness of Prime Minister's Questions) or a backdrop for Government policy announcements. The public does not feel closer to Parliament as a result of seeing it in action. If anything, surveys suggest that people who watch Parliament on television trust it less than those who do not; the same finding applies to C-Span viewers of Congress in the USA.[1]

Parliament as a mediated spectacle

As the nineteenth-century commentator Walter Bagehot observed, people are most likely to be deferential to power when it is inaccessible. As Parliament has become a mediated spectacle, shown rarely in its entirety, but more often in ten-second snippets on news bulletins and occasional live coverage of dramatic and atypical high-profile debates, the public has come to see it in a distorted form. MPs are concerned that the media spectacle of Parliament represents 'sensational highlights' (Roger Gale MP) and that 'they see the main confrontational aspects of Parliament rather than the day to day hard work of MPs' (David Lepper MP).[2]

Since cameras first entered the Commons coverage has declined, while the flow of MPs rushing towards the parliamentary broadcasting studios at 4 Millbank has increased. The locus of communicative power has shifted from the confined and rule-bound setting of the Commons chamber, where a speech might be heard by a few dozen colleagues, to the ambience of College Green or the BBC Westminster studio, with their promise of mass audiences.

Those who watch parliamentary coverage on television are, in general, older rather than younger, male rather than female, and broadsheet more than tabloid newspaper readers. When asked, the public says that Parliament should be available to watch on television, but few actually choose to do so and nearly half say that much of what is said in Parliament is difficult for them to understand.[3] In a non-deferential age, where procedural pomp and automatic respect have a declining place, many people regard Parliament, as seen on TV, as rather archaic, exclusive and irrelevant. As Peter Hain MP, the Leader of the House of Commons, has argued, 'The public, and particularly young people, now have less faith than ever in parliamentary democracy. We (politicians and media) who constitute the 'political class' conduct politics in a way that turns off our voters, readers, listeners and viewers ... And so the task for Parliament is to connect. Too many people believe that government is something that is done to them. Westminster must stop giving the impression of being a private club and instead give the public a greater sense of ownership'.[4]

The failure of the public to engage with the mediated spectacle of parliamentary theatre has given rise to a modernising agenda, the aim of which is to bring Parliament up to date. But what exactly does that mean? For some, the problem is procedural and cultural: Parliament goes about deliberation in a way that is alien to people who have grown up in an age of televisual discourse. In oral evidence to the House of Commons Modernisation Committee, Peter Riddell of *The Times* argued that 'People are not used to hearing long speeches any longer.... You yourselves do not sit and listen to seven hour debates .... It is...a format for discussion which is just weird for people, getting up and making long speeches. That is not how people naturally behave'.[5] It is this sense of cultural discordance between parliamentary and popular speech that is illuminated and accentuated by television coverage.

In an attempt to save political coverage from irredeemable unpopularity, Greg Dyke, the former Director General of the BBC, initiated a review in 2002, intended to find new ways of making political news and debate accessible to the disengaged public. In evidence to the House of Commons Media, Culture and Sport Select Committee in July 2002, Dyke stated that the BBC was seeking 'a way of bringing in different, younger people, people disenchanted with politics, without, crucially, alienating the by and large traditional, which tends to be over 50, audience because they are our heartland. We cannot afford to alienate or lose them so we have to keep our traditional programming to keep them, or a large chunk, while at the same time trying to change the programming to attract a younger audience.'

Inhabitants of 'the Westminster bubble' regard such efforts as inevitably undermining – or 'dumbing down' – the BBC's commitment to serious political coverage and analysis. In his 2004 MacTaggart Lecture at the Edinburgh Television Festival, John Humphrys rejected the notion that broadcasters have a responsibility to make politics more accessible: '… it's not our job to make it fun. It's a serious business and it's our job to report it seriously. We shouldn't be trying to lure people into politics by pretending that it's just another game show.'

Caught in an inelegant battle of rhetorical misrepresentations between the complacency of the Millbank elite and the alleged treachery of populists seeking to converge *Newsnight* and *Big Brother*, televised coverage of Parliament continues to recede into the late-night schedules, alongside French films and Open University re-runs.

Parliament as an interactive space

It is argued that new media, such as the internet and other digital information and communication technologies (ICT) could potentially take Parliament into a 'third media age' (print and broadcasting being the first and second) and support a new model of democratic governance based upon a more collaborative and dialogical relationship between parliamentarians and citizens.

First, the internet transcends some of the problems of distance. Distance is the historically intractable problem of all democracies: not just geographical distance, but also temporal distance – the problem of people in different time zones unable to speak to each other at the same time. The traditional justification for a representative democracy is that government and governed are inevitably separated by distances of space, time, cognition and attention. The internet, in allowing for communication based upon asynchronous co-presence, has the capacity to transcend at least some of those barriers. For example, instead of constituents having to visit physical surgeries, which for many is both inconvenient and intimidating, there can be private consultations *via* online surgeries; instead of parliamentary committees having to meet in one place, with witnesses travelling in to give their evidence, there is scope for taking evidence *via* video or instant messaging. Face-to-face communication is of course often superior and sometimes necessary. But virtual communication helps to dispel the image of Parliament and politicians always being 'out there', replacing it with one in which representatives are seen as always present and accessible, like supermarkets or the health service. It is a shift which changes radically the role that people will demand from politicians – and this calls for adaptations in parliamentary working structures and practices, as it has done in most modern businesses and public services.

The second key characteristic of the internet is the movement from bounded place to networks. We are, as Manuel Castells well described it, now living in a 'networked society' where the physical locations of our birth, our home and our work are less important than intangible connections, both global and local, between us and those who are connected to us through networks of communication, information, and trade. Increasingly, it is possible to opt into one network and out of another. The notion that one has a bounded place in life and that citizens should be represented within bounded spaces called constituencies is becoming an obsolete notion. This will have a profound effect on the future of elections and the future of political representation.

Thirdly, we are seeing a shift from transmission-based media to interactive media. Throughout the twentieth century mass communication media were in the business of message dissemination. Message receivers lacked opportunities to respond to message producers; in Professor Neil Postman's evocative phrase, this produced a 'one-way conversation.' The inherent feedback paths within digital media facilitate – and almost require – a two-way conversation. It is no longer feasible for politicians to send emails to their constituents without expecting emails to come back in return; a political party cannot put up a website with information without inviting visitors to comment on what is said. Interactive feedback provides a basis for democratic accountability. New media accountability draws upon rich, experiential and autonomous narratives which make political institutions accessible to the accounts of the represented.

The fourth characteristic of the internet is the least tangible. We might call it the transition from 'spectacle' to 'play'. Debord's critique of a political world in which people were being left increasingly as spectators upon their own lives, looking on, booing, cheering, shouting and hissing, and then walking away at the end of the show, is a fundamental challenge to the democratic claims of parliamentary democracies. With the emergence of media that people can use themselves – camcorders, videos, blogs – there has been a tendency towards the democratisation of public communication, with news stories emanating from the grass roots as well as the professional centre. With the internet, there is a sense in which everyone can now be a broadcaster and to some extent at least part of the ongoing performance of political life. Media organisations are increasingly interested in finding ways of bringing 'real' people into the political discussion, so widening the sphere of deliberation beyond the insulated portals of Parliament.

How has Parliament responded to these opportunities and challenges? In the classical antiquity of the internet (1994), Parliament's Information Committee published a report comparing its use of ICT with other parliaments and concluded that of eighteen European assemblies examined only Turkey had no parliamentary data network and only Denmark, Finland, Spain and the German *Bundesrat* had no live feed to members of parliamentary proceedings. The UK Parliament had neither a data network nor a live feed to members; it had no parliamentary funding for the purchase of IT equipment and no technical or training support offered by the parliamentary staff. The 1994 report recommended the establishment of a Parliamentary Data and Video Network (PDVN) which would have the benefits of providing MPs with direct access at any time to Library and other information services; allowing for the rapid transfer of information between MPs and their staff, and between Westminster and the MPs' constituencies; enabling MPs more adequately to oversee the actions of the Executive. The introduction of the PDVN has played a major role in increasing the access of MPs to information which was previously either centralised in Government Departments or the Commons Library, or spread physically between their parliamentary and constituency offices. The system gave MPs an impetus to go online and by 1998 96% of MPs reported using some form of ICT, with 70% connected to the PDVN.

The three main uses of IT systems by MPs are email between themselves, their staff and their constituents; access to the PDVN for information that they would previously have had to seek from a librarian; and access to Government Department websites and intranets.

For all of the benefits of MPs' adoption of ICT, these are arguably being used mainly to perpetuate existing power structures. PDVN is available to MPs, not those they represent, thus widening the gulf between the knowledge of professional politicians and the less informed position of outsiders.

The most important way in which the internet has been used to make parliamentary information more accessible to the public has been the creation of Parliament's website in 1996. In 2005 the site was still not particularly user-friendly and certainly not interactive: there was no scope for members of the public to register or discuss ideas. Compared to the website of any similarly sized company, www.parliament.uk gave a distinct impression of wishing to keep its users at arm's length.

The benefits of Parliament using ICT to communicate with their constituents are manifest: they help to create a more intelligently informed electorate which has an opportunity not simply to vote and speculate about the work of their representatives, but to vote on the basis of knowledge and to examine the record of their chosen representative or party for themselves. This publicity provides Parliament with much-needed legitimacy, in an age when credibility is increasingly associated with transparency. But for many MPs, the problem of coping with a growing flow of emails from their constituents results in their regarding ICT as a problem rather than a solution. MPs interviewed by Coleman and Spiller (2004) expressed concerns that:

- Email means you get contacted by people who otherwise would not bother.
- Not only does email make it easier to communicate, but it also creates higher expectations:
- People expect an email response – some even demand it.

The use of ICT by British MPs remains uneven. Coleman and Spiller's 2002 survey found that constituent correspondence was still overwhelmingly paper-based, with only 2% of MPs regularly conducting more than half their correspondence with constituents *via* email, one in six (16%) not using email at all, and the vast majority (72%) conducting less then a quarter of correspondence *via* email. Only one in twenty MPs reported receiving more than 50 emails per week and nearly three-quarters (73%) receive fewer than 25 emails per week. Two-thirds (67%) of MPs had a website. The later an MP entered Parliament the more likely they were to have a website. MPs entering Parliament after 1990 were 12% more likely to have their own website than those who entered since 1980 and 22% more likely than those who entered before 1980.[6] These trends can be expected to continue after the 2005 general election.

A more innovative and promising use of ICT by Parliament is in running online consultations. The first experiments in using the internet to facilitate public input to the UK Parliament began in 1998. Between then and 2002 ten online consultations were run by or on behalf of Parliament on a range of themes including domestic violence, family tax credits and stem-cell research. Instead of simply creating a web forum and inviting the public to have its say, rather like an online phone-in programme, these consultations were designed to recruit participants with experience or expertise in relation to specific policy issues. The objectives of these online consultations were to gather informed evidence from the public to help parliamentarians understand policy issues; recruit citizens whose evidence might be unheard or neglected in the usual course of parliamentary evidence-taking; enable participants to interact and learn from one another over an extended period of asynchronous discussion; enable participants to raise aspects of policies under discussion that might not otherwise have been considered; enable legislators to participate in the online discussion, raising questions and responding to citizens' comments, as time permits; and derive a fair, independent summary of views raised which can constitute official evidence to Parliament.

To take one example, the All-Party Domestic Violence Group commissioned the Hansard Society to run an online consultation with survivors of domestic violence. This was conducted in March 2000. Fifty-two per cent of participants had no knowledge of using the internet before they took part. Most of the participants were able to go online using computers in refuges. This had several advantages: the personal and often distressing stories they had to tell could be recounted in friendly and familiar surroundings; there were trained workers to help them if they needed personal support during or after posting their messages; IT help was close at hand – 60% of the women reported needing help in getting to the consultation website, and most of the time that was provided by refuge workers.

The online forum recorded an average of 1,574 hits per day. On average, 78 users visited the forum each weekday and 111 at weekends. Seventy-three per cent of the participants visited the site at least six times; 18% visited at least ten times. The average visitor session lasted 16 minutes and 31 seconds. One hundred and ninety-nine women registered and participated online, submitting 960 messages between them. Eighty-two per cent of messages to Womenspeak responded in some way to a previous message in the forum. Thirty-one messages (3.2% of all) were contributed by six MPs. Participants came from throughout England and Wales, with a demographically typical spread of ages and ethnic backgrounds. 10% of participants described themselves as being disabled; 6% were registered disabled. Fifty-eight per cent of the participants in the consultation had never been in contact with an MP before and 96% were not members of political parties. The majority of participants (77%) lived outside of London, so the internet effectively brought Parliament to them.

In a post-consultation survey a majority of participants (60%) reported that the consultation helped them to deal with their experiences of domestic violence. As a result of networking online, some participants made contacts with one another in the offline world. In the post-consultation survey, 24% of participants reported making new contacts and 92% reported learning something new as a result of reading other participants' messages. 68% of participants stated that they did not consider that the MPs who took part were interested in what they had to say and almost four out of ten (39%) were not satisfied with the contributions from MPs. Nonetheless, perhaps surprisingly, 94% of participants considered that the online consultation was a worthwhile exercise and 93% said that they would like to take part in future online consultations of this kind.

Following the relative success of these online consultations, the House of Commons Select Committee on Information produced a comprehensive report entitled *Digital Technology: Working for Parliament and the Public.*[7] Their recommendations amounted to a set of basic principles for the conduct of future online consultations. Everyone involved – consulters and consultees – should be clear at the outset about the purpose and terms of the consultation. Efforts should be made to recruit participating individuals and organisations with relevant experience, and to be socially inclusive, providing internet access and skills where necessary. Consultations should be interpreted or summarised independently, and participants should get feedback about any outcomes. Both consulters and consultees should expect to benefit from the experience, which should be systematically evaluated, but participants should understand that they were being asked to inform the thinking of legislators, not to make policy themselves.

In a similar vein the House of Commons Modernisation Committee commented, two years later, that 'there have now been several experiments with online consultation on an ad hoc basis, both by select committees and by all-party groups. They have generally been successful and have proved effective as a way of engaging members of the public in the work that we do and of giving a voice to those who would otherwise be excluded. We urge select committees and joint committees considering draft legislation to make online consultation a more regular aspect of their work'.[8]

Representation as conversation

According to the 2003 Oxford Internet Survey, most British people (61%) say that they frequently (22%) or every so often (39%) discuss politics with friends or family. But very few of them ever discuss politics with the people they elect to represent their interests and preferences. Most people (88%) have had no face-to-face contact with their MP within the past year. Three-quarters claim that within the past year they have never seen their MP on television, 80% that they have not written to their MP and 84% not to have visited their MP's website. There is a radical cultural disconnection between the ways politicians think, act and express themselves and the norms of everyday sociability.

This estrangement is manifested in a range of attitudes which underlie the contemporary crisis of public disengagement from official political institutions and processes. Whereas most people (79%) trust their local hospital, only a minority trust their local council (48%), the British Government (43%) or politicians (18%). Only 16% of the public trust political parties; 98.5% of British citizens are not party members and 14% express support for any party (compared with 44% in 1964.) Seventy-six per cent of the public believe that they have little or no power between elections and 66% agree that 'people like me have no say in what the government does.' In a 1999 survey by the US Council for Excellence in Government, almost two thirds (64%) of Americans agreed with the statement, 'I feel distant and disconnected from government'. Seventy-two per cent of the British public feel 'disconnected' from Parliament, with nearly half (46%) feeling 'very disconnected.' Over half of 35–44 year-olds (52%) and nearly half of 45–64 year-olds felt 'very disconnected' from Parliament. The vast majority (80%) of people who did not vote in the 2001 general election felt disconnected from Parliament.

Feelings of disconnection and political disengagement are intimately linked and will not be addressed by urging disconnected citizens to engage more dutifully. The task of democracy is to create connections which are authentic, meaningful and consequential. New media can play a crucial role in creating such connections, but technology alone produces no outcomes; the challenge is cultural and, as ever, Parliament must adapt.

Notes

1   Stephen Frantzich and John Sullivan, *The C-Span Revolution*, University of Oklahoma Press, 1996, pp. 249–51.
2   Quoted in Stephen Coleman, *Electronic Media, Parliament and the People*, Hansard Society, 1999.
3   *Ibid.*
4   Peter Hain, speech to the Parliamentary Press Gallery, 16 September 2003.
5   In Jean Seaton (ed.), *Politics and the Media: Harlots and Prerogatives at the Turn of the Millennium*, Blackwell, 1998, p. 17.

6 Stephen Coleman and Josephine Spiller, 'Exploring New media Effects on Representative Democracy', *Journal of Legislative Studies*, 11, January 2005.
7 House of Commons Information Committee, First Report, HC 1065, 2001–02: *Digital Technology: Working for Parliament and the Public*, HMSO, 2002.
8 Select Committee on Modernisation of the House of Commons, First Report, HC 368, 2003–04: *Connecting Parliament with the Public*, HMSO, 2004, para. 59.

Part VIII
Conclusion

22
Purpose and Prospects

Philip Giddings

There is no doubt that Parliament has changed substantially since the SPG was founded in 1964. Its composition, cultures and procedures are now very different from the portrait sketched by Michael Ryle in the opening chapter of this book. Nevertheless, much remains the same. The ambitions of reformers have not been fully realised, even if many of their particular proposals have been adopted. Anxiety about Parliament's relative powerlessness – that it has been increasingly marginalised by Government and ignored by the media – remains. Some of these anxieties reflect a failure, as some see it, to understand that Parliament is not about power, but influence. Thus Michael Ryle argues that Parliament's role lies not in taking and implementing decisions (that is the task of Her Majesty's Government) but in providing the public forum for debate between Government and people about how Government carries out its task.[1] It is in that critical forum, through dialogue and debate, that Parliament is able to exercise influence. But even from that perspective critical questions arise: how effective is Parliament's influence? is Government's response to criticism and dialogue adequate – and what can be done if it isn't? The critics' anxiety is that a government with a cohesive and disciplined majority has no incentive to respond positively – and that is why more progress has not been made to 'reform' Parliament. That view illustrates the central problem for debate when considering the future of Parliament: the role of party and party managers.

For the more ambitious reformers, the iron grip of the party managers, disguised as the 'usual channels', has continued to prevent any significant shift in the balance between legislature and executive. It would thus be easy to be gloomy about the prospects for Parliament, as we contemplate the future. But that prognosis itself is not new.

Parliament has been written off as an irrelevance before – not least in the period of the SPG's foundation. Yet in the four decades since then it has cautiously adapted to changing political and governmental realities, and on occasion (re-)discovered that it can indeed be the fulcrum of the British body politic. An attempt to sketch the prospects for an institution such as the Westminster Parliament therefore requires a balance between the reformists' optimism and the sceptics' gloom. It means analysing carefully what the institution actually is and how in its various modes it might develop.

One institution or several?

Too often the term 'Parliament' is used as a synonym for 'House of Commons'. But the Westminster Parliament consists of two chambers. Quite a lot of what is said of one chamber cannot be said of the other. That is obviously true about both composition and powers. That alone should make us circumspect in making judgements about Parliament as one institution. Even more important, however, are two other dualities, which divide both chambers and are built into the very fabric of the place, physically and culturally – the first between government and opposition, and the second between front-bench and back-bench.

To put the divisions in those terms is, of course, to overstate them. But a degree of overstatement helps to counter the implicit tendency of so much discussion to treat 'Parliament' as if it truly were a single, coherent institution. Rather, its complex, competitive and multi-layered nature must be fully taken into account in any credible analysis of its mode of operation, present or future. This complexity can easily be seen, for instance, when procedural changes are considered in the House of Commons. The interests of front and backbenchers, government and opposition, are frequently in conflict. Government backbenchers in particular have to wrestle with these tensions, such as between loyalty to their party and an interest in enhancing 'parliamentary scrutiny', or between commitment to seeing their party's legislative programme rapidly enacted and a desire to improve the quality of legislation by subjecting it to careful examination and amendment.

The key factor so often is party. Party loyalty is the glue which holds government front and backbenchers together – and yet it is also the separator dividing the majority party from the minority parties (including the cross-bench group in the Lords). 'Victory' for the Government is also victory for the majority party; conversely, a 'victory' for the

Opposition is a defeat for the governing party, as is only too apparent in the stately dances which are Lords' debates. In the Commons, when questions of confidence in Her Majesty's Government arise, the party stakes are very high indeed – indeed they could be no higher. Whether confidence need be engaged so frequently and so routinely is a crucial question for those wishing to loosen the grip of party managers. Whilst the majority party has such a tight grip, does it make sense to speak of 'Parliament' acting as a single, corporate institution? When we consider the effectiveness of the legislative process or of mechanisms for scrutiny and accountability, it makes more sense to look behind the term 'Parliament' or 'parliamentary' to their constituent (and sometimes competing) elements: governing and opposition parties; front and backbenches; the two chambers and their various types of committees. For in legislation and scrutiny 'Parliament' cannot be assumed to act as a cohesive entity.

The key roles

In this tele-visual age most people probably think of 'Parliament' as a place – the palace of Westminster – rather than as the institution located there; a place, moreover, with strong historical resonances but no great relevance to the average person, except perhaps as a tourist attraction. Yet the institution remains one of the focal points of the British system of government and politics. The essays in this volume illustrate the extent to which the institution performs more than one role. The United Kingdom's 'sovereign Parliament' is at the same time a representative assembly, a legislature, and a scrutineer of government and administration. As British constitutional doctrine has evolved over the last two centuries, each of those roles has acquired mythic status. As often as not, these myths obscure the reality of what Parliament does, not least because competing versions are held by different people. For instance in the debates about Britain and the European Union and about the role of the courts, the myth of parliamentary sovereignty plays a central but deeply confusing role (as earlier chapters have shown). In the controversies about the Commons committee systems and about reform of the House of Lords, competing understandings of Parliament's representative and legislative roles play a key part. If we wish to be clear about Parliament's future, it is therefore important that we tease out the implications of the fact that in each of these key roles, insofar as they continue, the Westminster Parliament no longer has a monopoly.

Competition in three key roles

A representative assembly

Historically, well before the rise of liberal democracy, Parliament was viewed as a representative assembly and its membership was selected for that purpose. Subsequently, democratic election replaced selection and patronage as the principal mode of recruitment of parliamentarians. The House of Commons, as the directly elected chamber, eventually became overwhelmingly dominant, so the practical function of representing the interests and peoples of the communities in the United Kingdom became overlain with the liberal democratic doctrine of representative government. The House of Commons was representative because it was the product of universal suffrage, the secret ballot, a competitive party system and a free press. Those were the processes which liberal democracy required, and by the end of the nineteenth century they were fully in place for men, though not until 1929 for women.

If democracy and representation were simply matters of constitutional provision, little more would need to be said. But, important as constitutional provisions are, representative democracy requires more. The deeply symbolic act of voting is vital, but it is only a beginning – a necessary but, as many a state emerging from authoritarian rule has discovered, not a sufficient condition. The debate about electoral systems makes the point very clearly. What is being transacted: approval of parties, policies, persons? unequivocal or conditional consent to the outcome? representation of communities, organised interests (social, economic, political)?, geographical areas, or political parties? Similar issues arise from the debate about the composition of Parliament: to what extent should it reflect the social composition of society? is it necessary to ensure that all voices in the community (more accurately, for a pluralist society, in its communities) can play their part in the formation of public policy?

Representation implies an intermediate role for parliamentarians, speaking on behalf of the people, parties and interests they represent. With the explosion of communications technology in the last twenty years the need for intermediaries is less compelling. Individual citizens, and especially groups, can speak directly for themselves through the internet and email, not to mention the many additional forms of broadcast and print media. As chapters 20 and 21 show, Westminster has been slow to adapt to this challenge. Moreover, in the age of subsidiarity, people may prefer to speak at and/or be represented in more local forums, including the devolved assemblies which, as Barry Winetrobe shows in chapter 18, are perceived to be more accessible to their citizens than Westminster. For the larger issues, it is likely to be the European Union, the World Trade Organisation, the G8 or the United Nations, to which citizens and groups want to address themselves – not to the Parliament of a medium-sized nation state. In short, Westminster is far from having a monopoly in representation. It has to compete, and that means making its processes and personnel far more accessible to the general public, as well as to the many specialist publics who want to influence the making and implementation of public policy.

During the years of the SPG's existence interest (or pressure) groups have seen significant growth in number and diversity. In most areas of public policy they have supplanted the political parties – in expertise, resources and the exercise of leverage over Whitehall. Many groups have membership numbers which dwarf those of the parties. A few, notably concerned with Europe, defence policy and the environment, have put up candidates in general elections. Parties continue to have hugely important roles in providing candidates for elections, campaigning and selecting leaders. But in articulating public views and contributing to the formation of public policy formation, as parties have weakened, so interest groups have thrived.

Parliament as legitimator

In the British system of government, Parliament is the Great Legitimator. It legitimates Her Majesty's Government, which is constitutionally required to retain the confidence of the House of Commons. Without that support a government would find it impossible to govern. Parliament legitimates legislation, brought before it mostly by Government for endorsement in primary or secondary form. It legitimates the policies and programmes which the Government presents for approval, especially those in spheres of activity (defence, foreign affairs – see chapter 17) in which legislation plays only a minor part. It legitimates the Government's proposals for taxation and expenditure. A Government with a substantial majority can normally take the Commons' endorsements for granted – but note the occasional exceptions which make the difference between 'normally' and 'always'. The House of Lords, however, is less biddable, unless the Government is willing and able successfully to invoke the provisions of the Parliament Act. Endorsement by the public's representatives conveys not only legal authority but also constitutional legitimacy.

Parliament's monopoly here has been the corner-stone of the doc-trine of parliamentary supremacy, and particularly of the primacy of the House of Commons as the elected chamber. But the question has to be faced, how long that position can be sustained in the light of the challenges to Westminster's representativeness and of the appar-ent disconnection of substantial sections of the public from parlia-mentary and party politics. Government itself increasingly uses extra-parliamentary means of consultation on policy issues and legis-lation. Opinion polling and, on some of the most contentious issues, referendums are alternative means of establishing what public opinion is. The television studio, radio phone-in, the website and the chat-room are considered by many to be more effective forums than Parliament for debating issues and representing the public's views. The alacrity with which Government ministers and the spokesmen of political parties accept invitations from these alternative forums indicates how low confidence in Westminster has fallen – except, perhaps, when, as with the Iraq War [see Chapter 17], the public per-ceives that the tight grip of the party machines on the Westminster process is slipping and that there is a real prospect of genuine debate and an unpredictable outcome.

Parliament as the inquest of the nation

In response to continuing poor confidence ratings in opinion polls for politicians generally, it has been pointed out that people give a much higher rating to their local MP individually. This is said to be related, in part, to the constituency member's grievance-redressing role, and it is supported by evidence of a substantial increase in MPs' post-bags, electronic and physical. It used to be argued that this was part of Parliament's role as the 'inquest of the nation', recalling in particular the Commons' insistence, in its tussles with Tudor and Stuart mon-archs, on 'redress of grievances before grant of supply' and, in con-temporary understanding of liberal democracy, on the importance of accountability of government to the governed.

However, the weakness of that linkage in the democratic chain was evident before the Study of Parliament Group was founded. It was given clear expression in the commitment of the Wilson Government elected in 1964 to setting up a Parliamentary Ombudsman scheme to supplement the work of MPs in dealing with constituents' complaints about maladministration. The subsequent widening and extension of the Ombudsman scheme across the public sector (see Chapter 6), and the development of complaints adjudicator schemes under the Major

Government's Citizen's Charter programme, underline the usefulness of these supplementary forms of grievance redressing mechanism. When the Government legislates to allow complainants direct access to the Ombudsman, rather than requiring them to route their cases through an MP, 'supplementary' will become 'alternative', though the strong link between the Ombudsman Office and Parliament will remain.[2]

Parallel to the expansion of Ombudsman schemes has been the development of judicial review, particularly following the amendment of the Supreme Court Rules (Order 53) in 1977[3] and the passage of the Supreme Court Act 1981, Section 31 of which regulates the process by which application for review can be made. The March 2000 edition of *Judge over Your Shoulder*, the Treasury Solicitor's guide to judicial review for government administrators, reported that between 1974 and 1998 the number of applications in England and Wales increased from 160 to 4,539.[4] This procedure is a powerful and effective means of seeking a remedy for the improper use of power by the government and its agents. The drawback is that in most circumstances it is available only to the very rich, who can afford to pay the legal costs themselves, or to those poor enough to qualify for legal aid. Since the passage of the Human Rights Act its potential ambit of application has considerably widened, although there has not been the flood of cases which some had anticipated.[5] The Court has available a full range of remedies in successful cases, including the power to quash or prohibit ministerial action, to issue injunctions or to grant damages. That is an armoury rather more formidable than a Select Committee or an MP asking a Parliamentary Question, but it can be deployed in far fewer instances, and only when alternative avenues have been exhausted. Nevertheless, the point remains that the judicial review procedure is a powerful and effective means of achieving redress, which cannot always be said of parliamentary action.

In addition to Ombudsman schemes and judicial review, Parliament faces another strong competitor in the business of dealing with citizens' grievances – the media. Television and radio 'consumer action' programmes, and similar columns and features in the print media, are often the first alternative to occur to the citizen frustrated by officialdom. Publicity is a powerful weapon – the mobilisation of shame, as the former Netherlands Ombudsman Marten Oosting called it. Some would say that for many citizens access to the media is a good deal easier than contacting their MP, the Ombudsman office or a law firm, to apply for judicial review. The increased resources now available to MPs for their constituency work have made it possible for many of them to improve their availability to their constituents. As mentioned earlier, so has email. But not all MPs welcome the increase in constituency welfare work which has resulted, even if it is one way in which Parliament directly connects with citizens.

Prospects for change

As the Study of Parliament Group's work over the last forty years has clearly shown, there has been no shortage of proposals for 'reform' or 'modernisation' or simply for incremental change to how Parliament in its various guises actually operates. There is no lack of inventiveness among the parliamentary community and outside commentators. What, then, inhibits the changes needed to re-connect our parliamentary institutions with the community? The problem is not that Parliament does not possess the necessary powers or procedures. It is a problem, rather, of culture: of the need to have the right people, with the right mindset and the appropriate resources. Changing the culture of an organisation, and *a fortiori* of a society, is very difficult. It is especially difficult when those who control the levers of power – in this case, party managers – perceive a change in culture to be a threat to their power, so that they will not therefore let go. The principal threat to a thriving parliamentary democracy in Britain is the tenacious grip of the party managers at Westminster.

People

If we look at those three requirements – the right people, with the right mindset and the appropriate resources – we can see how critical the parties are to the revival of Parliament, notwithstanding their decline relative to interest groups. Their 'recruitment' role goes far wider than the leadership cadre. Parties are the principal recruiting mechanism to almost the entire British political process: they choose and resource the candidates, seek to mobilise the voters, 'manage' the careers of those who are selected and, if successful at the ballot, elected. If a wider spectrum of British society is to be recruited into Parliament, so as to re-establish its connection with the majority of the people, then it is the parties who will have to adapt their behaviour to that purpose. What incentive is there for the parties to do this? It is perhaps one word – survival. Without that widening, the British political class will be built upon an increasingly narrow base, in competition with sectional and single-issue cause groups, until it finally loses contact altogether with the people it purports to govern and whose interests it should serve.

It should be admitted that there are *some* signs of a willingness to address the connectedness issue in the matters of gender and ethnicity. However, as the material in chapters 3, 4 and 5 shows, there is a *very* long way to go even with such obvious priorities. The deeper problem of preventing the professionalisation of politics from cutting off the people from their 'representatives' has yet to be grasped. An opportunity presents itself with the need to decide the future composition of the House of Lords. Regrettably, the Government is more concerned to prevent the House from gaining additional influence and thereby threatening to delay the passage of its legislation, than it is in improving the quality of legislation or addressing Parliament's democratic deficit. The one very clear message which came out of the consultations and evidence-gathering carried out by the Wakeham Commission was that the public did not want the second chamber of the British Parliament to be dominated by the political parties which control the House of Commons. The blockage to reform is that those who control those parties also control the process of House of Lords reform.

Mindset

How can the keys of party control be unlocked? This is the 'mindset' question, and it has two aspects. The first is how MPs perceive their basic role. Are they there to represent their constituents, or to further the party's programme (or, more sharply, the programme of its current leadership)? These are not inherently incompatible aims. Some, perhaps many, constituents may want their MP loyally to support the party in every aspect. On other hand, some, perhaps many, constituents may want party loyalty to give way to constituency interest, where these two conflict. Some constituents, further, may want a Member who will sometimes place his personal convictions above the claims of party, particularly if those claims are seen as a route to career advancement. Most constituents are not attracted by the (exaggerated) image of MPs as party hacks, dancing at the end of the whips' puppet strings. But most MPs are aware that they owe their election not to their own personal convictions, nor to their identification with the interests of the constituency, but to the fact that they are the candidate of their political party. They know, or think they know, that their prospects of achieving any political objectives at Westminster are more likely to be enhanced by maintaining good relations with their whips (that is, doing their bidding) than by rebelling against them. That is not an easy mindset to break.

The second aspect of the mindset question concerns the extent of the reach of party loyalty. This aspect surfaces from time to time, when MPs are debating so-called 'House of Commons matters', in which the Executive, and by implication party managers, should not interfere – for example, in the choice of the Speaker or membership of select committees. There is a strong element of fiction in this, since no Government which wants to ensure the passage of its business can ignore decisions which might affect its ability to achieve that objective. But the ability of MPs to change, chameleon-like, from party champion to consensus-politician when they transfer from the chamber to the (select) committee room, indicates that MPs can see that different mindsets are appropriate in different contexts. The rationale for the whipping system is ultimately to maximise the party's vote so as to keep the Government in office. Delivery of the main element of the party's programme will undoubtedly be central to that objective. But surely not every detail need be – as quickly becomes apparent when a minority government is in office and announces that it will only construe certain votes as votes of confidence.

The prevailing Westminster mindset is that *any* refusal to follow the party line is rebellion – and rebellion, with its concomitant 'discipline', prejudices a successful career. Yet there are rebellions and rebellions. The whips can terrorise the few, but must bend to the many. Indeed, a key part of their role is to inform Ministers and Shadow Ministers of the state of opinion in the parliamentary party, and particularly to give warning when the leadership's stance on a question cannot be sold. The change of mindset required here is that backbench MPs have to be prepared more often to stand their ground in response to pressure from the whips. In that way they can ensure that party leaderships and Governments become more responsive to opinions other than their own. As Philip Norton has shown, there has been a significant increase in dissent and rebellion in the last thirty years.[6] If enough backbenchers do that, then the iron grip of the party manager is broken. The key judgement is to be able to decide on those questions where a cohesive party line is essential, and those where it is not. Too often party managers play too safe.

The desire for a new style of politics was a notable feature of the campaign for devolution in Scotland, and it was widely believed that a changed electoral system and the consequential need for coalition would facilitate a new style. The degree to which such a style actually has evolved in Scotland and Wales is still an open question – and one which can be asked of Westminster also. One part of the dissatisfaction with 'the Westminster system' is its crude adversarialism. Another is the way in which first-past-the-post exaggerates the winner's margin, as with the Conservatives in 1983 and 1987, and Labour in 1997 and 2001. Too large a majority insulates ministers from effective parliamentary pressure and easily generates that 'arrogance of power' which ignores public opinion and steam-rollers opposition. We also know that with first-past-the-post there is a strong disincentive to vote in what are perceived to be safe seats; which point can support the argument that a change of electoral system would increase participation and regenerate parliament.

On the other side of the argument, critics of PR point out that it weakens the link between MPs and constituencies, it is more difficult to understand, and it can shift the power to decide who is to form the government from the electorate to the parties who would have to negotiate the coalitions – a very convincing argument against the use of party list forms of PR. The adoption of PR in Scotland and Wales gives an opportunity to assess the weight of those negative consequences in the British context. What needs to be added to the balance of advantage is the falling public confidence in the current Westminster system. The burden of proof is moving in favour of change, and such a change would have a considerable impact on Westminster's procedures and culture.

Another important consequence of devolution is that there is now more than one model of parliamentary government operating in the United Kingdom. The Scottish Parliament and the National Assembly for Wales show that parliaments can operate differently from Westminster, even though the Westminster model remains a very significant influence on the way the devolved assemblies are developing. In addition, devolution has shown the particular significance of party: the Scottish and Welsh Conservative, Labour and Liberal Democrat parties are different from the 'London parties' and, as the displaced Welsh Labour leader Alun Michael discovered, that difference has to be respected.

Resources

There is no doubt that significant advances have been made in the resourcing of Parliament and parliamentarians in the forty years since the SPG was established. MPs' salaries and allowances, the provision of office space, equipment, and the intranet, all illustrate this other side of the 'professionalisation' coin. The setting up of a research unit to provide some capacity for select committees marks a small start also in building up resources which should enable Parliament as an institution to challenge the Executive across a wider front than audit irregularities and maladministration. The development of the National Audit Office, the Office of the Parliamentary and Health Service Commissioner and now the Standards Commissioner, as discussed in chapter 15, contributed significantly to this. But in comparison with the huge resources available to the Government, backbench and Opposition parliamentary resources are puny. That imbalance is a constant threat to the real effectiveness of parliamentary scrutiny across the board – policy, legislation, and especially expenditure and administration.

In response to that line of argument parliamentarians are wont to point out that they have to be sensitive to likely adverse reaction from the electorate to the appearance that MPs are spending more on themselves. But the sensible response is to view such reaction as a challenge to make the case for resourcing the scrutiny and accountability of government. A very good case can be made, particularly in comparison with the resources available to other national legislatures, not to mention the European Parliament. Resources are not everything. A well-informed backbench MP or parliamentary committee is more likely than an ignorant one to mount an effective challenge to government – and thereby contribute more fully to good governance. What is true of scrutiny by Commons committees and backbench MPs is also true of scrutiny by groups and committees in the House of Lords. The obstacle in both cases is that the Government, in both its political and bureaucratic manifestations, is far from keen to subject itself to high quality criticism and challenge. Whilst the Government controls the parliamentary purse strings, it will prevent that development, albeit throwing the occasional bone in the direction of its advocates in the hope of buying them off.

Forty years on, can we be optimistic with the reformists about the prospects for Parliament, or must we accede to the gloomy prognosis of the sceptics? Forty years is a long time: eleven general elections, seven prime ministers, five changes of governing party. There has been ample opportunity for reform, and on some occasions, such as after the general election of 1979, hopes have been high. But the fundamental features of the Westminster system are still intact, the government whips remain in control and the reformers' ambitions have not been realised. On the other hand, notwithstanding the iron grip of the party managers, there have been some very significant changes, as the essays in this volume indicate. The situation is not one in which change is impossible; merely one in which change is gradual, incremental and largely piece-meal. In that respect it reflects the political culture of the United Kingdom for the last two centuries or more.

This reality is both a warning and an encouragement. Failing a sea-change in the party system or the attitudes of the major parties themselves, radical change at Westminster is very unlikely. Growing public disenchantment with national politics, especially among young people, the negative image of Parliament created by recurring allegations of 'sleaze', and a very low turn-out in the 2001 General Election made for a very worrying start to the new millennium. But there is some cause for hope. Change happens, even if the pace is often frustratingly slow. Patient, persistent, reasoned advocacy of the case for particular changes can over time lead to a change of attitude, so that the opportune moment – like the election of new governments in 1964, 1979 and 1997, or a finely balanced House of Commons as in 1974–79 – can be taken to effect *some* change. From both sides of the political spectrum (and the middle) there is no shortage of pungent criticism of Parliament's weakness, nor of proposals to improve its effectiveness. For the foreseeable future the prospect is that the pressure for change will continue – and so will the resistance to any possibility of weakening the controlling power of the Government's party managers. From time to time there will be minor advances in the cause of improving Parliament's effectiveness. On occasion there may be even a major advance, such as an agreed reform of the House of Lords. But until British political parties change, along with the mindsets of those elected to Parliament with their aid, the Parliament of Westminster will remain much as it was: the arena for the arts of party government.

Notes

1 J. A. G. Griffith and M. Ryle, *Parliament*, Second Edition, Sweet & Maxwell, paras 1–009, 1–0127, and 1–031.
2 The Government accepted the principle in its response to the *Review of the Public Sector Ombudsmen in England: A Report by the Cabinet Office*, April 2000 – see HC Deb 20 July 2001 Col 465W. The long delay in implementation suggests 'if' may be more appropriate than 'when'.
3 SI 1980 No 2000.
4 Treasury Solicitor, *The Judge over Your Shoulder: A Guide to Judicial Review for UK Government Administrators*, March 2000, p. 1. Over half the applications were immigration cases. Only 22.4% – still a substantial number – of the applications resulted in full hearings. The first edition of the guide was published in 1987.
5 Public Law Project, *The Impact of the Human Rights Act on judicial review: an empirical Research Study*, June 2003.
6 See, for example, Philip Norton, *The Commons in Perspective*, Martin Robertson, 1981, pp. 225–235.

Appendix: Publications by the Study of Parliament Group, 1964–2004

A   Books

Britain in the European Union
Edited by Philip Giddings and Gavin Drewry
Macmillan Press Ltd, 2004
ISBN 14039 0451 0 (hbk) 14039 0452 9 (pbk)

Conduct Unbecoming – the Regulation of Parliamentary Behaviour
Edited by Oonagh Gay and Patricia Leopold
Politico's Publishing, 2004
ISBN 1 842750 55 0

The Deregulation Procedure: An Evaluation
David Miers
Hansard Society for Parliamentary Government, 1999
ISBN 0 900432 52 7

The Law and Parliament
Edited by Dawn Oliver and Gavin Drewry
Butterworths, 1998
ISBN 0 406 98092 6

Westminster and Europe: the Impact of the European Union on the Westminster Parliament
Edited by Philip Giddings and Gavin Drewry
Macmillan Press Ltd, 1996
ISBN 0 333 64980 X

Parliamentary Accountability: A Study of Parliament and Executive Agencies
Edited by Philip Giddings
Macmillan Press Ltd, 199?
ISBN 0 333 63201 X

The House of Lords at work
Edited by Donald Shell and David Beamish
Oxford University Press, 1993
ISBN 0 19 827762 8

Parliamentary Questions
Edited by Mark Franklin and Philip Norton
Oxford University Press, 1993
ISBN 0 19 827317 7

Parliament and International Relations
Edited by Charles Carstairs and Richard Ware
Open University Press, 1991
ISBN 0 335 09698 0

Parliament and Pressure Politics
Edited by Michael Rush
Oxford University Press, 1990
ISBN 0 19 827576 5

The New Select Committees, second edition
Edited by Gavin Drewry
Oxford University Press, 1989
ISBN 0 19 822784 1

The Commons under Scrutiny
Edited by Michael Ryle and Peter G Richards
Routledge, 1988
ISBN 0 415 01147 7

The New Select Committees: A study of the 1979 Reforms
Edited by Gavin Drewry
Oxford University Press, 1985
ISBN 0 19 822785 X

The Study of Parliament Group: The First Twenty-one Years
Dermot Englefield
Study of Parliament Group, 1985
ISBN 0 9510485 0 3

The House of Commons: Services and Facilities, 1972–1982
Edited by Michael Rush
No. 614
Policy Studies Institute, 1983
ISBN 0 853 74221 9

The Commons Today [a revised edition of *The Commons in the Seventies*]
Edited by Stuart A. Walkland and Michael Ryle
Fontana Paperbacks, 1981

Parliament and Economic Affairs in Britain, France, Italy and the Netherlands
Edited by David Coombes and Stuart A. Walkland
Heinemann, 1980
(Part II: 'Parliament and the Economy in Great Britain' is by members of the
Group)

The House of Commons in the Twentieth Century
Edited by Stuart A. Walkland
Oxford University Press, 1979
ISBN 0 19 827193 X

Westminster and Devolution
Prepared by members of the Study of Parliament Group
Vol. XLIV No. 579
Policy Studies Institute, 1978

The Commons in the Seventies
Edited by Stuart A. Walkland and Michael Ryle
Fontana, 1977
ISBN 0 006 34497 6

Specialist Committees in the British Parliament: the experience of a decade
By members of the Study of Parliament Group [edited by P. G. Richards]
Vol. XLII No. 564
Political and Economic Planning, 1976

The House of Commons Services and Facilities
Edited by Michael Rush and Malcolm Shaw
for Political and Economic Planning and the Study of Parliament Group
Allen and Unwin, 1974

Parliamentary Scrutiny of Government Bills
J. A. G. Griffith
for Political and Economic Planning and the Study of Parliament Group
Allen and Unwin, 1974
ISBN 0 04328 008 0

Westminster to Brussels: the significance for Parliament of Accession to the European Community
Political and Economic Planning in association with the Hansard Society and the Study of Parliament Group
[written by David Coombes, Max Beloff and Nevil Johnson]
PEP Broadsheet 540, 1973

Commission on the Constitution: Research Papers 5: Aspects of Parliamentary Reform
By members of the Study of Parliament Group
HMSO, 1973

The Member of Parliament and his information
Anthony Barker and Michael Rush
for Political and Economic Planning and the Study of Parliament Group
Allen and Unwin, 1970

The Commons in Transition
Edited by A. Harry Hanson and Bernard Crick
Fontana, 1970

Reforming the Commons
By members of the Study of Parliament Group
Vol. XXXI No. 491
Political and Economic Planning, 1965

B   Articles

'The Deregulation Procedure: an expanding role'
David Miers
Public Law [1999] 477–503

'Lobbying Parliament'
Michael Rush
Parliamentary Affairs 43, 1990, pp. 141–8

'Party Committees in the House of Commons'
Philip Norton
Parliamentary Affairs 36, No 1, 1983, pp. 7–27

'Private Bill Procedure: A case for Reform'
The Study of Parliament Group [written by Peter G. Richards]
Public Law [1981] pp. 206–227

C   Evidence

Except where otherwise stated, all select committees were of the House of Commons.

Deregulation Committee, 1st Special Report, Session 1998–99, HC 324
The Future of the Deregulation Procedure
Oral evidence (30 March 1999) and Annex to Report (both by David Miers, arising out of work of Delegated Legislation Study Group)

Select Committee on Procedure, 4th Report, Session 1998–99, HC 185
Procedural consequences of devolution
Evidence of 10 February (pp. 15–20 written and 20–31 oral) and Appendix 28 (pp. 138–41)

Select Committee on Standards and Privileges, 13th Report, Session 1997–98, HC 633
Appeal procedures: A consultative document
Appendix 12

Select Committee on Procedure, 4th Report, Session 1995–96, HC 152
Delegated legislation
Appendix 7 (pp. 67–72)

Treasury and Civil Service Committee, 5th Report, Session 1992–93, HC 583
The Government's proposals for budgetary reform
Appendix 10 (pp. 43–8)

House of Lords Select Committee on the Committee Work of the House, Report, Session 1991–92, HL 35-II
pp. 250–2 (written: Michael Rush)

Select Committee on Procedure, 2nd Report, Session 1989–90, HC 19-II
The Working of the Select Committee System
pp. 160–6 (written), pp. 167–68 (oral) (by Michael Rush, drawing on work for SPG)
pp. 202–6 (written: Gavin Drewry), pp. 231–8 (oral) (by Gavin Drewry and Philip Giddings with Peter Hennessy)

Select Committee on Procedure, 4th Report, Session 1988–89, HC 622-II
The Scrutiny of European Legislation
Appendix 15 (p. 141) (by Gavin Drewry after consultations with SPG)
Select Committee on Members' Interests, Minutes of Evidence, Session 1989–90, HC 283
(evidence actually given on 14 June 1988)

Parliamentary Lobbying
pp. 26–30 (written), pp. 30–43 (oral) (by Michael Rush, Colin Seymour-Ure, Philip Norton and Michael Shaw appearing in individual capacities but based on SPG research)

also Third Report, Session 1990–91, HC 586

Parliamentary Lobbying
Appendix 1 (p. 1) (Michael Rush)
Select Committee on Procedure, 2nd Report, Session 1986–87, HC 350
The use of time on the floor of the House
Appendix 20 (pp. 29–32)

Select Committee on Procedure, 2nd Report, Session 1984–85, HC 49-II
Public Bill Procedure
pp. 72–78 (written), pp. 79–93 (oral: Philip Norton and Nevil Johnson)

Select Committee on Procedure (Finance), Report, Session 1982–83, HC 24-III
Appendix 10 (pp. 10–17) (by Ann Robinson 'after consultation with members of the Study of Parliament Group')

Select Committee on Procedure, 1st Report, Session 1977–78, HC 588-III
Appendix 1, pp. 1–20
Select Committee on House of Commons (Services), 8th Report, Session 1976–77, HC 509
Services for the Public
Appendices 1 and 2, pp. 88–94

Select Committee on Assistance to Private Members, Report, Session 1974–75, HC 375
Appendix 21, pp. 112–118
Select Committee on Procedure, 2nd Report, Session 1970–71, HC 538
The Process of Legislation
Appendix 6, pp. 304–9
(by A. H. Hanson, D. Coombes and S. A. Walkland on behalf of the Academic Members of the Study of Parliament Group)

Select Committee on Procedure, 2nd Special Report, Session 1969–70, HC 302
Parliamentary Scrutiny of Taxation
Appendix 9, pp. 181–8

Select Committee on Parliamentary Privilege, Report, Session 1967–68, HC 34
Appendix V, pp. 187–95

Select Committee on Procedure, 6th Report, Session 1966–67, HC 539
Public Bill Procedure etc.
Appendices 3 and 4: pp. 88–99

Select Committee on Procedure, 1st Report, Session 1966–67, HC 153
The times of sittings of the House
pp. 48–50 (written: Sir Edward Fellowes), 50–65 (oral: Sir Edward Fellowes and Bernard Crick)

Select Committee on Procedure, Report, Session 1965–66, HC 122
Financial Procedure
pp. 74–5 (written, extracts) (This consists of paragraphs 11 and 20 of the written evidence of 1965.)

Select Committee on Procedure, 4th Report, Session 1964–65, HC 303
pp. 51–68 (oral: P. A. Bromhead, A. H. Hanson and H. Wiseman), Appendix 2, pp. 131–142 (written)

Bibliography

Note: this is a list of the works referred to in the text, not a comprehensive bibliography of the literature on Parliament.

Books

N. Bamforth and P. Leyland (eds), *Public Law in a Multi-Layered Constitution*, Oxford: Hart Publishing, 2003.

S. Barnett and E. Seymour, *A Shrinking Iceberg Travelling South...: Changing Trends in British Television*, London: University of Westminster, 1999.

S. H. Beer, *Modern British Politics: A Study of Parties and Pressure Groups*, London: Faber, 1965.

R. Blackburn and A. Kennon, *Parliament: Functions, Practice and Procedure*, 2nd edition, London: Sweet & Maxwell, 2003.

D. and G. Butler, *Twentieth Century British Political Facts, 1900–2000*, London: Macmillan, 2000.

D. Butler and D. Kavanagh, *The British General Election of 2001*, London: Palgrave, 2002.

D. N. Chester and N. Bowring, *Questions in Parliament*, Oxford: Clarendon Press, 1962.

S. Coleman, *Electronic Media, Parliament and the People*, London: Hansard Society, 1999.

B. Crick, *The Reform of Parliament*, London: Weidenfeld & Nicolson, 1964.

G. Drewry (ed.), *The New Select Committees: A Study of the 1979 Reforms*, Oxford: Clarendon Press for the Study of Parliament Group, 1985.

M. Eagle and J. Lovenduski, *High Time or High Tide for Labour Women*, London: The Fabian Society, 1998.

Erskine May, *Parliamentary Practice*, Sir William McKay, KCB, (ed.), 23rd edition, London: Lexis Nexis, February 2004.

T. Erskine May, *Treatise on the Law, Privileges, Proceedings and Usage of Parliament*, 1st edition, London: 1844.

M. Franklin and P. Norton (eds), *Parliamentary Questions*, Oxford: Clarendon Press, 1993.

S. Frantzich and J. Sullivan, *The C-Span Revolution*, Norman, Oklahoma: University of Oklahoma Press, 1996.

L. Friedman, *Total Justice*, New York: Russell Sage Foundation, 1985.

O. Gay and B. K. Winetrobe, *Officers of Parliament: Developing the Role*, London: Constitution Unit, 2003.

O. Gay and P. Leopold, *Conduct Unbecoming: The Regulation of Parliamentary Behaviour*, London: Politico's, 2004.

P. Giddings (ed.), *Parliamentary Accountability: A Study of Parliament and Executive Agencies*, London: Macmillan, 1995.

P. Giddings and G. Drewry (eds), *Westminster and Europe: the Impact of the European Union on the Westminster Parliament*, London: Macmillan, 1996.

P. Giddings and G. Drewry (eds), *Britain in the European Union: Law, Policy and Parliament*, Basingstoke: Palgrave, 2004.

J. A. G. Griffith, *Parliamentary Scrutiny of Government Bills*, London: G. Allen & Unwin, 1974.

J. A. G. Griffith and M. Ryle, *Parliament: function, practice and procedures*, London: Sweet & Maxwell, 1989.

R. Gregory and P. Giddings, *The Ombudsman, the Citizen and Parliament*, London: Politico's, 2002.

Hansard Society, *Making the Law: Report of the Hansard Society Commission on the Legislative Process*, London: Hansard Society, 1992.

Hansard Society, *Report of the Commission on Parliamentary Scrutiny: The Challenge for Parliament – Making Government Accountable*, London: Vacher/ Dod, 2001.

Hansard Society, *Parliament at the Apex: Parliamentary Scrutiny and Regulatory Bodies*, London: Hansard Society, 2003.

R. Harris, *Good and Faithful Servant*, London: Faber, 1991.

R. Hazell and A. Trench (ed.), Has Devolution made a Difference? The State of the Nations 2004, Exeter: Imprint Academic, January 2004.

B. Ingham, *Kill the Messenger*, London: HarperCollins, 1991.

I. Jennings, *Parliament*, Second Edition, Cambridge: CUP, 1957.

D. Judge, *The Parliamentary State*, London: Sage, 1993.

Lord Lester of Herne Hill and D. Pannick (eds), *Human Rights Law and Practice*, 2nd ed., London: Butterworths, 2004.

A. L. Lowell, *The Government of England*, 1919.

P. Norris and J. Lovendeski, *Political Recruitment: Gender, Race and Class in the British Parliament*, Cambridge: Cambridge University Press, 1995.

P. Norton, *Dissension in the House of Commons 1945–74*, London: Macmillan, 1975.

P. Norton (ed.), *The House of Lords in the 1980s*, Oxford: Basil Blackwell, 1985.

P. Oborne, *Alastair Campbell: New Labour and the Rise of the Media Class*, London: Aurum Press, 1999.

E. C. Page, *Governing by Numbers: Delegated Legislation and Everyday Policy-making*, Oxford: Hart Publishing, February 2001.

I. Richard and D. Welfare, *Unfinished Business: Reforming the Lords*, London: Vintage, 1999.

R. Rose, *The Prime Minister in a Shrinking World*, Cambridge: Polity, 2001.

A. Roth and B. Criddle, *Parliamentary Profiles*, various volumes, 1998–2001.

M. Rush, *The Role of the Member of Parliament since 1868: From Gentlemen to Players*, Oxford: OUP, 2001.

M. Rush, *Parliament Today*, Manchester: Manchester University Press, April 2005.

M. Ryle and P. G. Richards (eds), *The Commons under Scrutiny*, London: Routledge, 1988.

J. Seaton (ed.), *Politics and the Media: Harlots and Prerogatives at the Turn of the Millennium*, Oxford: Blackwell, 1998.

C. Seymour-Ure, *The British Press and Broadcasting*, 2nd edn, Oxford: Blackwell, 1996.

C. Seymour-Ure, *Prime Ministers and the Media*, Oxford: Blackwell, 2003.

D. Shell and D. Beamish, *The House of Lords at Work*, Oxford: Clarendon Press, 1993.

C. Skelcher, S. Weir, and L. Wilson, *Advance of the Quango State*. London: Local Government Information Unit, 2003.

J. Squires and M. Wickham-Jones, *Women in Parliament*, Manchester: Equal Opportunities Commission, 2001.

S. A. Walkland, *The Legislative Process in Great Britain*, London: Allen & Unwin, 1968.

S. A. Walkland and M. Ryle (eds), *The Commons Today*, London: Fontana/Collins, 1981.

H. Wallace and W. Wallace (eds), *Policy-Making in the European Union*, Oxford: OUP, 2000.

Articles

S. Childs and J. Wilthey, 'Sex and the Signing of Early Day Motions in the 1997 Parliament', *Political Studies*, 52, 2004.

S. Coleman and J. Spiller, 'Exploring New Media Effects on Representative Democracy', *Journal of Legislative Studies*, 11, 2005.

P. Cowley and S. Childs, 'Too Spineless to Rebel? New Labour's Women MPs', *British Journal of Political Science*, 33, 2003.

P. Cowley and M. Stuart, 'More Bleak House than Great Expectations', *Parliamentary Affairs*, 57, 2003.

P. Cowley and M. Stuart, '"In Place of Strife": the PLP in Government, 1997–2001', *Political Studies*, 51, 2003.

M. Elliott 'Parliamentary sovereignty and the new constitutional order: legislative freedom, political reality and convention', 22 *Legal Studies*, 340, 2002.

D. Feldman, 'Parliamentary Scrutiny of legislation and human rights', *Public Law*, 313, 2002.

D. Feldman, 'The Impact of Human Rights on the Legislative Process', 25 *Statute Law Review*, 91, 2004.

M. Flinders, 'The Politics of Public-Private Partnerships', *British Journal of Politics and International Relations*, Vol. 7.

M. Flinders, 'Icebergs and MPs: Delegated Governance and Parliament', *Parliamentary Affairs*, Vol. 57, 767–784.

M. Flinders, 'Distributed Public Governance in Britain', *Public Administration*, Vol. 82, 883–909.

R. Gregory and G. Drewry, 'Barlow Clowes and the Ombudsman', Parts I and II, *Public Law*, Summer and Autumn 1991.

W. B. Gwyn, 'The British PCA: Ombudsman or Ombudsmouse?', *Journal of Politics*, 35, 1973.

P. Hennessy, 'An End to the Poverty of Aspirations? Parliament since 1979', First History of Parliament Lecture, Attlee Suite, London, Portcullis House, 25 November 2004.

Lord Irvine of Lairg, QC, 'Judges and Decision Makers: The Theory and Practice of Wednesbury Review', *Public Law*, 59–78, 1996.

A. Kennon, 'Pre-legislative scrutiny of draft bills', *Public Law*, 478, 2004.

Sir J. Laws, 'Law and Democracy', *Public Law*, 72, 1995.

J. Lovenduski, 'Gender politics: a breakthrough for women?', *Parliamentary Affairs*, 50, 1997.

D. Marsh and M. Read, 'British Private Members' Balloted Bills: A Lottery with Few Winners, Small Prizes, but High Administrative Cost', Essex Papers in Politics and Government, University of Essex, 1985.

J. C. McNeill, 'Is the reformed House of Lords a more representative chamber?', Unpublished Undergraduate Dissertation, University of Hull: Department of Politics and International Studies, 2003.

P. Norton, 'Party Cohesion in the House of Lords', paper presented to the Sixth Workshop of Parliamentary Scholars and Parliamentarians, Wroxton College, Banbury, 31 July–1 August 2004.

J. Rasmussen, 'Female political career patterns and leadership disabilities in Britain', *Polity*, 13, 1981.

Lord Woolf, 'Droit public – English style', *Public Law*, 57, 1995.

T. Wright, 'Prospects for Parliamentary Reform', *Parliamentary Affairs*, 57, 4.

Government Publications

Lord Butler, *Review of Intelligence on Weapons of Mass Destruction*, HC 898, 2003–04, 14 July 2004.

P. Collcutt and M. Hourihan, *Review of the Public Sector Ombudsmen in England*, Cabinet Office, April 2000.

C. Haskins, *Rural Delivery Review*, Department of the Environment, Food and Rural Affairs, October 2003.

Committee on Standards in Public Life, *Standards of Conduct in the House of Commons*, Eighth Report Cm 5663, HMSO, November 2002.

Department for Constitutional Affairs, *Constitutional Reform: a new way of appointing judges* CP 10/03, 2003.

Intelligence and Security Committee, Report on *Iraqi Weapons of Mass Destruction – Intelligence and Assessments*, Cm 5972, TSO, September 2003.

Lord Hutton, *Report of the Inquiry into the Circumstances Surrounding the Death of Dr David Kelly CMG*, HC 247, 2003–04, 28 January 2004.

Lord Nolan, *Committee on Standards in Public Life, First Report*, Cm 2850-I and II, HMSO, 1995.

B. Phillis (Chairman), *An Independent Review of Government Communications*, Cabinet Office, January 2004.

Lord Renton, *The Preparation of Legislation*, Cmnd 6053, HMSO, 1975.

Lord Richard, *Report of a Commission on the Powers and Electoral Arrangements of the National Assembly for Wales*, TSO, 31 March 2004.

Top Salaries Review Body, *First Report: Ministers of the Crown and Members of Parliament*, Cmnd. 4836, HMSO, December 1971.

Top Salaries Review Body, *Report No. 20*, Cmnd. 8881-II, HMSO, May 1983.

Top Salaries Review Body, *Report No. 38*, Cm. 3330-II, HMSO, July 1996.

HM Treasury, *Audit and Accountability for Central Government: the Government's response to Lord Sharman's report 'Holding to Account'*, Cm 5456, TSO, March 2002.

Lord Wakeham, Royal Commission on the Reform of the House of Lords, *A House for the Future*, Cm 4534, HMSO, January 2000.

D. Wanless, *Securing Good Health for the Whole Population*, HM Treasury, February 2004.

House of Commons Papers

House of Commons (Administration): Report to Mr Speaker, HC 624, 1974–75, HMSO, 1975.

House of Commons Services: Report to the House of Common: Commission (the Ibbs Report), HC 38, 1990–91, HMSO, 1990.

Parliamentary Commissioner for Administration, Third Report, 1967–68, HC 54, HMSO, December 1967.

Review of the Administrative Services of the House of Commons: Report to the Speaker by Sir Edmund Compton, HC 254, HMSO, 1974.

Review of Management and Services: Report to the House of Commons Commission (the Braithwaite Report), HC 745, 1998–99, HMSO, 1999.

Standing Orders of the House of Commons, TSO, January 2003.

House of Commons Committees

Education and Skills Select Committee, *The Work of the Committee in 2002*, HC 359, 2002–03, TSO, 2003.

European Scrutiny Committee, *European Scrutiny in the Commons*, Thirtieth Report of 2001–02, HC 152, TSO, June 2002.

Foreign Affairs Committee, *Sierra Leone: Exchange of Correspondence with the Foreign Secretary*, First Special Report of 1997–98, HC 760, HMSO, May 1998; and, *Sierra Leone: Further Exchange of Correspondence with the Foreign Secretary*, Second Special Report of 1997–98, HC 852, HMSO, June 1998.

Foreign Affairs Committee, *The Decision to go to War in Iraq*, HC 813, HC 1025 and HC 1044, 2002–03, TSO, 2003.

Home Affairs Committee, *The Work of the Committee in 2002*, HC 336, 2002–03, TSO, 2003.

Information Committee, First Report, HC 1065, 2001–02: *Digital Technology: Working for Parliament and the Public*, HMSO, 2002.

Liaison Committee, *Shifting the Balance: Select Committees and the Executive*, First Report of Session 1999–2000, HC 300, HMSO, March 2000.

Liaison Committee, *Shifting the Balance: Unfinished Business*, First Report of Session 2000–01, HC 321, HMSO, March 2001.

Liaison Committee, *Oral Evidence on 21 January 2003*, HC 334-I, 2002–03, TSO, February 2003.

Modernisation Committee, *The Legislative Process*, First Report of Session 1997–98, HC 190, HMSO, July 1997.

Modernisation Committee, *Explanatory Material for Bills*, Second Report 1997–98, HC 389, HMSO, December 1997.

Modernisation Committee, *Select Committees*, First Report of Session 2001–02, HC 224, HMSO, February 2002.

Modernisation Committee, *Scrutiny of European Matters in the House of Commons: Government Memorandum from the Leader of the House of Commons*, HC 508, 2003–04, TSO, April 2004.

Modernisation Committee, *Connecting Parliament with the Public*, First Report of Session 2003–04, HC 368, TSO, June 2004.

PCA Select Committee, First Report of Session 1990–91, HC 129, HMSO, 1991.

PCA Select Committee, *Compensation to Farmers for Slaughtered Poultry*, Third Report of Session 1992–93, HC 593, HMSO, April 1993.

Procedure Committee, Fourth Report, 1964–65, HC 303, HMSO, 1965.

Procedure Committee, First Report, Session 1977–78, HC 588, HMSO, 1978.

Procedure Committee, *The Working of the Select Committee System*, Second Report of Session 1989–90, HC 19, HMSO, 1990.

Procedure Committee, *European Business*, Third Report of 1996–97, HC 77, HMSO, 1997.

Procedure Committee, *Delegated Legislation*, HC 152, 1995–96, 1996.

Procedure Committee, *The procedural consequences of devolution*, Fourth Report of 1998–99, HC 185, HMSO, May 1999.

Procedure Committee, *Delegated Legislation*, First Report of 1999–200, HC 48, HMSO, March 2000.

Procedure Committee, *Parliamentary Questions*, Third Report of Session 2001–02, HC 622, TSO, 2002.

Public Administration Committee, *Quangos*, Sixth Report of Session 1998–99, HC 209, HMSO, November 1999.

Public Administration Select Committee, *Review of Public Sector Ombudsmen in England*, Third Report of Session 1999–2000, HC 612, HMSO, August 2000.

Public Administration Select Committee, *Mapping the Quango State*, Fifth Report of 2000–2001, HC 367, HMSO, March 2001.

Public Administration Select Committee, *Government by Appointment: Opening Up the Patronage State*, Fourth Report of Session 2002–3, HC 165, HMSO, July 2003.

Scottish Affairs Committee, *The operation of multi-layer democracy*, Second Report of 1997–98, HC 460, HMSO, December 1998.

Select Committee on Sittings of the House, HC 22, 1991–92.

Welsh Affairs Committee, *The primary legislative process as it affects Wales*, Fourth Report of 2002–3, HC 79, TSO, March 2003.

Welsh Affairs Committee, *Draft Transport (Wales) Bill*, Fourth Report of 2003–4, HC 759, TSO, July 2004.

House of Lords Committees

Constitution Committee, *Devolution: Inter-Institutional Relations in the United Kingdom*, Second Report of 2002–03, HL 28, TSO, January 2003.

Constitution Committee: Sixth Report of the Committee, 2003–04, *The Regulatory State: Ensuring its Accountability*, HL 68, TSO, 6 May 2004.

Constitution Committee: Fourteenth Report of the Committee, 2003–04 *Parliament and the Legislative Process*, HL 173, TSO, November 2004.

Constitution Committee, *Annual Report*, Seventeenth Report of 2003–04, HL 194, HMSO, November 2004.

European Union Committee, *Annual Report 2004*, Thirty-Second Report of 2003–04, HL 186, HMSO, November 2004.

Joint Committees

Joint Committee on Human Rights, *The Case for a Human Rights Commission* HL Paper 67/HC 489 Sixth Report of Session 2002–3, TSO, March 2003.

Joint Committee on Human Rights, *Scrutiny of Bills: Second Progress Report*, Fourth Report of 2003–04, HL 34/HC 303, February 2004.

Joint Committee on Human Rights, *The Meaning of Public Authority under the Human Rights Act*, Seventh Report of 2003–04, HL 39, HC 382, TSO, March 2004.

Joint Committee on Human Rights, *Commission for Equality and Human Rights: Structure, Functions and Powers*, Eleventh Report of 2003–04, HL 78/HC 536, TSO, May 2004.

Joint Committee on Human Rights, *Commission for Equality and Human Rights: The Government's White Paper*, Sixteenth Report of 2003–4, HL 156/HC 998, TSO, August 2004.

Joint Committee on Human Rights, *The Children Bill*, HL 161/HC 537 of 2003–04, TSO, September 2004.

Index